1928 Citroen with "H" historic registration plate.

MOTORING IN SPAIN

by

Brian J Deller.

The ideal reference for English speaking RESIDENTS and VISITORS to Spain who own, rent or operate vehicles, including motorcycles.

Third Edition

bjdeller @ spainvia.com

DISCLAIMER

This book, the third in the line, is intended as a guide for the English speaking visitor to, or resident in, Spain to assist them in quickly becoming acquainted with the driving and owning of private motor vehicles in Spain, including rental cars, motorcycles and small trucks. It is not intended to be used as a reference book for litigation. The contents of this book cannot be used as a basis for any claim against the author or any other party associated with it. It is intended to save the readers much money and stress.

First printed February 2004.
Second Edition, September 2005
Third Edition, November 2007.

Copyright © September, 2003/2005/2007 Author, Brian John Deller.

ISBN No. 978-84 - 611- 9278- 6 (2007 Edition.)

Design and layout by the author. Published by the author.

Printed in Spain by: -

P. R. Grafis, Fuengirola, Malaga, Spain.

It is a criminal offence to reproduce, photocopy or transmit any part or the whole of this book, in any form whatsoever without the written permission of the author/publisher.

Author's E-mail address: bjdeller@spainvia.com

(Please put "Motoring in Spain query" in email subject line.)

For updates and other new information, visit the web site at: -

www.spainvia.com/motoringinspain.htm

This book is the only one of its kind (advice on Spain) and it is regularly updated on the author's web-site.

MOTORING IN SPAIN

Introduction to Third Edition.

Following the great succeses of the first two editions, this edition again updates the information necessary for the English speaker to comfortably and economically own and operate a motor-vehicle in Spain.   Much of the new information is based on questions received from readers of not only the books, but the weekly articles published in two leading English language newspapers published in Spain, and regular radio spots, one as the Motoring Correspondent of REM.FM Radio based on the Costa del Sol, but broadcasting from the Gran Canarias to Valencia Province, Madrid, and other areas.   Like the other books, this edition is intended to be read and then carried in the car so it is available for roadside references and emergencies, such as an accident where the driver's report may not be in English. A translation of this universal form is at the back of this book and it has already been reported by some readers as being found essential after an accident here in Spain.

As before, changes to the laws and other news items that occur after the publication of this edition are to be found at the author's web-site. I have included instructions for those who do not normally use a computer, where they can go to an Internet cafe and see the updates as well as print them out.   Please see page 9.   For those wary of this now "old" technology, it is very easy.

Another new plus is the availability of a hands-on service for those who need help in transferring registrations and all other administration matters with owning a vehiclein Spain.   Please see pages 287 - 288.

This book is not intended to be a fully comprehensive "driving lesson manual" although, as a result of many letters received by the author, some basic rules are explained. I have also included some historical facts to show how the laws have developed in recent years. Some minor repetition of information is deliberate to get a needed message through or to save having to jump from page to page. Spain is near the top of the EU countries with high death and serious injury rates on the roads, although big improvements have occurred in 2005/2006 and the government is involved in a campaign to reduce the still high rates even further. With this in mind, it is essential that drivers know the rules to avoid the expense and trauma of fines and Court appearances.

Brian Deller, Malaga, SPAIN

THE AUTHOR THANKS THE HELP OF THE PROFESSIONALS NAMED BELOW: -

Don Jose Luis Martinez Hens, *Abogado* (Barrister).

Sr. Martinez has a legal practice with the office based in Fuengirola on the Costa del Sol. Jose Luis is fully fluent in English and he is experienced in all types of Spanish legal matters including motoring litigation, civil matters, lease and property transfers and conveyancing.

Office 1. Calle Capitan 12, Local 4, 29640 Fuengirola, Malaga, Spain.

Tel. (0034) 952 582 930: Fax (0034) 952 470 919

Mobile (in English) (0034) 658-316-516. E-Mail, Jlmhens@terra.es

SPECIALISED SERVICE ON THE COSTA DEL SOL.

An experienced expert in all matters pertaining to motoring and residence matters. With contacts at the Malaga Trafico, Sr. Jamie Cruz, who is fluent in English, is able to offer a quick service on the subjects covered in this book very quickly at a fair price. He has been in business since 1999. See pages 287 - 288 for more details.

Office: Calle Camilo Jose Cela, No 3, Opposite the Zoo entrance in Fuengirola 29640, Malaga.
Tel. 952 59 35 00: Mobile 616-673-556

A PROFESSIONAL WIFE.
Thanks also to my lovely wife, Beverley, who kept the coffees and sandwiches coming so the work continued painlessly, sometimes into the night, but as I approach my 70th birthday, like many others I believe I have found the secret of keeping the years at bay. What is it? Have something to get up for every day, and something to go to bed for every night.

THANKS ALSO TO THE MANY BUYERS OF PREVIOUS EDITIONS OF THIS BOOK, FOR THEIR KIND THANKS FOR MY WRITING IT, AND FOR THEIR SUPPORT.

AND TO YOU TOO, DEAR READER, THE "NEW CONCERNED" MOTORIST IN SPAIN.

4

The author and publisher, Brian J Deller.

I have long qualified for pension, but having found retirement boring, I have written this book to satisfy the real need for it in Spain.

Joining the RAF as an aircraft-apprentice at the age of 16, after finding out I was red/green colour-blind and could not take up flying, I spent thirteen years specialising in aircraft engine systems of all types. This was followed by three years with Rolls-Royce Aero-Engines, mainly in the USA, until that company went into liquidation in 1970/1. I then spent five years with earthmoving equipment manufacturer JCB, travelling to especially the Far East, Australia & New Zealand, working on dealer-development. In 1975, I was offered employment during a business visit to South Africa, and as a result my family and I moved there in 1976, staying until 1999, as by then, the terrible crime situation there made everyday a dangerous existence. Spain has become the last home.

I have been involved in a lot of voluntary charity work, especially with amateur acting, and also the training of motorcyclists of all ages on how to ride safely, a task started with the RAC-ACU scheme in the UK. Two years were spent as a police reservist where, working with the after effects following serious road accidents (including personally advising relatives of deaths), proved conclusively the lack of good sense that many of us seem to practice as far as driving is concerned, especially driving drunk or "drugged", these being also a major problem in Spain.

Spain was chosen as the "escape" destination in 1999 because my wife Beverley had often visited this country as a child/teenager and loved the Spanish way of life. This book has been written (and updated now twice due to its success) as a result of my experiences driving here, and the accepted fact that most foreign visitors and residents are ignorant of the many motoring differences here to especially the UK, even many of those who have lived here for ten years or more. For the football fans, Beverley's father, Don Hazledine, once played for Derby County.

In my younger days up to age 45, I used to race motorcycles in organised races on road tracks and in cross-country events, eventually getting involved in the organisation of racing in South Africa and elsewhere. I also write weekly columns for the Round Town News and the Costa Del Sol News, and I am the motoring correspondent for the popular radio stations REM.FM, broadcasting to most of Spain in English and Coastline Radio covering the eastern Malaga province.

In every society, there are people who think they know it all. I admit that I do not, but learning is what makes life worth living and I hope you all experience the same pleasure. Enjoy the book, and you can contact me by E-mail or phone if you have a question or advice on *Motoring in Spain* not covered in the book or my web-site. Remember that updates and other information are in the web-site.

E-mail to: bjdeller@spainvia.com or Tel. (0034) 666-888-870

(Please note "Motoring in Spain" on E-mails to avoid SPAM deletion.)

Web Site at: www.spainvia.com/

Contents in Alphabetical Order   Page No.

KEEPING THE INFORMATION UP TO DATE.

With any book of this type, it is important that the information is kept up to date, so to supplement your book, I have a web-site at:

www.spainvia.com/motoringinspain.htm

For those unfamiliar with computers, here are step by step instructions on how to get to the updates. It as easy as reading a book.

Find someone who has a computer connected to the Internet. If not, go to an Internet cafe where it is not expensive to buy say 30 minutes (about 2 - 5 Euros plus a coffee?). If you can, ask someone to help you the first time as it will only take a few seconds to find my web-site. Go to the Internet browser programme. Do not be shy to ask for help!

In the "address" line at the top of the screen, type "www.spainvia.com". Make sure that you have spelt it correctly with the full-stops. Then press Enter or use the mouse to click on the "Go" button on the right of the address line. You should see within a few seconds, a page called "Via de Vida - Way of Life". You are now in my web site.

Use the mouse to place the arrow pointer on the screen over the book cover picture, "*Motoring in Spain*". Again, if in doubt the first time, ask someone to show you how. Click the left hand button on the mouse. You will then go through to the page, which will open other pages with more information on *Motoring in Spain*.

At the bottom of this page, you will see another menu list "Update Pages", giving the pages of information based on a month and the year. Start at the top, and go through each page to read the updates. You can print the pages (if the cafe has this facility) which can then be read at home and carried with the book in the car if you wish. There is also a list of many of the bookshops selling the book as well as copies of Press reviews. As far as I know, this book is the only one of its kind (information on Spain in English) which is backed up with this facility. It makes the need for a relatively expensive annual update unnecessary and gives the buyers of the book much better value for money.

I do not agree that people who are over 50 should be "scared" of computers. After all, I learnt how to write and maintain my own web-site at 62. It is as easy as writing a letter as long as you overcome your personal fears.

DEFINITIONS AND GENERAL INFORMATION.

Please note that the age limits refer to Spanish licence regulations and also apply to foreign EU <u>residents</u> with EU licences, e.g. UK or Irish, etc.

Driver (*Conductor*/a). The person who is in control or responsible for the vehicle, including those "animal-powered", while on the public highways, even when not in motion. It can by definition, include anyone with a domestic animal (dog) on the road. However the owner is also responsible for the vehicle in certain circumstances.

Pedestrian (*Peatón/ona*). A person who uses the public highway, including footpaths, while on foot. These users are subject to the same Laws as all road users.

Trafico. The Government department that is responsible for all matters related to road traffic in Spain. It is part of the *Ministerio del Interior* (Interior Ministry).

Vehicle Ownership and Insurance Documents. If visiting Spain in your vehicle, your normal proof of ownership papers must be carried at all times in the vehicle as well as your driving licence. If you are driving a Spanish registered vehicle, including a rental vehicle where the papers should be supplied by the rental company (in the glove compartment?), you should carry: -

⇒ *PERMISO DE CIRCULACIÓN.* Shows the registered owner of the vehicle inluding his/her current address on the Trafico computer.

⇒ The **CERTIFICATE OF INSURANCE** issued by the insurance company. Payment must be up to date or, if paid by monthly stop order, proof carried that it is, eg a Bank statement.

⇒ As applicable, if the vehicle is more than four years old (two years for service vehicles, taxis and rental cars), it must have been tested for roadworthiness called the ITV (in UK, MOT), with the TEST STICKER RECEIPT on the upper right side of the windscreen. For motorcycles, the "free period" is five years (unless they are used for rentals), and after four years for cars, the test is then needed every two years until ten, then every year. The date (month/year) of the next due test date is noted on the sticker. In practice, the author sees many cars that should have the sticker, but there is often none to be seen on the windscreen. A possible cause for a fine of up to €300 but usually much less but still a pain to pay!

If a foreign-plated vehicle, it must have the current roadworthiness certificate (MOT, or other equivalent) with the vehicle.

PLEASE NOTE. Loss of vehicle original documents usually means an ITV check of the vehicle to ensure that the loss is genuine.

⇒ The *TARJETA DE INSPECCION TECHNICA DE VEHICULOS* (legal technical specification of the car, as supplied by the EU licensed manufacturer). This card is also used to record the ITV inspections on the reverse side.

⇒ You should also carry the standard accident report form, the *DECLARACIÓN AMISTOSA DE ACCIDENTE DE AUTOMÓVIL* ("agreed friendly statement of facts about a motor vehicle accident") supplied by your insurance company. If involved in an accident, the details can be legally binding in Court if signed by all drivers involved in an accident. The details must be correct in this form which is usually to be completed in Spanish unless your broker speaks English and will help with any translations needed. The form layout is standard thoughout the EU. A copy of this form, and notes on using it, in English is at the back of this book in case of need at the side of the road.

⇒ In addition, if towing (or carrying a vehicle), the documents relating to those vehicles should also be carried ready to show to an authorised official. In the case of a towed vehicle over 750 Kg MAM, the same documents are as if it is a motor vehicle. For "carried vehicles" on a low-bed, for example, proof of ownership or legal papers for the carriage as well.

⇒ Driving Licence (DL) *(PERMISO DE CONDUCCIÓN)*. It is legal to drive on your foreign EU type driving licence in Spain, even if you are resident here, but the conditions that apply to the Spanish drivers still apply to you if you are resident here for more than 6 months (183 days) in each calendar year, such as a medicals at age 45 years, (see DL page 124) and proof of residence. According to the EU Directive, you do not have to register your foreign EU licence at Trafico but it does have benefits as described later in this book. If you wish to change to a Spanish DL, it is easy and how to do it is at the back of this book. There is a lot of information on driving licences in this book some of which covers the rules on towing. The benefit of registration of the DL includes being advised of any renewals due to expiry dates or medicals by post, along with a temporary licence to use so the renewal can be done easily by mail.

⇒ If you are resident in Spain, you may obtain a Spanish licence without "losing" the right to a British/Irish document if you return to the UK, etc. However, it is an offence to have more than one driving licence regardless of where it is issued unless they are for different classifications or unless one is an International Driving Licence (IDL) which must always be accompanied by the original current licence. My web-site and this book has further information on IDLs.

⇒ An identification document for the driver/s such as a *RESIDENCIA* or from March 2007 a **CERTIFICATE OF RESIDENCE,** NIE or passport. If you have a driving licence with your photo on it, most authorities will accept this, but, as a visitor you should carry your passport with you anyway, or, as I do, good certified photocopies of all documents.

⇒ The receipt for the current year's payment of the local tax similar to the Road Fund tax elsewhere but paid to the local ayuntamiento (municipal council), and called in Spain the IMPUESTO MUNICIPAL SOBRE VEHICULOS DE TRACCION MECANICA.

Please note that the advantage of having a Spanish licence is that you will receive in the mail a letter advising you when it is about to expire giving you three month's notice, along with a temporary DL to use as you must send in your original licence. If you fail,to renew your licence for any classification on or before the date shown in the licence, after four years you are not able to renew it without a full driving school and test procedure. Obviously, from date of expiry where you have not renewed it, you are no longer legally allowed to drive.

You should also be aware as a resident here in Spain, that if you use your foreign EU driving licence without taking the medicals as the Spanish have to, and you are involved in a serious accident, if the other party's legal team or the police discover that you have not had the mandatory medical examinations, you could be described as not having a current driving licence. So although your UK licence, etc. may say it expires when you are 70 years of age, IN SPAIN IT IS NO LONGER LEGAL IF YOU HAVE NOT TAKEN THE MEDICAL. I know that a lot of the roadside police and Guardia Civil officers may not know this fact but if you have an accident where it goes to Court, a smart lawyer for the other driver is likely to know. The result could be that you are guilty regardless of who caused the accident because your DL was not current.

A copy of the official advice letter showing this is on my web-site (in Spanish).

⇒ <u>Non-EU citizens</u> must have an International Driver's Licence usually but not neccessarily, issued in their home country along with their valid normal foreign licence.

⇒ <u>RENTAL CARS</u>. The rental car must have the same vehicle documents. More information on rental cars documentation and legal needs is explained later in this book.

CLUNK, CLICK EVERY TRIP!

Trafico reports that during the Easter 2007 holiday week, 48% of those killed on the roads in motor vehicles in Spain were <u>not wearing seat-belts</u>, and later the same year, summer 2007, 60% of drivers and passengers in touring cars and small vans that died in road accidents were NOT wearing belts. One must be appalled at these terrible and very sad figures and wonder about the mentality of such people who after all the publicity about the deaths, fines and penalty points for this offence, which after all is meant to save lives, still do not get into THE HABIT of Clunking and Clicking every time they get behind the wheel and before they start the engine. And for making sure that all passengers have done the same, especially children. So please "belt up" everyone in the vehicle every trip, no matter how short. The more mature UK drivers will recognise the slogan above. Please be warned, the police are very serious about this offence and do not hesitate to give a stiff fine and take away your penalty points. Several years ago, I was in a car that turned over twice on a dirt road in South Africa after a total brake failure going down a steep hill to a T-junction. I was wearing a belt and after the car literally stopped rolling over twice, with the driver's door flying open and the roof collapsing a bit, I got out without even a bruise and just shook the broken glass out of my shirt. Needed a cup of strong, sweet tea though. Do not be frightened to speak nicely to those who are stupid enough to ignore this safety rule. You are doing them a big favour, and if they are in your vehicle, saving you and possibly them from the probability of a fine and loss of penalty points if caught.

BUYING FUEL IN SPAIN.

One of the first benefits that the British visitor will find is that fuel is much cheaper in Spain than in the UK, especially the difference in cost between petrol and diesel, and that is one reason why diesel cars are so popular in Spain. Well over 50% of new cars sold each year in Spain are now diesel powered. The following is information about buying fuel in Spain at the *gasolineras.*

These are the types of motor fuels in Spain. Each supplier has their own brand name for them: -

⇒	95-octane petrol (*Gasolina*) unleaded (*Sin Plomo*), commonest used.

⇒	Diesel (*Gasoleo*), standard good quality fuel for all diesel cars, turbo and non-turbo engines.

⇒	Super 98-octane petrol unleaded (*Gasolina, sin plomo*), for high performance cars.

⇒	Diesel (BP Ultimate, Repsol, etc). Claimed higher quality fuel for a few cents more per litre. Tests show it is cleaner and gives better fuel consumption.

⇒	97 octane Super with a lead replacement chemical for older cars.

⇒	Gasoloeo "B" Diesel, cheap lower quality fuel for older engines. Rare now and usually in small country garages. About 3/4-price of standard diesel, and was the only diesel fuel sold about 10 years ago. Now intended for industrial and old machine agricultural use. Be careful not to fill up you modern vehicle with this diesel fuel. It will damage your engine with much black smoke from the exhaust.

It is necessary to ensure that you use the correct fuel for your car if it is a rental (assuming you are familiar with your own car). Most rental cars have the fuel needed noted on a sticker next to the filler cap. As elsewhere in the EU, the service station hoses have colour codes for the different fuels and different size nozzles for petrol and diesel . If you use the wrong fuel, you will damage the car and be charged for the repairs if a rental car.   On a petrol car, this involves a new catalyser, on a diesel, usually a new expensive pump, plus other expensive items and maybe engine top-end repairs. On both petrol and diesel, the repairs are very expensive.

In Spain, as in most of Europe, in most service stations, you may be expected to fill your tank yourself, and then go to a cash desk to pay. A receipt will be given if asked for - (*Un recibo, por favor*—say it as " oon rethibo, por fabor").   Unless you have adult and fit strong passengers left in the car, *do not leave the keys* in the car or even the doors unlocked while you pay as it is not unknown for thieves to steal the car or its contents, especially at the first filling station near the airports.   And if your car is taken in this way, THERE WILL BE A PROBLEM WITH ANY INSURANCE CLAIM. Also it is against the law to use your mobile phone while in the fuelling area.

While on the subject, beware of anyone trying to distract your attention at any time with for example, telling you that your tyre is flat even while you are driving and sometimes they may be dressed as policemen but in a plain unmarked car. Often they are responsible for the damage. While you are taking your luggage out to get the spare tyre, they steal it and drive off. (I know that it has been written elsewhere in this book, but the author knows of someone who has been "caught" twice).

TRUST NOBODY.

Due to some drivers filling up and speeding off without paying, some stations need you to pay about €50 before they will let you fill-up or a specified amount which is then controlled from the cash desk, usually during the late hours and at night. So if the pump does not work, this is often the reason. There will be a notice at the pump, but it is usually in Spanish (of course!).

You are not allowed to use your mobile phone, or any similar radio emitting device, while filling up. You do not have to switch it off; just do not answer it if it rings.

Diesel fuel is about 5- 8% cheaper than 95 unleaded, and when the extra economy of the modern turbo-diesel engine-car is considered, the overall added fuel economy in running a diesel in Spain can be as much as 20 to 30% with little usable difference in normal on-road performance. As in other countries, many garages have a shop at which you may buy newspapers, wines, bread, and other quick food; many on the autovias also have a cafe serving hot meals and drinks. Many urban stations also have car washes, either drive through, or with a three stage (soap, wax and wash) hand-held high-flow gun in special bays. Also there are self-use vacuum cleaners, as well as the usual water and air points.

In many Provinces in Spain especially Andalucia, it is illegal to wash your vehicle in the street (to save water and for safety reasons in the narrow streets), so these services at service stations or special wash-bays are very useful, quick and cheap to use, and the water is often re-used after filtering. They also have the benefit, or should have, of having de-mineralised water for the final wash as the tap water in some Provinces, especially in parts of Andalucia, is very "limey" and can leave streaks on the bodywork if not immediately wiped clean. However, in Malaga City, not all of Malaga Province yet, but planned at several of the costas to overcome water shortages with all the golf courses and holiday makers in summer, they are now using de-salinated water from specially constructed factories. The water is virtually pure with no mineral content.

ROAD TYPES. (MORE DETAILS ARE IN THE SIGNS PAGES).

⇒ A *CALLE (cai-ye)* and an *AVENIDA* are roads/streets/avenues, where normally, there are speed limits of 50 kph (31 mph), unless otherwise signed, usually lower. They are mostly residential. Common prefixes are C/... for *Calle* & *Avda.* for Avenue. An urban residential road without pedestrian paths usually has a 20kph (12 mph) speed limit <u>even if there are no signs</u>, and when passing any pedestrian, you must give a gap of at least 1-1/2 metres (or 4-1/2 feet). Remember this also if a vehicle hits you as a pedestrian.

⇒ A *PASAJE* (pasa-ke) is a passage; not usually open to motor traffic.

⇒ A *PASEO MARITIMO (paseyo maree-teemo)* is a road alongside a beach and may be open or closed to traffic.

⇒ A *CARRETERA* is a main trunk road or often a by-pass if near a town; it can be a 4-lane with a centre divider. It can also be a national road. The limits are up to a usually posted 100 kph (62 mph). A *carretera* may change into an *AUTOVIA* when leaving the city limits and will be signed as such similar to the motorway signs in Britain, etc. If a three lane with a central lane for overtaking, you should turn on your headlights for safety so the cars travelling the other way can see you are approaching them.

⇒ An *AUTOVIA* is a "fast" dual four-lane carriageway (at least two each way) and is usually a national road. It is usually to motorway standards and prefixed "A"..

⇒ An *AUTOPISTA* is a motorway-classed road, which is often a toll-road (*PEAJE* or pe-a-kay), built as a high-speed motorway/freeway/expressway. It is identified with a number prefixed "AP". The limit for most vehicles is 120 kph, although you may see expensive cars doing expensive speeds (if they are caught). On the toll roads, rates are often increased in summer (doubled?) on the holiday routes. They are usually quite empty out of season as the Spanish, as elsewhere, do not like paying tolls and there is usually an alternative route. There is more detailed information on Toll roads in this book. Please refer to the pages 56 - 59.

⇒ A *TRAVESIA* is a through-way main road in a small town where traffic has to use to stay on the main road. Caution is advised as they are favourite spots for mobile speed traps.

Roads are signed by not only the national Spanish route number eg. N or A, but also local and European route numbers: -

⇒ Road Prefix e.g. "N" followed by a number. BG= background colour.

⇒ Type of road. (More on road types in the signs pages)

E (red BG)	European network number. Often continues into adjoining EU country.
A (Blue BG)	Autopista or Autovia. (Motorway standards)
AP (Blue BG)	Can be a toll road (*Peaje*)
N (Red BG)	National. A Provincial main trunk road. If followed by a Roman number (e.g."N - IV"), the road will continue into the next Province.
D (Yellow BG)	Provisional destination or diversion (*desvio*) road. (Usually due to Road works.)

Notes:

1. If a road is 6,5 metres (19, 7 feet) or less, it is officially a "narrow road".
2. If a lane is 3 metres (9, 8 feet) or less, it is legally a narrow lane. This usually causes signs denoting rights of way when two vehicles meet head on, and restrictions on overtaking.
3. A "road" is anywhere public or private that is open to the public. Thus a commercial car park is legally a road subject to the same laws as anywhere else on public roads. For example, learners are not allowed to be taught there without a qualified instructor and vehicle. Safety and insurance are the main considerations.
4. The hard shoulder is legally part of the road but is intended for emergency use only (autovias, peajes and carreteras). It is not to be used for parking, use of a mobile phone, etc.
5. Hard shoulders may be used by vehicles with a MAM of up to 3.500 Kg when they are unable to travel fast so blocking traffic. An example would be scooters and quadricycles.
6. Permanent lanes for the use of taxis and buses (in cities) and special vehicles everywhere are not to be used by other traffic (except police, fire vehicles and ambulances).
7. Hard shoulders are not strong enough to support heavy vehicles, 3.500 KG plus. They are not allowed to travel on them. Basically hard shoulders are to support the main roadways to resist deterioration of the surface by heavy traffic.
8. In some areas there are lanes reserved specifically for bicycles. They are clearly marked both with signs on posts and painted on the lanes.
9. Roundabouts are special usually busy junctions to allow traffic to change direction without the use of traffic lights. See page 112 for more information.

ROADS TYPES, CONTINUED.

10. A Lay-by is an area for vehicles to park for a specific purpose without obstructing traffic and is signed as such. See traffic signs pages.

11. Emergency braking areas are sections of the road to the right that have deep gravel and protection walls in them so a vehicle with failing brakes can pull in and stop safely.

12. Split traffic circles are not referred to as roundabouts by the Spanish authorities. More on these on page 110-113.

13. Railway crossings are where the road passes over railway lines and the entrance is controlled by usually bar-gates. There are accidents every year in Spain where vehicles try to "beat the train". Signs are on posts and on the roads. Please refer to signs pages.

14. Speed bumps. Most in Spain are very dangerous especially those steel formed for scooters with small diameter wheels. These also damage/wear excessively vehicle suspensions. They must have signs warning of them in good time on the approach.

15. Depression. Where the road has a "formed ditch" to allow water to cross it when it rains. Must also be well signed on the approach.

16. Road islands. These are marked with cross hatches painted in white on the road. Despite what you may see, vehicles are not allowed to park on them and penalty points will be lost for offenders. They are designed to channel traffic to the correct entrance or exit at that point and to give good visibilty. The only vehicles allowed to travel on these areas are those as on hard shoulders and people walking with animals.

17. Separator or median. A safety barrier between the opposing directions on a road to avoid head-on collisions. They direct out of control vehicles back into the correct direction of travel. Many are now made of sections of precast concrete positively joined together to stop heavy vehicles seperating them, or possibly the corrugated steel strips on wooden posts known commercially as "Armco". Both are dangerous to motorcycle riders.

18. Emergency lane or shoulder. On rural roads this is the area that may be partly tarred or dirt but levelled so a vehicle can drive (driver has lost control?) onto it. There may be a drainage ditch at the side.

19. Central reservation or median. A wide strip of grassed land with no barriers (but perhaps a drainage ditch) between two opposing directions of travel. Bushes may be planted to not only reduce headlight glare, but to slow down a vehicle that has left the road. The area is usually wide enough so a vehicle can avoid entering the other opposing lanes.

20. Red and White Chequerboard painted on a steep downhill road. Indicates the emergency braking and stopping area on the right is ahead. Gives notice to a driver so he/she can start the emergency stopping in good time.

21. Pedestrian areas are places, elevated or not, where pedestrians have sole right of way. Parking on or in a pedestrian way/area can lose the driver points.

22. Thick white lines. As in other countries and you are not allowed to turn left across these unless there is a DOTTED LINE BREAK in the solid white line at the turning point. Often you can go to a roundabout a short distance further on and come back to make a safe turn.

23. At city junctions, the normal "cross-hatch pattern " painted in yellow on the road is often to be found. You are not allowed to drive onto this area until you can see that you can definitely exit it. If the traffic lights change and you cannot move thus blocking the junction, it could mean a €300 fine from the local policeman who is watching for such drivers who seem to be ignorant of the Law.

GENERAL SPEED LIMITS FOR VEHICLES AND OTHER INFORMATION

(Please also refer to the pages on traffic signs.)

<u>Referring to the table on next page:</u>

1. The speed limits on non-autovias are often varied for a short section where, for example there may be a series of slow curves. Instead of recommending a safe speed, the actual speed limit is reduced and shown by the "must do" white circle, red border, black number sign. Speed traps at these points if it is a known accident black spot, may occur.

2. The maximum posted speed may be legally exceeded by up to 20 kph if needed to safely pass another vehicle where the traffic is two way, e.g. not on an autovia.

3. The minimum allowed speed is half that of normal traffic in the same class except where signed.

4. All terrain vehicles (ATVs) are restricted to what the Technical Specification Card states unless the speed must be lower due to restrictions on the specific vehicle e.g. carrying a dangerous product.

<u>Additional Notes.</u>

⟹ Probationer drivers. During the first year after passing the test, new drivers are restricted to a maximum speed anywhere of 80 kph. In town it is 50 kph and any transgression can result in the order for a retest. (It is recognised that many younger drivers often are liable to have accidents after passing the test due to over-confidence.)

⟹ Buses authorised to carry standing passengers are restricted to 80 kph maximum and a minimum of half that speed.

⟹ When driving on a three-lane road where the centre lane is for overtaking in both directions, the vehicle's dipped headlights are to be on as a safety precaution. (No one seems to know this!)

⟹ There are other road signs such as large lit boards (and in tunnels), road markings and temporary road signs such as the yellow background road works that supercede the overall speed limit as signed previously on that road.

⟹ The maximum speed for cycles (yes), three wheeled mopeds, light quadricycles (no B-licence required), and vehicles for handicapped persons on the road (not the foot-paths) is limited to 45 kph (28 mph). However, cyclists may exceed 45 kph on roads where it is safe to do so on the open roads, but not in urban and residencial areas.

⟹ Some drivers have disabilities that have resulted in a legal restriction on their maximum speed they can drive. Having only one eye is one such cause.

⟹ If a speed restriction is painted on the road in a specific lane, the restriction only refers to that lane.

⟹ You must not drive too slowly for your vehicle and the conditions. It is an offence and a cause of a significant number of accidents each year and can attract a fine and/or penalty points.

TABLE OF THE MAXIMUM AND MINIMUM SPEED LIMITS IN SPAIN

Roads / Vehicles	Autopista (Peajes) and Autovias. Max & Min speeds	Roads for cars only. Conventional roads with a tarred hard shoulder width of 1, 5 m and at least two lanes in either direction and with an additional centre lane for overtaking.	Other conventional roads	Built up areas. Towns and City Roads In-Town highways.
Motorcycles and private cars	120 -- 60	100 -- 50 (2)	90 -- 45 (2)	50 -- 25
Buses Adaptable mixed vehicles	100 -- 60	90 -- 45	80 -- 40	50 -- 25
Goods vehicles and vans Articulated vehicles	90 -- 60	80 -- 40	70 -- 35	50 -- 25
Automobiles with a trailer less than or equal to 750 kg.	90 -- 60	80 -- 40	70 -- 35	50 -- 25
Other automobiles with a trailer	80 -- 60	80 -- 40	70 -- 35	50 -- 25
Newly qualified drivers (first year)	80 -- 60	80 (3)	80 (5) & (3)	50 -- 25
Special vehicles without brake lights with a trailer and agricultural cultivators		25	25	25
Other special vehicles such as earthmoving machinery.		40	40	40
Those that can reach 60 kph on level ground	70 -- 60	70 -- 35	70 -- 35	50 -- 25
Three wheeled vehicles and light quadricycles	70 -- 60	70 -- 35	70 -- 35	50 -- 25
Cycles, two and three wheeled mopeds, quadricycles and vehicles for handicapped people.		45	45	45

⇒ If travelling on an autovia or autopista (toll road) and your vehicle has problems but you can still travel, you must leave at the next exit.

⇒ You must not approach road junctions faster than 50 kph (in the absence of signs with a lower number) where you do not have clear visibility of traffic from all directions.

⇒ Small pueblos (villages) often have a speed limit sign close to or on the name sign of the village on the entry roads. This is for the whole village except where otherwised signed. Where it is before the sign by say 50 metres, it only applies up to the sign and is a slow down area but if no other speed limit sign is evident, this limit still applies as it is the standard for residential areas.

⇒ Where there are no pavements in a residential area, unless otherwise signed the legal limit is 20 kph (12 mph) and pedestrians always have priority.

⇒ Where there are signs with a lower limit to 50 kph, and showing, for example, children playing, extreme caution is necesary with special regard to childen playing in the roads.

⇒ Cyclist must be given a wide berth when being passed and if necessary speed lowered to allow for an emergency. An accident with a cyclist usually is blamed on the motorist.

⇒ When a vehicle cannot reach the miniumum allowed speed for its class and the road, the emergency lights (4-way flashers) must be turned on.

⇒ If when travelling, usually on the open roads, the traffic ahead slows rapidly or stops, it is expected that you will operate the emergency lights to warn following traffic to avoid a collision. This must save a lot of rear end collisions being caused by bad drivers.

⇒ If you expect to travel at low speeds on escort duty (abnormal load, etc) your vehicle is expected to show a large sign on the roof stating "V-21"or "V-22" to warn other traffic.

⇒ When a maximum speed sign is on a danger warning sign, the speed returns to the normal for that road when the end of danger sign appears.

⇒ In the absence of a speed limit sign on autovias, the maximum speed will automatically be 80 kph. Normally it is 120 kph with signs every kilometre or so.

⇒ The following vehicles must reduce their speed by 10 kph when on intercity roads:
- Cars and buses carrying school students.
- Vehicles transporting minors (buses).
- Vehicles transporting hazardous materials.

⇒ Vehicles transporting hazardous materials must also reduce the speed below the posted limits in towns by 10 kph.

⇒ Most people do not obey this but if TOWING, the maximum speeds allowed are 80 or 90 kph depending on the vehicle and road type. See speed table on page 21.

CHECKING YOUR VEHICLE SPEEDOMETER FOR ACCURACY USING A STOP WATCH.

By dividing 3 600 seconds by the speed being checked over one kilometre, you will see whether or not your speedometer is accurate. Most speedometers are not accurate at higher speeds and generally over-read: that is they read that you are going faster than you actually are. This means that you can exceed the speed limit according to your speedometer by about 5% depending on your vehicle, without actually breaking the Law, but if you want to be sure, you can easily check your speed using the Km sign-posts on most *autopistas/autovias*. For the equivalent mph, multiply the kilometre speed by 0,61 or use the conversion table on next page.

EXAMPLE: Speed being checked with stopwatch between kilometre signs = 100 kph. Drive your vehicle to set your speedo-reading to a constant indicated 100 kph (or 62 mph). In this example, the actual watch reading is 37,5 seconds.

3.600 / 37,5 = 96 kph.   The true speed is 96 kph.

EXAMPLE TIMINGS over One Kilometre.

True Speed, kph	Secs/Km	True Speed, kph	Secs/Km
35	103	80	45
50	72	90	40
60	60	100	36
70	51,5	120	30

For safety's sake, always do this check on an "empty" road.

To check KPH speeds if you have a classic older car with an MPH Speedometer, refer to next page.

SPEED CONVERSION TABLES.

To convert <u>kph to mph</u> or <u>mph to kph</u>, select speed in mph or kph (X) in centre columns, and read in next column for converted speed.

MPH	X	KPH		MPH	X	KPH
18,6	30	48,3		86,9	140	225,3
21,7	35	56,3		90,0	145	233,3
24,8	40	64,4		93,2	150	241,4
21,7	35	56,3		96,3	155	249,4
31,1	50	80,5		99,4	160	257,4
34,2	55	88,5		102,5	165	265,5
37,3	60	96,5		105,6	170	273,5
40,4	65	104,6		108,7	175	281,6
43,5	70	112,6		111,8	180	289,6
46,6	75	120,7		114,9	185	297,7
49,7	80	128,7		118,0	190	305,7
52,8	85	136,8		121,1	195	313,8
55,9	90	144,8		124,2	200	321,8
59,0	95	152,9		130,4	210	337,9
62,1	100	160,9		133,5	215	345,9
65,2	105	168,9		136,6	220	354,0
68,3	110	177,0		139,7	225	362,0
71,4	115	185,0		142,8	230	370,1
74,5	120	193,1		145,9	235	378,1
77,6	125	201,1		149,0	240	386,2
80,7	130	209,2		152,1	245	394,2
83,8	135	217,2		155,3	250	402,3

SPEED CAMERAS IN SPAIN.

In 2001, Spain was the third worst in the (old) EU for deaths and injuries on the roads, but a concerted effort seems to paying off, although there is still a way to go. There are eventually expected to be 500 speed cameras in Spain, with many fixed, and quite a few mobile. Unlike for example, the UK where the cameras are thought by many to be money grabbing devices, the Spanish ones are sited in known accident black spots only. The fixed cameras can be located by going the government Trafico web-site where maps show exactly where they are. This web site address is at (click) and then click on the province you will be travelling through.

http://www.dgt.es/trafico/radares/radares.htm

Naturally, it is in Spanish, but is easy to follow if you do not understand this language and if going on a long journey, it is an easy matter to mark on your map where they are. Remember that *ascendente* means increasing and *descendente* means decreasing. They refer to the way you are travelling when the Km markers where the cameras are noted in the web site. E.g. 128, 34 *ascendente* means that the Km markers are reading 128, 129, 130 etc, as you drive and the fixed camera is at the 128, 34 position on the road.

NAVIGATION SYSTEMS AND RADAR TRAPS.

As we all should know now, as noted above, there is an increasing network of fixed radar cameras around Spain, and the location of each one is recorded in the Trafico web site, where we can all go and note down before our journeys. We also should know that it is illegal in Spain to have a device that receives and warns drivers of a radar traps ahead where the information is purely by the receipt of the radar gun signal, but it is not illegal to have a navigation device in your car where the places where the radar traps are situated and are noted in the software and then warn the driver that he/she is about to approach that zone by using Global Positioning Systems. When you think about it, why should it be illegal because not only arc the traps noted in the Trafico web-site, but large signs are set up on the approach in good time so it would be very difficult to justify banning the warning of these traps this way. Buy shares in the companies making these systems? Maybe not because although it is illegal to use a "held to the ear" mobile phone in Spain, by far the most drivers have not bought hands free kits for their vehicles, especially delivery vans, and can be seen daily in large numbers still using them illegally. But many are buying "SatNav" systems.

For those who have, be warned that the type that is held to the windscreen with a suction cup and that leaves a witness mark on the glass when it is removed, cars are being broken into as most drivers place the SatNav in the glove compartment. The same applies to those with a fixed cradle that a portable SatNav drops into. Trafico warns owners to take care.

USEFUL PHONE NUMBERS

At the national numbers, there will be someone who speaks English. and able to help you. Please note that the numbers will connect you to the local nearest authority. It is suggested that you put the emergency ones in your mobile.

Emergency (same as UK 999 or USA 911)	**112**
National number for the Guardia Civil. Accidents on the "out of town" roads.	**062**
Local Police. Urban accidents.	**092**
National Police. (For a serious crime).	**091**

Consulates and Embassies.

Locality	British	Irish
Alicante	965 21 60 22	
Balearics	971 36 33 73	
Balearics	971 30 18 16	
Barcelona	376 355 660	934 91 50 21
Bilbao	944 15 76 00	944 23 04 14
Fuengirola, Malaga		952 47 51 08
Las Palmas	928 26 25 08	928 29 77 28
Madrid	915 24 97 00	914 36 40 93
Malaga	952 35 23 00	
Mallorca	971 71 24 45	971 71 82 29
Santander	942 22 00 00	
Seville		954 21 63 61
Tenerife	922 28 68 63	922 24 56 71
Vigo, Galicia	986 43 71 33	

INTERNATIONAL CLASSIFICATION OF VEHICLES.

The following table shows the international classification of vehicles with a brief description. (MAM = Maximum Authorised Mass, or legal fully loaded weight).

Vehicles for persons	Vehicles for goods	Trailers
Category M Vehicles with at least 4 wheels used to transport people	Category N Motor vehicles with 4 wheels used to transport goods.	Category O Trailer including semi-trailer
Category M1 Not more than 8 seats plus the driver's.	Category N1 As above, MAM not exceeding 3,5 tonnes	Category O1 Trailers and light semi-trailers, MAM up to 750 kg.
Category M2 More than 8-seats not including the driver's MAM not exceeding 5 tonnes	Category N2 MAM over 3,5 tons, but not more than 12 tons.	Category O2 MAM over 750 kg, up to 3,5 tons.
Category M3 More than 8-seats not incl. the driver's. MAM over 5-tonnes	Category N3 MAM above 12 tonnes	Category O3 MAM over 3,5 tons, up to 10 tonnes.
		Category O4 MAM over 12-tonnes

AXLE WEIGHTS In order to prevent damage to the road surfaces, in conjunction with manufacturers' specifications, the maximum loads on any vehicle must not be more than the figures below on all roads in the EU. Some owners of heavy goods vehicles grossly overload their vehicles causing danger not only to themselves and delays to other road users.

The maximum weight per axle on heavy goods vehicles (HGVs) in Spain is: -

Axles used to power the vehicle	11,5 tonnes
Non-powered axles	10 tonnes

This means that if a HGV has six axles with one driven axle, the MAM cannot be more than (5 x 10) + (1 x 11,5) = 61,5 tonnes which also must not be more that the permitted MAM for the vehicle. The limits in the UK are less, and have been the cause of controversy where Continental-based trucks damage UK highways.

Please note that in Spain a moped or scooter with an engine up to 49 cc is not considered to be a motor-vehicle.

ACCIDENT RATES ON THE ROADS IN SPAIN

Spain can be a dangerous place to drive, although the worst places are, as everywhere else, the big cities and their urban areas due to the density of traffic. The *Ministerio del Interior*, of which Trafico is a department, is currently involved in a concerted campaign to improve the statistics and in the last few years, there has been a great improvement.

However there is a long way to go because looking around every day, many Laws are still just ignored by drivers. The obvious ones are using a mobile phone while at the wheel and riding a scooter or small moto without a crash helmet. I think that many of us have had near misses caused by the idiots who still concentrate on their mobile phone, held to the ear, not even using a hands-free set up: I know I have. And while we all think that it is the scooter rider's fault if he / she wants to kill themselves, if they involve you, it is going to cost you not only money, but a lot of emotional stress. We all just do not need it.

Too many of the deaths are reported to be pedestrians, so please remember the golden rule when leaving a junction <u>in a vehicle</u> or <u>crossing the road on foot</u>,

LOOK BOTH WAYS TWICE

and please make it a habit. Many of the UK and Irish pedestrians have been killed or injured because the person <u>looked the wrong way once</u> before stepping into the road or pulling out from an intersection in their vehicle.

Another common fault is driving too fast in the narrow roads where pedestrians are common. If there is no obvious restriction sign, remember that in the pueblos (villages) the name sign of the village on the road entering it often has a speed sign over or near the name sign indicating the overall speed limit in the village. Where there are no footpaths there is automatically a legal limit of 20 kph unless it is signed otherwise, eg 10 or 30 kph (6 or 20 mph). There is a legal requirement to give pedestrians a clearance of 1,5 metres (4-1/2 feet) when you pass them.

MAIN CAUSES OF ACCIDENTS IN SPAIN.

The following are the main causes of traffic accidents in Spain (in 2006) according to the research carried out by Trafico.

- Distractions such as lighting a cigarette or using a mobile phone, eating, naughty children, etc. are the main cause of road traffic accidents in Spain;.
- Excessive speed is the second cause.
- 70% to 80% of accidents are due to human errors.
- There are about 5,500 deaths and 150,000 injuries on Spain's roads every year, but except for the summer months in 2007, the rates have dropped possibly due to speed cameras.
- It costs each Spanish adult resident about €400 a year for accidents on the roads.
- The total cost is €16,000 million euros (£11 034 483 759).
- 55% of traffic accidents occur on motorways and dual carriageways.
- 45% of traffic accidents happen in built-up areas.
- Excessive speed means there are 5 times more deaths on motorways and dual carriageways than in built-up areas.
- But injuries are more severe in built-up areas (pedestrians?).
- Pedestrian deaths are more likely than survival if the vehicle speed is above 55kph (33 mph).
- Above 80 kph (50 mph) most pedestrians hit by a vehicle die. (Look both ways when crossing the streets.)
- About 700 pedestrians die in Spain each year, that is one 1 every 12 hours.
- Most accidents occur on straight stretches of road, not bends.
- The older the vehicle, the more likely a mechanical failure is to occur.
- Main vehicle failures that occur are due to lighting, steering, brakes, excess vehicle weight and, above all else, the poor state of tyres.
- Excessive speed is responsible for 1 of every 5 accidents that cause at least one death.
- Over 40% of Spaniards admit having driven whilst drunk,
- And between 30 and 50% of mortal accidents are caused by drunk drivers.

TABLE SHOWING DOWNWARD TREND IN ACCIDENT DEATH RATES.

Type of Vehicle	Total Victims - Deaths			
	2003	2004	Diff. Numbers (+) / -	% -Variation
Bicycle	58	66	8	+13,79
Moped/scooter (up to 49 cc)	169	143	- 26	- 15.38
Motorcycle (49 cc plus)	230	272	42	+18,26
Cars	2.608	2.176	- 432	- 16,56
Vans	268	248	- 20	- 7,46
Autobuses	19	3	- 16	- 84,21
Trucks, Rigid.	72	65	- 7	- 9,72
Articulated trucks	117	115	- 2	- 1,71
Other vehicles	94	97	3	+3,19
Pedestrians	394	326	- 68	- 17,26
Totals	4.029	3.511	- 518	- 12,86

While most classifications show an improvement, motorcycles (motos) especially show an alarming increase and, after Trafico analysis, has led to the raising of the starting age for moto-riders from 14 to 16 years to start late in 2005. Bicycle rider deaths have also increased, and the Laws introduced in 2004 hope to lessen these, which appear to be mainly due to collisions with motor vehicles. Drivers having to give way to cyclists, especially at road junctions and roundabouts, is now one of the Laws, and, as a vehicle driver, a collision with a cyclist will be difficult to defend.

YOU HAVE A SERIOUS PROBLEM IF YOU AN ACCIDENT WITH A CYCLIST.

RENTAL VEHICLES - GENERAL ADVICE

In Andalucia alone, according to an official survey in 2003, on average each year, over 800.000 vehicle-weeks (one car for a week) are rented by customers who speak English. The following is noted for your attention to consider as important when you collect, use and return your vehicle.

⇒ Make sure that the vehicle cost covers all that you need, remembering that in Spain you can be forced to pay injury damages by the Criminal Court as well as a civil Court. This means that if you injure or kill someone while you are driving drunk (for example), the <u>Criminal Court</u>, while sentencing you for the offence of driving under the influence, can also award damages to the victims.

⇒ When you collect your rental car, you will be tired after the journey, excited that you have arrived, and generally just want to take possession of the vehicle and get on your way. Be prepared to stay "cool" and follow the check list procedures noted here to save money and possible future stress.

⇒ Check there is at least one approved reflective jacket - *chaleco* (preferably two) and this must be <u>kept in the passenger section</u> of the car so it can be put on <u>before getting out</u>, day and night, outside of urban areas (these being a 50 kph speed limit and with street-lighting). Do not accept the car without these as <u>you</u> will be fined if stopped, not the rental company. They must supply the jacket, no arguments. They are cheap enough although you may be asked for a cash deposit for all legal accessories that will be returned.

⇒ Check there is a spare lamp (bulb) kit for the car, with, if needed, a tool to change them at the side of the road. The tool is usually a small screwdriver but you may be expected to use it if stopped by the police because a lamp or bulb has failed. Unable to change it means about a €90 fine paid on the spot if you do not live in Spain.

⇒ If you wear glasses for driving, have a spare pair in the car. You may be asked to show them to a policeman.

⇒ You must have your <u>driving licence and identification with you at all times</u>, unlike the UK. No licence - you will most likely have to leave the car at the side of the road and be fined, <u>and</u> possibly lose penalty points. It happens all too frequently and the EU is arranging for the transference of points penalties to the driver's home country.

⇒ Drivers were expected to have "bail bonds" until recently. These were (usually) insured capital amounts that could be left with the police or Court to ensure that you turned up fro the subsequent legal proceedings thus avoiding a period in jail. As an EU citizen, they are no longer needed as, if necessary, extradition is not a problem now.

⇒ Make sure that the fuel level in the tank is "as taken". Some rental companies supply the car with a full tank and it must be returned as such, others, the tank can be empty when returned as it was when collected. Remember to fill up quickly if nearly empty. Some readers have complained that as much as €80 has been debited from their credit card after they have returned the car. Another reason to get the return paperwork signed that the vehicle is OK.

BE CAREFUL OF THIEVES AT ALL SERVICE AREAS.

There are thieves who wait at airports, Malaga and Murcia are noted for the problem, who check likely targets and then follow them to the first fuel-service station. They then have tricks to divert your attention away from your vehicle so they can then steal luggage or handbags, etc. especially if you are on your own. Lock the car before you pay the bill at the cash desk. Do not leave the keys in the car. TRUST NO ONE.

SPECIAL NOTE FOR RENTAL CAR FINANCES.

Please remember that the rental company has your credit card number (perhaps?) and may debit your card after you have returned the car for any damage not found when it was returned.

GET THE RELEASE FORM SIGNED AND TAKE THE COPY BEFORE YOU LEAVE.

Also under Spanish Law, your rental agent has to give your full details to the police in the event of any traffic offence being committed while the car was in your "charge", such as going through a camera trap at excess speed, etc.

INSTRUCTIONS (LAWS) ON USE OF CHILDS' SEATS.

All instructions refer to the compulsory EU-CE approved child's seats and carry-cots. All children must be carried in a manner to ensure a maximum chance of survival in the event of an accident, and even when a vehicle is forced to make a sudden stop. For this reason, all people in vehicles up to nine seats including the driver, must wear an approved seat-belt if fitted and in the case of children, approved seats specially designed for this purpose. Devices such as airbags are also a great benefit but not if they injure the child, so child's carry cots must not be placed in the front.

The following information advises the driver in Spain (and the EU), even for rental cars, what is needed for children. It is best that you advise the company at the time of booking the vehicle if you will need the equipment.

⇒ Up to age 9 months and up to 10 Kg, a carrycot must be used laid across the rear seat and <u>secured with cars's safety belt/s</u> or any specially approved attachment.

⇒ From 10 Kg to 13 Kg, and up to 2-years old, a child's car seat fitted in the rear with the child facing rearwards.

⇒ From 9 Kg to 18 Kg and from 9 months to 3 years old, child's seat facing front or rearwards, fitted in the rear of the car and secured as in the seat's instructions.

⇒ From 15 to 25 Kg, and 3 to 6 years old, use a seat adaptor (elevator) to lift child up to fit comfortably with, if necessary, a CE-EU approved seat belt adaptor.

⇒ From 22 to 36 Kg, and 6 to 12 years old, use a seat elevator so that child is comfortably protected using the normal car seat belts correctly fitted.

In all cases, the driver must exercise common sense in ensuring that the child has adequate protection in the event of any sudden stop, or the best chance of surviving a crash. With this in mind, children up to the age of 12 years are not allowed to sit in the front seat, but if your child is big e.g. 1,5 metres tall at this age and fits the standard seat belts <u>comfortably</u>, the police are not likely to take any action. Also, if there are no airbags in the front, the police may not insist on the rear seat rule being obeyed for the child seat, but you could still be stopped for a check. Make sure that there are no loose objects on the rear shelf. These can cause injury in a crash and this is a simple precaution that is not often taken.

The author sees cars every day with children with no seat belts, and it is a shame when a child is killed or injured because of the stupidity of the driver, who by Law, is responsible in all cases. As I prepare this book, the Press reports three children killed in one accident in Spain. None were wearing seat belts or seated in approved seats but just allowed to "run around" in the car. There has been recent Trafico reports that that 1 in 3 drivers stopped in road blocks were not wearing a seat belt and this will automatically earn a fine of about €300 plus three points. It is also a sobering thought that over a holiday period in 2007, 60% of the people in cars and small buses that were killed were not wearing seat belts, so please be warned: the police are very strict about this law.

Rental Car Checks, - Continued.

Also in the Semana Santa week (Easter) in 2007, 48% of the people killed in Spain WERE NOT WEARING SEAT BELTS. We should all wonder what is wrong with people who are so stupid, remembering that many were passengers. It is the driver's responsibility to ensure that all in the vehicle correctly wear seat belts, and that the children are in approved seats as described in this book.

But many people, sadly mostly Spanish, with the most precious "possession" they are ever likely to have, their children, do not take this precaution. Shame on them!

⇒ Check that you have a copy of the Insurance Report Form in English if you are not fluent in Spanish. The one in the rental car will most likely be in Spanish. This is important if you have an accident where the other driver does not speak English and a copy of the form in ENGLISH is in the back of this book. (You are warned not to sign the accident form unless you are 100% confident that it the information is correct as even if you are not at fault, you could be deemed to be so, if the other driver's description is a lie and you sign the form agreeing to it.)

⇒ Exterior bodywork for damage. Before accepting the vehicle, report every mark in writing on the form. Some companies may charge you for respraying a whole panel (€150+) for a small mark on the paintwork.

⇒ Plastic wheel trims, most companies now remove them as they can be stolen or fall off and you are then subsequently charged for replacing them. You will also be identified as a rental car-user by potential thieves because the car has no wheel trims. These thieves target tourists because they know they are "green" and excited as well as probably tired, and also may be leaving the country soon so identification of the thieves at a later date is difficult.

⇒ Engine oil and radiator levels. Check these with the agent present if possible. The author has collected cars with very low oil level (and high oil consumption), and you are charged for any engine damage caused. The check is easy to do and worthwhile TRUST NOBODY.

⇒ After you have left the pick-up point, check exhaust is clear with engine running "hard": no excessive blue or black smoke from the exhaust. You could be accused of damaging the engine when you return the vehicle. If you are concerned, report it to the depot as soon as possible.

⇒ You may be asked for a returnable deposit (€30?)for the mandatory triangles, spare lighting bulb kit and yellow jackets. Remember to allow time to get your cash back when returning the vehicle, as well as having it checked for (no?) damage.

⇒ <u>CHECK TYRE PRESSURES AS SOON AS POSSIBLE</u>. The author has rented cars in many parts of the world, and experience shows that, in as much as 80% of cases the tyres are under-inflated, often dangerously so, even though the rental company clerk has insisted that the tyres have "just been checked". As in any country, as the driver, you are responsible in the event of an accident. If you are not sure of the pressure, 200 kpa or 2 bars (32 psi) is safe unless you are heavily laden, then 220 to 240 kpa. A tyre pressure comparison chart is in this book.

⇒ All tyres have a wear block on them to show when they should be changed. The law states that the tyre must have minimum of 1, 6 mm depth of tread across the width of the tyre and around all the circumference. If it is the rainy season (September to May) make sure the tyres have good tread depth, much more than the minimum if possible. Independent tyre testing has shown that in wet weather on roads awash with water, 3 mm is a better bet for safety. Reject the car if you are not happy as I have done several times. It is amazing how quickly they find another car, often almost new. It is your life or holiday at stake.

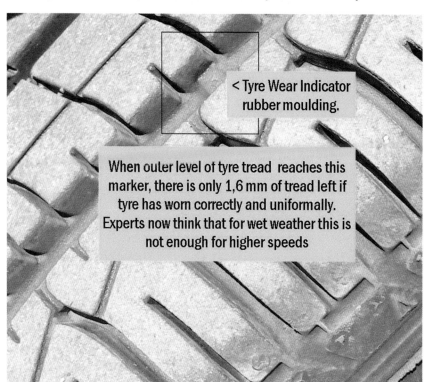

< Tyre Wear Indicator rubber moulding.

When outer level of tyre tread reaches this marker, there is only 1,6 mm of tread left if tyre has worn correctly and uniformally. Experts now think that for wet weather this is not enough for higher speeds

With a tread depth of even 2 mm, in heavy rain, speeds have to be kept very low (not more than 90 kph–55 mph) to avoid sliding or "aquaplaning" in an emergency. ABS braking systems (an acronym for Anti-locking Braking System) will not stop you "floating" (aquaplaning) on the rain-water covered roads, nor will they allow you to stop more quickly except in certain circumstances.

While mentioning ABS braking systems, many drivers think that they can allow you to brake in a shorter distance.   This is not strictly true, except perhaps on a very wet or greasy road where the driver is not a trained expert.   The main advantage of ABS is that you can maintain steering control while braking heavily, even on a mixed road surface (tar and dirt?).   On a slippery road, especially after it rains after a long dry period, instead of sliding out of control off the road, you can still steer the car hopefully away from other traffic, but the tyres ability to grip the road and stop you in a shorter distance because of the ABS braking system is mostly a fallacy, especially if you are an advanced driver.

For those who do not know what ABS brakes are, there is more on them and other safety devices in this book in the Tyre Section on pages 79 - 82.

VEHICLE ENGINE CAM DRIVE BELTS.

Most vehicles have one of two different methods of driving the timing cam from the crankshaft to the head/s in the engine. One is by a chain similar to that used on bicycles and this is by far the oldest. But it is expensive to incorporate in an engine and is a source of noise when it gets worn along with the need to change the sprockets in the drive chain. A newer device and by far the most common now is the "Kelvar" fabric and steel toothed-belt which is cheaper to make, quieter in operation and easy to change when it is worn. As the belt must ensure that the valves in the engine open in time with the corresponding position of the crankshaft, any failure is catastrophic and will cause the engine to stop at the road side with an expensive repair needed to the cylinder head and maybe the pistons.

Manufacturers state two options where the belt must be changed as a service item, and they are MILEAGE and AGE. Most service garages recognise the mileage need but many (most) forget the age need because most cars exceed this recommended figure before the age change becomes due. But this is no excuse for the acknowledged trained experts for missing this service item to the customer's expensive disadvantage.

One retired reader who does a small mileage each year with his bought new Ford Mondeo had a failure at 67.000 km after 8-1/2 years of ownership. The Ford handbook specified 105.000 km OR five years for the life of the toothed drive-belt. As the car had been serviced only by the local Ford agency (Costa Blanca), when the belt broke the car was GRUAed to them for a repair for which he was duly charged about €3.500 as it was deemed to be out of warranty. After writing to me for advice, I said that he must get the bill for the repair reversed and get his money back plus expenses as the Ford agency service department had failed in their professional work by not following the Ford recommended service periods and it was their task to advise the customer of the need. The reader advised that the need for change had not been discussed at any time.

Why put this in a book about the laws you may ask? It is right that customers who take a vehicle to the experts who often charge a lot of money for their services to EXPECT ONLY THE BEST.

Most cars now have these belts and I can think of at least five people whom I have advised in the last 15 years while in their cars that the mileage is close to change time for the belt and a few months later they have been stuck at the side of the road with an expensive failure. Our Ford Focus diesel has a life of 105.000 km and five years. The advisor at the Ford agency where we bought the car new in 2001, says that they have diesel cars that have 150.000 km without a failure. Nevertheless, at 125.000 km, and just over five years of age, we had ours changed for the peace of mind it brings. It cost under €200.

How is your car doing? A failure can cost €3 to 4.000.

THE POLICE FORCES IN SPAIN

There are several types of police authorities in Spain. They are: -

⇒ National Police (*Policía Nacional*). This is the police force mainly concerned with serious crimes, and the detectives who investigate murder, etc., belong to the *Policía Nacional*. They have a police station, called a *comisaria*, in the larger towns, and like all policemen in Spain (and as it should be in all countries now with the terror and drug gang problems), they are armed. If you are not officially employed in Spain, the foreigner's residence (residencia and NIE) registration is carried out at certain branches of these stations, but ask locally. Their uniforms are brown, but many detectives wear "civvies". In 2006, it was announced that the national police and the Guardia Civil were to be combined but we have yet to see that finalised at time of printing.

⇒ Local Municipal Police (*Policia Municipal* or *Policia Local*). These are employed by the local councils (*ayuntamientos*) and stay in that area for most of their lives or until they leave the job. They are responsible more for the minor problems in their area including local traffic control. They are recognised by their dark blue uniforms and often wear black & white chequered hats on duty in the streets. My wife says that they are usually worth looking at.

⇒ *Guardia Civil.* This force is national and also specialises in country areas where there is no *Policia Local*, as well as the big towns on specific duties. This force also patrols the national highways controlling traffic as well as all the other policing duties, as well as guarding the borders and at points of entry to Spain such as airports. They often ride powerful motorcycles, in pairs on the main roads, have some mechanical knowledge and are trained in first aid. You will also see their (usually 4 x 4) vehicles on the highways, or driving along the beaches looking for drug-smugglers and illegal immigrants, or parked somewhere observing traffic. They also operate helicopters and high-speed boats. Many of the routes from Africa used by drug smugglers and illegal immigrants to Europe are through Spain. They will assist you in an emergency, as well as carry out tests for driving under the influence of alcohol or drugs. Originally part of the army, they live in barracks mainly, with their families, and so are protected from the personal threats of criminals. They are dressed in green uniforms, and in "dress" uniform, wear the distinctive shiny odd-shaped hats. They where part of the military forces in Spain from the days of Franco but soon will be integrated with the National Police.

⇒ In Catalunya, the autonomous province in the north west of Spain, the police are known there as the *Mosso d'Esquadra*, or *Mossos* for short. They are a civilian (non-military) police force that like the policia local elsewhere, attend to minor crime in the towns, especially in Barcelona.

POLICE FORCES (Continued)

It is encouraging to know that the Spanish police forces are continuously being increased in numbers due now to the reported increases in crime caused by, as reported in the Press, Eastern European immigrants but is is interesting to note that in Anadaliucia, 50% of the prisoners in the jails are foreigners; and they are reported not to be "luxury hotels" as in some countries. Drug dealing, burglary and car theft (and theft from cars) is increasing, especially the stealing of luxury cars by organised foreign gangs who seem to get caught more often than not though. However, the drive at present is to reduce the high death and injury rates on the Spanish roads and it is working.

It is possible to report crimes now via the Internet and when you are settled, it is worth contacting the foreigner's department at your local ayuntamiento to find out how to do it. In Barcelona for example, the web address is www.policiadecatalunya.net; then go to "Accés a l'oficina virtual de denúncias" in the middle of the page and then click on the English flag. Note the conditions of reporting. You will be given a reference number and you must go to the local police station within 72 hours to sign the denuncia (report). Check with your local foreigner's department for your local access and how to do it.

HI-TECH TRAFFIC POLICING HAS ARRIVED.

Trafico is from August 2007, using Personal Digital Assistants (PDA) and mobile phone systems to speed up checks and policing at the road-side by the Gardia Civil initially and then other police forces where the Trafico computer records can be accessed directly at the side of the road to check on a driver or a vehicle and to record and print out any fines or orders issued as the result of an offence being committed. Or even if there are outstanding fines that have not been paid, etc. A PDA is a hand-held mini-computer which will have the various forms on the screen where one piece of information can be inserted, and the record, if any, on the Trafico system will complete the details. If, for example, a registration number is inserted and the record shows that the car is a blue Ford, but the car stopped is a green Renault, it wiil be seen that there is a major problem existing e.g. the car may be stolen.

The system is part of the Trafico new programme called Programa de Informatización de Denuncias with the acronym PRIDE. If the driving licence is a fake or the driver has been banned from driving, etc. an immediate arrest would result, as well as the vehicle documents being false In fact the advantages list can be quite comprehensive and we all benefit - unless you are an offender, of course.

If the driver is resident in Spain, and this can be picked up in several ways at the roadside, and he/ she is driving an foreign registered vehicle, the system will generate the fine and penalty points, and tell the system that the vehicle should be on the Trafico records as re-registered onto Spanish plates within 30 days as is the Law, the normal time allowed for such action. If not, the police have the correct address where another multa (fine) can be sent. Also, the system can generate a list of vehicles for the GC and the police to look out for.

Using this new system, with the in-car and motorcycle laptop computers also supplied, it will be possible to pay the fine at the roadside now (remember that this an admission of guilt though), but Trafico state that change for any cash offered will not be available. If the offender decides to plead guilty, the advantage of the 30% discount that is offered if the fine is paid within 14 days applies and payment can also be made with approved common credit or debit cards. As is the law at this time, if you do not pay at the roadside, and elect to go to Court, you may do so and you have 14 days to advise the issuing authority of your intended course of action, but if you are a foreigner with no provable property ownership in Spain, you will have to pay on the spot anyway and engage a lawyer. If you are unable to do so, your vehicle will be impounded until the fine is paid or if a serious offence needing a Court case, an arrest may be made. With the Juicio Rapido (rapid justice system) this could be within days.

The PDA device also has a global positioning system built in so it will record the actual place as well as the time of any offence and it also works off the short range radio system known as Bluetooth so it can be carried away from the police vehicle (car or motorcycle) for up to about 15 metres. The vehicles are also equipped with small printers so the multa or fine can be issued in a printed state thus obviating the need to write it out in perhaps poor light, and avoiding mistakes.

CHECKING SPEEDING FROM HELICOPTERS

Back in the 1960s when I was working in the USA, I had 60 miles (100Km) to travel to work each day across the tarred Mojave desert roads in a 130 mph Chevrolet Camaro. Every so often there would be a wide, painted white line across the road, and these were used for timing speeders by the California Highway Patrol using helicopters and light aircraft. They would then radio ahead to a police car to stop the offenders to book them. I never was stopped. Now, in Spain we go several steps further with helicopters fitted with radar cameras that can trap speeders in areas where there are fast roads but not much traffic. We are told that they can even read the number plates as far away as a kilometre. Why buy a fast car now? The golden ages of motoring appear to be over for the sporting drivers which included me just a few years ago especially on my very fast motorcycles and those expensive cars that are still being uprated with horsepower enough to power a small aircraft.

Glossary of Useful Non-Technical terms.

Spanish Term	English Meaning	Notes
Abogado.	Lawyer or Solicitor.	The one you hopefully do not have to approach with a problem.
Asistencia en viajes.	Roadside assistance (for breakdown or accident on holiday, etc.).	Help by your insurance company, etc. who supplies you with the telephone number.
Automoviles Inspeccion Tecnica de Vehículos.	Listings are in the local Yellow Pages, or in the Trafico web site for ITV test station addresses.	Where you take your vehicle for technical safety testing. (In UK– MOT).
Ayuntamiento	Town / city council.	
Baja de matrícula. Can be done by the breakdown truck (GRUA) driver for you.	Vehicle scrapping certificate (accident or old age).	Mandatory to prevent the vehicle being rebuilt.
Bonificación.	No Claims Bonus	Insurance classification
Centros de Reconocimento Médico para Conductores.	A small clinic where you go for a medical for a driving licence.	Near the *Trafico* Offices, but usually there is a registered one in each larger town. See Trafico web-site for addresses and page 145.
Certificado de equivalencia.	Was a translation issued by the RACE to accompany your foreign, EU driving licence. See also International Driving Licences.	See Driving Licence pages. No longer needed for EU licences with "ring of stars" on them.
Certificado Internacional de Seguro de Automóvil.	Was known as the "Green Card".	90 days cover for other EU countries as in policy.

Caballos de vapor (CV).	Horsepower/bhp (actual).	From the French calculation method.
Código de circulación.	Spanish Highway Code.	
Costa *or* Gasto de defensa.	Legal expense.	Supplied with most insurance policies.
Declaración jurada.	Sworn statement.	
Empadronamiento, Nota de, *or* Certificado de Empadronamiento.	Electoral register, Noted on the... This is important to do as you need this form to obtain some documents such as a Spanish driving licence, or to buy a new car in Spain, etc.	Often asked for as proof of residence in a your local area. Obtained at local town hall at usually <u>no cost.</u> Take your *escritura* or rental contract to obtain this simple document, as well as NIE/NIF and passport. Also see back of book.
Franquicia.	Voluntary insurance excess as in policy.	You pay this first amount for any damage.
Garantía: Sin garantía.	Guarantee: Without guarantee	Sin = "without", e.g. *sin plomo*: unleaded petrol.
Gestor and gestoria	Business and legal advice agent and agency.	A legally qualified and registered advisor for all matters related to business and some legal, but not as highly qualified as a lawyer. Usually also a notary.
Homolgamación	Homolgamation. An approved specification used to standardise vehicles (or signs, etc) technically in the EU.	
Hoja de Reclamación	Book held by most retail outlets for official complaints against the company . You keep a copy. Can be inEnglish.	

Limitado.	limited (insurance cover?).	
Impuesto municipal sobre vehículos de tracción mecánica.	Annual "Road Tax" paid at your local Town Hall (*Ayuntamiento*).	Must be usually paid from March and before end of
Impuesto sobre la circulación.	Special vehicle registration tax. Not IVA / VAT.	Tax on a new vehicle. Being changed in 2008 to reflect exhaust emissions.
Impuesto Sobre Transmisiones Patrimoniales y Actos Jurídicos Documentados.	Transfer tax, 4% of the deemed value, by the authorities, of the vehicle.	Used when selling and buying a vehicle. The tax is usually paid by the buyer.
Incendio y robo.	Fire and theft, as in Third Party, Fire and Theft	Insurance cover
Inspección Tecnica de Vehíclos (ITV)	The vehicle roadworthy test procedure.	In Spain, any car over the mandatory periods is subjected to a technical test at an ITV official test centre. See pages in this book for periods.
Jefatura provincial de Trafico. Adminsters all to do with the traffic in Spain.	Provincial Traffic Office. Also called just "Trafico". web site; www.dgt.es	Where you may register a vehicle including change of ownership, obtain a driving licence, pay fines, etc.
Marca or matricula.	Car registration number.	
Matriculación.	Registration (of motor vehicle).	
Multa.	Traffic fine or penalty.	
Norma	Rule or regulation based on Law.	
Oficina Municipla de Informacion al Consumidor	Local office, often in the council building, where local prices can be checked and any complaints processed.	
Permisso de circulación.	Driving licence.	Also " *Carnet de Conducir*"
Potencia fiscal.	Fiscal horsepower. Noted on the Tarjeta de inspección técnica de vehículos.	Formula used to calculate road tax. Detailed in this book on page???

Precintado	Sealed.	Example, when Customs "seal" a motor vehicle for a period of time?
Real Automóvil Club de España. (RACE). Say it "rathay".	Royal Automobile Club of Spain.	Equivalent of the RAC or AA, etc. in the UK. See page 262.
Residencia. Used to mean a card issued by the government to all foreigners who legally are resident in Spain. Now EU residents only need to register locally and receive a simple certificate.	Residence permission. When you live in Spain for more than six months each year, i.e. you officially live in Spain, not your country of origin.	In this context. Now an A4 sheet of paper issued as a receipt by the local authority.
Se alquila.	"For rent" - notice.	
Se vende.	"For sale" - notice.	
Segundo mano *or* usado	Secondhand.	
Seguro de ocupantes.	Driver and passenger insurance.	Optional cover for injury and time off work.
Seguro obligatorio.	Compulsory insurance cover.	Third party is the minimum.
Solicitud de Carnet del Permiso de Conducir.	Application for a Driving Licence.	Form TASA 2,4 at the *Trafico* office. See page 142.

Tarjeta de inspección técnica de vehículos.	Technical specification card issued for a new vehicle, and stamped on rear at time of the road-worthy tests during the ITV (MOT).	You also get a stick-on certificate which is placed on the top right hand side of your windscreen with the date due for the next test. Different colour for each year.
Todo riesgo.	Comprehensive insurance (all risks).	
Toquen Claxon	Sound your Horn, usually a sign with these words.	On sharp narrow bends, etc.
Vehículo De Ocasión	"Bargain vehicle" (on a sale).	Usually seen in dealerships and adverts.
Vigilantes Jurados.	Security Guards.	Usually armed.

ENGLISH	SPANISH	Notes
Accident Report Form issued by Insurance Companies. See back of this book.	Declaración Amistosa de Accidente de Automóvil. Also know as the Decl. de Siniestro de Automovil...	Completed by both or more drivers after an accident and sent to the Insurance companies ASAP.
Annual Road Tax, usually paid at your local Town Hall (*Ayuntamiento*)	Impuesto municipal sobre vehículos de tracción mecánica.	Pay it in months from March to June (varies). Penalty for late payments.
Bargain vehicle, or Chance to buy a bargain vehicle.	Vehículo De Ocasión	Usually seen in motor dealerships and adverts.

Lawyer	Abogado	
Business and legal advisory <u>agent</u> and <u>agency</u>.	Gestor and gestoria.	A legally qualified and registered advisor for all matters related to business, but not as highly qualified as a lawyer. Can also be a notary.
Card issued when you first buy your vehicle, and stamped at time of the road-worthy tests during the ITV. Must carry in vehicle.	Tarjeta de inspección técnica de vehículos.	You also get a sticky label which is placed on the top right hand side of your windscreen with the date due for the next test. Different colour each year.
Certificate (translation) issued by the RACE to accompany Non-EU foreign and non-"ring of stars" EU driving licences.	Certificado de equivalencia.	Not needed if an EU citizen with correct driving licence. See licence pages.
Electorial register, Noted on the...	Empadronamiento. (Nota, or Certificado de Empadronamiento.)	Form showing proof of residence in a local area. Take your *escritura* or rental contract to the town hall to obtain this free, simple, useful document.
Comprehensive insurance (all risks).	Todo riesgo.	
Compulsory insurance cover.	Seguro obligatorio.	Third party is the minimum. (Riesgo tercero)
Driver and passenger insurance.	Seguro de ocupantes.	Optional cover for injury and time off work.

Driving licence.	Permiso de conducción.	Also "*Carnet de Conducir*"
Driving Licence Application.	Solicitud de Carnet del Permiso de Conducir	The driving school does this as part of the training and driving test.
Electorial register. It is important that you do apply at the local ouncil (ayuntamiento) if you are resident or have property in Spain.	Empadronamiento, Nota, or Certificado de,	Form showing proof of residence in a local area. Take your escritura or rental contract to the town hall to obtain this simple document.
Fire and Theft, as in Third Party, Fire and Theft.	Incendio y Robo.	
Fiscal horsepower.	Potencia fiscal.	Used to calculate the annual road tax.
"For rent", - notice.	"Se alquila".	
"For sale", - notice	"Se vende".	
Guarantee: Without guarantee	Garantía: Sin garantía	
Homolgamation	Homolgamación	A specification used to standardise vehicles technically, and some road signs.
Horsepower (actual).	Caballos de vapor (CV).	Method of showing engine power. (also bhp or Kw).

Was known as a "Green Card". Normally valid for 90 days each year unless otherwise arranged.	Certificado Internacional de Seguro de Automóvil.	Extended cover for other EU countries. See insurance pages 222-231.
Lawyer or Solicitor.	Abogado.	Advocat = Barrister
Legal expense.	Defensa Penal.	
Listing in the local Yellow Pages for ITV test stations.	Automoviles Inspeccion Tecnica de Vehiculos	All national addresses are in the Trafico web site www.dgt.es
Medical for a Driving Licence. See page101.	Centro de Reconocimiento Médico para Conductores.	Usually near the *Trafico* Offices or in local town. Listed in the Trafico web site.
No Claims Bonus.	Bonificacíon.	
Registration (of motor vehicle)	Matriculación	
Provincial Traffic Office.	Jefatura Provincial de Trafico. ("El Trafico")	Where you may register a vehicle including change of ownership, obtain a driving licence, pay fines, etc.
Registration number (of motor vehicle)	Matricula or marca.	
Registration tax.	Impuesto sobre la circulacion	Is 7% or 12% depending on engine capacity. Changing in 2008. See page 253.

Residence Permit.	Residencia, since March 2007, called a residence certificate.	In this context, it means the card issued to register you as a Spanish resident. Must be renewed every five years.
Roadside assistance (on holiday, etc.).	Asistencia en viajes.	Roadside help by your insurance company or RAC, etc. Emergency telephone number is supplied on a card for you wallet.
Royal Automobile Club of Spain.	Real Automóvil Club de España. RACE.	Equivalent of the RAC or AA in the UK.
Sealed.	Precintado.	When Customs seal a motor vehicle so it cannot be used for a period of time.
Secondhand (vehicle).	Segundo mano.	
Security guards.	Vigilantes jurados.	
Sound your horn.	Toquen Claxon	Sign seen on narrow bends.
Spanish Highway Code.	Código de circulación.	
Sworn statement.	Declaración jurada.	
The roadworthy test procedure.	Inspección Tecnica de Vehíclos (ITV)	In Spain, the tests for roadworthyness carried out at government inspections sites. Listed in the Trafico web site.
Town/city council.	Ayuntamiento.	Pay your "road tax" and local taxes here.

Traffic fine or penalty.	Multa.	
Transfer tax, 4% of the deemed value (by the tax office or Hacienda) of the vehicle. They have their own list of values.	Impuesto Sobre Transmisiones Patrimoniales y Actos Jurídicos Documentados.	Used when selling and buying a vehicle. The tax is usually paid by the buyer.
Unlimited (cover).	Ilimitado.	
Vehicle scrapping certificate.	Baja de matrícula.	Mandatory to prevent the vehicle being rebuilt or you suffering costs due to subsequent criminal activities by others.
Vehicle transfer, tax form (Form 620). Covered in more detail in the last pages in this book.	Compra-venta de vehículos usados entre particulares.	Used to pay tax (4% on current value of vehicle) on transfer of ownership. Cannot register change without this being paid. Obtained from the *Hacienda* tax office or a tobacconist (*tabac*) shop.
Voluntary insurance excess.	Franquicia.	You pay this first amount for damage.
Wheel clamps.	Cepos	Used to immobilise a vehicle for parking in an illegal area.

SURVIVING THE N340 AND SIMILAR DANGEROUS ROADS,
AND OTHER SUGGESTED TIPS FOR SAFE DRIVING IN SPAIN

The A7/N340 coast road on the Costa del Sol and on the Costa Blanca (it runs all round the coastal areas of Spain) is often described as the most dangerous road in Spain (even Europe) and I have seen too many shunt-type accidents where the several cars hit the ones in front causing backups of several kilometres and sometimes two hours of stop-start motoring, proving that keeping the 2-second distance advanced driving rule (more in the wet) from the vehicle in front, is vital on this road, as on all others such as the N332 on the Costa Blanca. My advice (and the taxi driver's) for the Costa del Sol 4-lane N340, is that in medium to heavy traffic, stay in the "fast" lane at traffic speed (usually 100 kph) keeping 2 + seconds from the vehicle in front. Many visitors think that as it is a four-lane dual carriageway, it is an autovia or motorway: but it is not. In most places, Fuengirola to Estepona, to enter the road, you have to accelerate from a STOP sign to 100 + kph in one metre, so special care is needed, including, in my opinion, treating the road as a two lane (one each way) road with an extended slip road on the right where slow traffic (80 kph or less) can stay or safely enter and exit without upsetting the flow of the main lane, the left hand "fast" one.

This allows vehicles to get on and off the A7/N340 safely in the right hand lane and for you to avoid a "rear-ender". We had a lady neighbour who holidays here whose car was written off on entering the A7/N340 where another car rammed her from behind. It does not matter whose fault it was (except to the victims): injuries and unnecessary material damage was caused, not to mention the fear of driving again. Ignore the few bad drivers who "bully" you to get past, unless of course there is no vehicle at all in front of you, then if safe, move over. The toll roads are generally very much safer as the few accidents on these roads being usually due to high-speed tyre failures (tyres too soft?) or poor driving skills.

THE TWO SECOND RULE. For those unfamiliar with this approved rule, it is a foolproof method for judging a safe distance to follow the vehicle in front when you are in a traffic stream. It is foolproof because the faster you go, the greater the gap-distance to the vehicle in front. For very wet or slippery roads, the time is increased to 4 or even more seconds. The distance left is enough for you to stop safely (if you are awake) even if the vehicle in front stops suddenly, but all good drivers look ahead to vehicles further on to judge what is likely to happen, don't we?

Simply note the car in front passing a fixed marker such as a post at the side of the road, then count "one thousand and one: one thousand and two" under your breath at a normal rate, this representing two seconds. (Try it with your watch, but not while at the wheel!). If you pass that same marker in less that the 2 seconds you are probably too close. In the wet, use a 3-second or even 4-second rule if the roads are really bad and your vehicle is fully loaded.

The idea is that you can relax and drive in the traffic stream, secure that if the driver in front has to stop suddenly, you can do so also without any sudden actions where you have to "change your pants", or end up exchanging personal details if you are far too close and meet suddenly. Also your wife will keep quiet: well mine does.

If you have not practiced this before, try it and be amazed at how much space there is in the gap in front. And you can drive without the stress of continual braking saving fuel and brakes/tyres.

I always say you can tell which drivers who have hit the rear end of another car that has stopped quickly as they then in the future leave a great distance in the gap for years afterwards so let us hope we do not bump into each other on this, or any other road. Do not get upset when another vehicle pulls out and enters your gap in front. You are the good driver and he is only taking advantage of your driving skills to get into the main stream, and next time it may be your turn. The Spanish Law states that, on the open road, you must always leave an adequate space for another vehicle to comfortably pull into the gap between you and the vehicle in front.

Another important general driving tip is when you are waiting to overtake another slower vehicle on a main two-way road, usually a truck where you have limited vision, keep back at least FIVE OR MORE CAR LENGTHS, especially if you have a RH drive steering wheel (UK?) car, and then when you are intending to overtake and can easily see that the other side will soon be clear and safe even if a single vehicle is approaching but you can judge when to pull out and accelerate while it is still coming with the space in front still there to pull back into if necessary. Signal your intention well in advance, and start accelerating before you pull out so that you are overtaking the other vehicle with a 20-plus kph speed advantage which is legally allowed out of town. So many drivers "hug" the back of the vehicle in front, and then expect to be able to accelerate instantly to get by, but the time spent in the other lane can be four to five times as much as executing the manouevre correctly as recommended by advanced driving schools.

I must admit to getting upset (but not in a rage) at drivers who hug the rear of the vehicle in front, especially if it is a bus or large truck where they cannot see ahead, and think that they can just pull out when the road is clear, accelerating from a low speed and being "exposed" in the opposite lane for about five times longer that they should be. I get upset because I am usually already driving in that lane overtaking at about 20 to 40 kph faster having seen the safe opportunity. Usually though a blast on my horn is enough to send them back into their "safe haven" about 2 to 5 metres behind the truck, but they must curse me for their poor driving skills.

Watch out though that the driver directly behind the slow moving vehicle does not pull out without looking in his/her mirror. I have lost count of the number of times over the years when I have had to flash lights and blow my horn because I am overtaking a badly trained or lazy driver, with my much faster speed advantage because of the above, where he/she will pull out, often without signalling, when I am just about alongside. Many drivers think that as they are at the head of the queue they have the right to go first. Not true! The one overtaking and already in the overtaking lane has preference. A driver can only enter another lane if it is safe to do so, and if someone is already in that lane overtaking, it is definitely not safe to change lanes then. The advantage here is that you are on the other side of the road for about a quarter of the time compared with the inexperienced or "too lazy to learn advanced driving" vehicle, and the Law allows you on the intercity roads (90 to 120 kph speed limits) to speed by up to plus 20 kph over the speed limit to achieve this safe manoeuvre.

Another safety point on a four lane careterra/highway (not an *autovia*) with sharp blind bends in it, is never change lanes while entering or while in them, especially to the right hand one until you can see at least 100 metres ahead in that lane. Again, on the N340, I have seen cars travelling at the speed limit, move over because they are being bullied by a bad driver, only to find that they have to brake sharply because there is a slow moving vehicle just around the sharp bend or a vehicle is pulling out through a Stop sign onto the A7/N340. Do not be bullied. It encourages the bad driver to do it all the time.

Please always remember that Trafico's statistics have also shown that slow driving has been one of the 5 reasons for serious accidents, and still is a serious problem. Slow driving is moving at about 75% or less of the speed limit on an otherwise open road in safe conditions out of the residencial areas. Excessive speed in the wrong places is another, of course, but there are many experienced and competent drivers who can drive safely on the open road, when conditions permit, at speeds in excess of the posted speed limits as long as their vehicle is in good order and they are fit and able to do so. In my opinion, supported by a Trafico report in May 2005, it is far more dangerous to drive at 65 kph in a 50 kph zone (plus 30%), that at 140 kph in a 120 kph zone (plus 17%).

Most of you reading this will say "I knew all that!", but if it saves one reader from an unecessary accident, I feel OK about including the above in this book. As a result of the articles in the Press and radio programmes I do, I have been surprised at some of the seemingly basic questions I have been asked about driving, so there appears to be a popular need for the above. Perhaps it is because so many of us took the driving test many years ago and need a refresher course now?

And as I have been told many times in my life and passed it on to others, there are no stupid questions.

T-JUNCTIONS ON MAIN RURAL ROADS. Many T-junctions in Spain have "slip roads" to allow the avoidance of other vehicles colliding with a vehicle that is stopped or travelling very slowly either turning off the main road or on to it. They are usually, but not always depending on the traffic densities, on rural roads with speed limits of 80 to 100 kph normally, although for the junction, a "must do" speed limit sign reduces speeds to about 60 kph as indicated.

⟹ Traffic coming towards the reader, if turning left (right to the reader) may enter the slow down middle slip road and wait until there are no vehicles going the other way in the RH lane. Traffic continuing on the road towards the reader can do so without having to stop and wait.

⟹ Traffic coming out of the minor road can cross over into the centre slip road, and either wait until the main road lane is clear or use it to accelerate up to the speed limit thus avoiding traffic having to slow down. The opposite direction works in the same way.

54

SNOW CHAINS AND SOCKS AND DRIVING ON SNOW.

It is essential, both sensibly AND by law in Spain to carry and fit the auxiliary devices to tyres that enhance the tyre's grip on slippery roads where there is snow. The treads clog up with snow that is around freezing point and leave you with a smooth tread surface that is unable to grip, but with a "movable tread" formed by the chains or a "sock", the snow is automatically broken free so there is some reasonable grip to keep your vehicle going. Also, cars with front wheel drive are much better for these conditions because the weight of the engine is over the driving and steering wheels. Of course four wheel drive is even better, but they often still need chains of socks fitting. Normally you only need to fit them to the driving wheels that are being powered by the engine/transmission, but it is better to fit to all wheels if the roads have steep cambers.

You may also use studs, the tungsten steel "teeth" that can be fitted to the tread on suitable tyres and are used especially for driving on ice, but they are not so necessary in Spain, only mainly the countries where it does not go above freezing for months and the roads may have "black" ice on them.

Full details on the different types of chains and socks and what tyres they may be used with is in the web site.

http://www.roofbox.co.uk/snowhome.html

For example, we have a Ford Focus with 196 x 60H x 15 tyres fitted and due to the fact that chains could hit and damage the suspension parts and especially the brake pipes, you cannot use chains, and this is noted in the Operator Manual. But you can use snow socks.

For those who are travelling to the Sierra Nevada or driving through northern Spain in winter, this is important reading.

THE TOLL ROADS IN SPAIN

Spain has a a good network of roads, especially since entering the EU, and much of the cash for developing these roads has been provided by the EU. Many of these roads are toll roads (or *peajes*). A map of many of the toll roads in Spain can be seen at the website www.viat.es and on the next page but one. Each road has a gated entrance / exit where payment is made for the use of the road, and this payment may be made in three ways: -

- With cash at one of the booths. Often involves queuing. Available booths have a green arrow over them. Those closed have a red cross.
- By credit card through a gate right of the cash booths. Most credit cards are accepted. Can only be used by cars.
- Through a gate where, if you have made arrangements to obtain one, an on-board *televisor* which is an electronic remote about the size of a standard cigarette packet. It triggers an automatic sensor to open the barrier, simultaneously debiting your Bank account as previously arranged. The viat.es web-site shows how it works. Maximum speed through the gate is 40 kph.

Approaching the toll collection area, you will see signs advising which lane or barrier gate gate to use depending on how you want to pay. They are as follows: -

The toll lane for auto-payment with an OBE sensor only. Called "VIA-T" for "via telepeaje"

The toll lane for credit cards AND the OBE sensor.

 This toll booth accepts cash, credit cards and the OBE auto-sensor. You see this sign on the approach before the tool booth area. Some are sensibly advising well in advance, how much the toll is, and what credit cards may be used. If no "T" symbol, you must pay by card or cash.

On the Costa Blanca, the toll road is called the A7/E15. On this road you will get a ticket when you start with the name of the enter point noted. When you exit, you are charged for the distance between these two points.

Eventually, all the toll roads in Spain will use the VIA-T system of payment until, if the EU plans are satisfied, the EU satellite GPS system called Galileo comes on line and cars will have a transponder so that they can just drive through the toll booths with their owner's bank account being automatically debited as with the current system. But people will have to manage their Bank accounts well to avoid overdraft charges

No. passes per month	Discount %
From 1 to 10	0
From 11 to 15	5
From 16 to 20	10
From 21 to 25	20
From 26 to 30	30
From 31 to 35	40
From 36 upwards	50

If you use an on board sensor (OBE or Televisor), you will receive a discount on the total cost for the month depending on the number of times you use the road during that month. At the time of preparing this book the published discount rates for Via Telepeaje are as in the table left.

Most of the toll roads greatly increase the charges at holiday times and periods such as June to September. This is a shame because, in my (logical?) opinion the theory should be that to ensure the best road safety by reducing traffic on the older roads that the toll roads have by-passed, the rate should be the same all year, or better still, paid for out of general taxation. But, of course, it is a commercial decision as the toll roads have been financed by private investment, not the government.

To arrange for the use of a *televisor*, contact your own local bank. If it does not support the system you can check which Banks do by going to the web site www.vial.es, and click on "COMO COSEGUIRLO". If you have access to a PC with a broadband Internet connection, you may download a presentation from this site, in English, which will give you all the information you would need. This web site also shows a map of the toll roads in Spain, copied on the next page.

There is also more information on the Costa del Sol toll roads at: -
www.autopistadelsol.com and www.aseta.es/index.html

The Spanish toll road system map is on the next page.

MAP SHOWING THE TOLL ROADS IN SPAIN AS AT JULY 2005

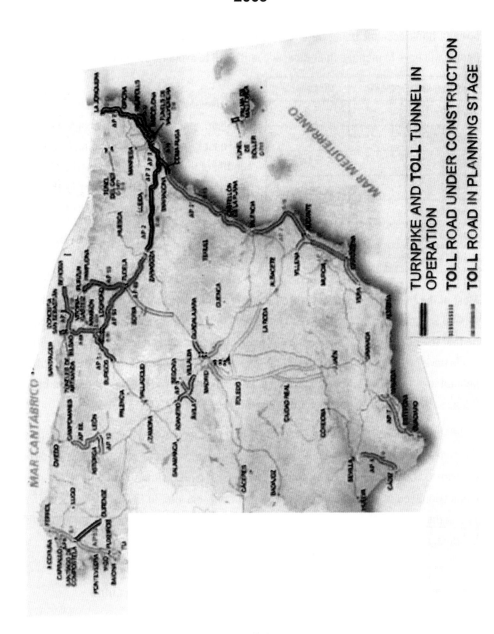

ACCEPTED CREDIT CARDS FOR TOLL PAYMENTS

These Banks will also organise payment through the transponder sensor system. Please contact your local branch for details. More may be added to this list later.

Penalties, Traffic Fines (*Multas*).

As in any country, a system of fines for is used to "punish" driver/riders/pedestrians who break the Law, and, as in any other country, ignorance of the Law is no excuse. Fortunately in Spain, it is not yet considered a necessary source of income for the authorities, although we have been advised that the number of speed cameras is to eventually increase up to 500 nationally, especially for use at peak holiday times. However the fixed ones can be located as they are listed on the Trafico web site at: www.dgt.es/trafico/radares/radares.htm. The Trafico web site shows only the fixed cameras, not the mobile ones but the site now also shows all the proposed ones at this time. When going on a journey to new territory, it pays to check where they are and mark them on a map especially if you do not have the device called a "SatNav" where, if the software is up to date, it will warn you where they are. I remind you again that radar detecting devices that receive the speed trap signal, or especially send out a signal that corrupts the speed camera signal, are not allowed in Spain (or France).

The Spanish policing authorities are human, and especially in the tourist areas, tolerant of those visitors who may not be aware of minor local Laws, they will exercise discretion if the driver is polite when stopped, and if the misdemeanour causes no serious danger to other road users just issue a warning: unless the driver is drunk or using drugs, using a mobile phone illegally or not wearing a seat-belt, of course. All "No-Nos".

Fines, or *multas*, are set to discourage offenders from repeating offences and can spoil a visitor's holiday. Offences are set as minor (*leve*), serious (*grave*), and very serious (*muy grave*). The levels of fines are now published and are as follows, minor offences can carry a fine of up to €300, serious, € 3.000, and very serious, depending on the Court. You would lose your licence on the spot for the muy grave. More on following pages.

The new Laws in Spain specify that you can now be fined for <u>following the vehicle in front too closely</u>, the fines being from €300 upwards (depending on the officer), as well as lose penalty points. As our BMW was badly smashed in 2001 from the rear by a Mercedes driver (we crash only with the most expensive cars) I happily agree with this Law. Tailgating is an annoying and dangerous habit and when you have lost one car to one such driver, let alone the risks to life and limb, with the associated costs, inconvenience and especially stress, it is understandable to get very annoyed with the bad drivers who do it. My wife gets very nervous now when someone does it to us and I suffer her telling me to do something about it (?). As a visitor, if you cannot pay on the spot or you may pay by cash or credit card as you will be escorted to a Bank cash-point or an open Bank to withdraw the cash (no cheques, etc.) and if you are unable to do this, you may have your vehicle impounded until the fine is paid.   Due to the many sometimes months of delay between the offence and the Court case if the defendant decides to take this route, the authorities are planning to insist on the fines being paid at the road side, even for the Spanish, as the administration and delays are causing havoc. This is how it is done now in Portugal.   A driver thus treated can still go to Court but as this can be months further on, the onus is on the driver to get the fine, and the penalty points loss, reversed.

On the 1st. July 2006, the new penalty points system was introduced, and this is discussed in detail later in this book.   If you have property in Spain, then you can currently be issued with the summons called a *boletin de denuncia*, and you can pay when you get home.   The fine must be paid within 30 days (30% discount if within 10 days). You may pay the fine from any post office (*correos*) using a P.O. money order (*giro postal*) or at the local *Trafico* office, which may not be so local, or if a *policia local multa*, issued by the local police, at the local police station (not the *comiseria*).

A new development announced is the discussion for co-operation between Spain and the UK to allow access to each other's motoring databases to trace foreigners who commit offences where they are not stopped by the police, such as camera speed traps and parking, etc. and then return home without paying.   As in the UK, the authorities do not seem to be able to control the recently reported 2 million cars/drivers without insurance in Spain, road tax payment and driving licences, so perhaps we should be a bit sceptical about the scheme. I call these people "parasites", for we end up paying their costs when they cause an accident.

ALWAYS MAKE SURE YOU GET A RECEIPT FOR PAYMENT.

DRINKING AND DRIVING IN SPAIN.

Between 30 and 50% of mortal accidents are caused by drunk drivers

I am of the opinion that drinking substantial amounts of alcohol within 12 hours before driving, especially where the amount is so high that the driver is still drunk the next morning should be totally banned. In fact, in my opinion for reasons of experience where, as a reservist (volunteer) policeman some years ago, I have had to attend to many accident scenes where deaths have occurred due to drink and driving: It would be much better if all drinking and driving is banned as so many people just do not know when to stop: so why start if you know you have to drive? Why even go out with the car if you know you are going to drink excessively? The same applies to drug-takers, and in my opinion, where anyone is caught over the drink limit, or drugged, the vehicle should be confiscated; –for good.

As a volunteer police reservist in years gone by, I have, on eight occasions in the early hours of the morning, had to wake up parents, wives or relatives to tell them that their loved one / s was killed in a stupid and unnecessary road accident the night before due to an excess of alcohol. I have made too many cups of coffee in strangers' kitchens, and had grieving females crying on my shoulder. We humans do terrible things to ourselves and each other!

It is only by admitting to these unnecessary tragedies that I feel justified in making that statement on banning any drinking and driving. Many years ago in the Royal Air Force, I had young friends killed or seriously maimed and their careers wrecked by drunken car drivers who were then subsequently fined a trifling amount (£10 - 15?) for being drunk in charge of a motor vehicle. My friends were mainly on motorcycles but some were in cars.

In Spain, the limits are much lower than in some other European Union countries, especially the UK. Still, far too may Spaniards (and visitors) die or are seriously injured each year due to drunken, or drugged, drivers behind the wheel. It is worth noting that in the first two years following the issue of the driving licence, the maximum is 0,15 mg per litre of blood or half the normal allowance.

THIS APPLIES TO FOREIGN VISITORS AS WELL.

IT IS REALLY NO SECRET. THE BEST THING IS NOT TO DRINK AND DRIVE AT ALL.

On the next page is the table for alcohol limits allowed while in charge of a motor vehicle or as a road user. This includes pedestrians, etc. The visitors from Britain will note that the limits are some 40% lower than in the UK so please beware. Due to the ongoing and current high accident rates with drunk drivers, the authorities will show no mercy. More than 50% over the limit will most likely mean being arrested and licence confiscation until the appearance in Court and with the recently approved penalties, a jail sentence is inevitable. 140% over the set limit and it is certain arrest and jail plus driving licence confiscation. And the jails in Spain are as they should be, not "country hotels".

ALCOHOL CONSUMPTION LIMITS FOR DRIVERS

DRIVER'S CLASSIFICATIONS	MAX. ALCOHOL LEVEL RATES	
Please note the quantities are: - Mg/l = milligrames per litre of air—breathalysed. g/l = grammes per litre of blood by sample.	IN EXHALED AIR Mg/litre	IN BLOOD Gr/litre
All drivers are forbidden to be in charge of any vehicle with levels of alcohol exceeding>	0,25 mg/l	0,5 g/l
For transport vehicles of more than a Maximum Authorised Mass of 3.500 kg, not more than >	0,15	0,3
Drivers of vehicles with more than nine seats, and those who drive school buses, dangerous goods, public service vehicles, emergency services, and special services. Not more than >	0,15	0,3
Drivers of any vehicle in the two years following the issue of their first permit / licence to drive, not more than >	0,15	0,3

Please note that the standard alcohol limit is about 60% that of the UK

As in many other countries, drivers of public service vehicles rightly have lower limits. Due to the continuing battles to reduce accidents where alcohol and drugs have played a part, the authorities have regular blitzes to catch offenders who often when involved in an accident, kill or maim innocent people, sometimes pedestrians. But in Spain, the sentences are severe for such offences and long jail sentences and damage payouts are common. And in my opinion, so they should be as well as the sentences being served full time, with no "get out of jail card" because the jails are full.....

If you are stopped by the authorities and asked to give a breathalyser sample or carry out a sobriety test and you refuse, as elsewhere in the world, refusal will result in a charge of civil disobedience, which often carries a harsher penalty than being found over the limit.

The penalties now approved to be from 2004 as modified from late 2007 and listed on the next pages, include up to six months in jail, stiff fines and community service. The decisons are made by usually the arresting officers as is normal everywhere. You can have your licence confiscated by the police officer on the spot (failing the breathalyser/drug test machine) as a precaution so you may not drive until the case is settled, not just until you are sober without engaging a lawyer to fight your case. You will also be arrested and spend at least one night in jail, and, as a visitor your country's relevant driving licencing office may be advised of the proven offence so the sentence can be also "in force" at home. The authorities are starting a scheme now working in Portugal where your penalty starts right away if it is serious and although you can still go to Court, this getting tough is because there are too many drivers who flagrantly break the laws every day, with many who previously have been charged and are waiting for the Court case committing the same offences again during that waiting period.

CIVIL DAMAGES - PLEASE BE WARNED.

As already stated, the Criminal Courts in Spain can, and often do, award substantial damages to the plaintiff, especially in the event of a motor accident. These damages, which to many are an excellent idea as they obviate any need for the victims to have the necessary cash to start a civil case, are limited to up to about €350.000 for personal injuries and up to about €100.000 for damage to assets. Please remember though that the other party can still take out a civil case if the injury/damage costs were actually far higher. If you are the guilty party, your insurance will cover the legal policy amounts, but anything over this, you are liable to pay out of your assets, plus any excess legal costs. An example would be where a driver does not insist on any passenger (the driver's family members are not generally covered by the driver's third-party injury insurance) wearing a seat belt, or if the driver is drunk, or his / her car has faulty tyres. This is because the injuries would have been deemed to have been far less serious, or not at all if the person/s had been wearing the seat belt/s, not drunk, bad tyres, etc. Another note is that the driver is the one reponsible and fined, plus penalty point action taken, if any passenger does not have a seat-belt fitted in the event of being stopped in a road check, but I have heard of adult passengers being fined also.

Also, the owner of the vehicle can also be liable for these costs where the driver is not the owner but is driving the vehicle <u>with</u> the owner's permission.

Summary of Laws Introduced in 2004.

Changes and additions to the Penal Code came into effect from October 2004. They include those for drunken or drugged drivers and <u>can be given in addition</u> to penalties under the new points system depending on the Court (see pages 67 to 72): -

⇒   Up to six months in jail, and / or

⇒   a fine of 6 to 12 monthly salaries, and / or,

⇒   31 to 90 days community service, and / or

⇒   the driving licence being suspended, which also may mean having to take the driving test again to regain it.

⇒   Drivers without insurance face heavy fines as well as suspension and or penalty points.

Where reckless driving is involved, the penalties include jail from 6 months to two years and licence suspended from 1 to 6 years. Reckless driving includes speeding excessively as noted in the table in this book. Please see following lists of penalty points and offences in this chapter.

ALL "GUILTY" CASES WILL ALSO HAVE AN EXPENSIVE EFFECT WITH INCREASED INSURANCE PREMIUMS.

Unlike the UK where speeding penalty points have been largely discounted by the insurance companies as a reason for increasing premiums, this is not the case in Spain.

2007 - MODIFICATION OF THE MOTORING PENAL CODE ANNOUNCED.

The Spanish Ministry of the Interior and Ministry of Justice have announced that the penalties for the offences listed below are to be increased in severity from summer 2007. The alcohol limits currently used, as shown in this book still apply, but when the rate exceeds 1, 2 gr/litre of blood (140% over the limit), then the added minimum penalties listed below will be set by the Court. There are no minimum rates set for drug abuse which means that the mere presence of illegal drugs (or prescription drugs that are known to affect driving) found will constitute an offence.

	At this Time	From 2007
Alcohol & Drug Offences Driving under the influence of alcohol or drugs	Possible penalties awarded by the Court: prison sentence from 3 to 6 months, or a from 6 to 12 months, and/or community service from 31 to 90 days, and losing the driving licence for 1 to 4 years.	Driving under the influence of more than 1.2 gr/litre of alcohol or under the influence of drugs, prison from 3 to 6 months or from 6 to 12 months, and/or community service for 31 to 90 days.
Speeding. Currently, as in the table in this book.	Driving recklessly or at proportionately high speeds for the established limit, prison 6 months to 2 years, and loss of licence from 1 to 6 years.	More than 50 kph over the limit in an urban area, and 70 kph in an inter-urban area, prison from 3 to 6 months or 6 to 12 months, and/or community service for 31 to 90 days.
Driving dangerously	Driving any vehicle in such a way to be a danger to all road users, 6 to 2 years in prison and loss of licence from 1 to 6 years.	Reckless or dangerous driving, 2 to 5 years in prison.
Driving without a licence	Administrative offence.	6 months in prison or 12 to 24 months and community service of 31 to 90 days.

While the authority at the road-side has the choice of what actual penalty to charge the erring driver with, this can be changed by his boss or treated with severity within the Law by the Court at a later date, but the road-side police, depending on the seriousness of the offence can still confiscate the driving licence and / or the vehicle, and take the driver to the local jail, resident or tourist visitor.

PENALTY POINTS FOR TRAFFIC VIOLATIONS
- EFFECTIVE JULY 1st 2006.
THE DETAILS INCLUDING FINES AND APPEALS PROCEDURES.

This system ONLY applies if you drive in Spain using a Spanish driving licence. Drivers caught with a foreign EU driving licence, depending on the severity of the offence, may be fined if you can prove Spanish residence (nearest cash point, if not) or your driving licence confiscated on the spot if the offence is serious enough. If resident with a foreign EU DL, the points will be added to Trafico's records and when they are all lost, the banning will apply as with Spanish DL holders.

However, from March 2007, the EU has approved the transferring of fines and sentences, including penalty point's losses between participating EU States, the UK, Ireland and Spain included, where the sentences will apply in the country where the driving licence is issued as well as the whole of the EU. But there are no signs that this is happening yet.

However, like all good intentions, it will take time to set up the administration, especially in many of the newer EU States. But from August 2007, the police & GC are being issued with Personal Digital devices that connect with the Trafico records at the road-side.

HOW MANY POINTS DOES EACH DRIVER HAVE?
If you have had a driving licence for three years plus, you are credited with 12 points. If less than three years, or if you have got your licence back after being banned for having lost all your points, you start with eight points.

GOOD DRIVERS
After three years of "no penalty points loss" driving, you will receive an extra two points to your credit. After that, each three years you will receive one point up to a maximum of 15. So it will then be possible to lose 12 points but not your licence.

OFFENDERS
WHAT HAPPENS WHEN YOU LOSE ALL YOUR POINTS?
You automatically lose your licence starting within the periods stated below. You will be able to obtain a new one after successfully completing a course and a theory test organised by the provincial traffic department (Jefatura de Trafico). The courses have been arranged at about 200 driving schools around Spain (listed in the Trafico web site), and the offender has to pay the costs. Naturally, the courses are mainly in Spanish. Your new licence will then have eight points credit.

If you do not lose any more points in the following two years you will recover the full 12 points. If you lost your licence due to very serious offences (incurring the loss of six point penalties) you will have to wait three years to recover the 12 points.

Cont.

In addition, if you commit serious or very serious offences you could have your licence taken away regardless of the number of points left on it as was, and still is, the law before the new penalty points system started.

HOW LONG UNTIL YOU RECOVER YOUR LICENCE?
In the case of professional drivers, after three months the first time and after six the second time. A professional driver would be a taxi driver, HGV, bus drivers, etc.
In other cases six months the first time and twelve the second.
In all cases, drivers will have to attend a special course that may be tailored for the offence and pass a new driving test depending on the sentence.

ARE POINTS LOST ON THE SPOT?
No. Points are lost when the punishment has been fixed (Sanción firme) this is:
When you do not appeal against it (Recurso Administrativo) to the issuing authority, e.g. Guardia Civil, Policia Local, etc, or the Provincial Trafico Office within 15 days of your being notified of the offence – if you appeal, then you are notified if the appeal has been approved or denied (Notificación de Resolución). If you appeal, you then have first the "Body" to whom the defence has been submitted who will study the evidence and either allow the defence, in which case the charge will be cancelled, or reject the evidence in which case the full reasons must be given in writing to the claimant driver. It is all "lawyer work" for most drivers.

However, Trafico is considering changing this rule in 2008 as there are very big delays and backups in the Courts as drivers contest and appeal the charges as is their right. For the serious charges, the licence confiscation may start immediately to force the driver to ensure that the Court case starts as soon as possible (at his/her expense using a lawyer).

The advice (resolution) must state whether the appeal has been finalised, meaning that is the end of the matter and you are either guilty or innocent, or whether you may be allowed to go further to Court to contest the charges. The notice with all information justifying your defence may be sent by registered post or submitted by hand in which case you are advised to get an official dated receipt. It is best to use a lawyer (abogado) at this stage.
The bodies (Guardia Civil, etc) authorised to issue fines must do so within:

⇒	Minor (leve) offences .	3 months.
⇒	Serious (grave).	6 months
⇒	Very Serious (muy grave).	12 months.

-- from the day of the alleged offence. If they have not been issued within these time scales, they automatically are withdrawn or expired. However, these terms can be legally extended by such administrative actions as, for example, time taken locating the offending driver due to the address on the Trafico (or foreign EU records such as the UK-DVLA) computer system not being correct.

However, if during such an extension, a period of six months elapses, the charges will be expired, although left on file, <u>except if due to</u>:

⇒ The driver is responsible for the delays.

⇒ The process is suspended pending the case being transferred to a Court hearing for any reason.

The issuing authority or Trafico has one year then to demand the completion of the sentence or any payment, licence confiscation, etc.

<u>APPEALS PROCEDURE.</u>

In respect of any charges made by the issuing authority, the charged may apply to the Ministerio del Interior (MDI) with a "recurso de alzada", and the MDI will then use their influence to settle any dispute that the charged may have with Trafico. Note that Trafico is a department of the Ministerio Del Interior. This must be done within one month of the sentence. The decision then is final and it ends the administration stage of the offence, but there is one last action that can be made, called the "recurso de reposición" against the issuing office which must be made within one month of sentence, or a recurso contencioso-administrativo directly against the issuing administration including the office of the mayor or town hall if applicable, I.e. the authority is a policia local.

The fines for penalty notices are not to be paid until they are made final after all the appeals mentioned above. This is important as to do so before can mean an admission of guilt.

Where to pay (include a copy of the multa/sentence form):

⇒ The collection office of the issuing authority.

⇒ Trafico, either by registered post or by hand.

⇒ A participating Bank where collections are made on behalf of the issuing authority.

<u>PAYMENT PERIODS.</u>

⇒ If paid within <u>15 working-days</u> of the first charge, a 30% discount applies. This then assumes admission of guilt.

⇒ If paid within 15 work-days of the final resolution date (after the appeals have been rejected by the Court), then a 15% discount applies.

⇒ If not paid within the above time period, then a *procedimiento de apremio* will begin where personal goods will be valued and recorded ready for their seizing in lieu of the debt amount which will then be advised at that time. This amount will include all the costs associated with the procedure.

Cont.

⇒ As well as the seizing of personal goods, bank accounts may also be seized plus any pending tax rebates.

⇒ If the sentence included suspension of your driving licence this must also be handed over until the payment of fines, or any period of loss of the licence has been satisfied.

CAN I FIND OUT HOW MANY POINTS I MAY HAVE?

The DGT website (www.dgt.es) will have a section allowing you to do so at: https://puntos.dgt.es/tramites/permisos/ppp_sin_cert.htm. You will need a password or the date of the offence/s to obtain the information.

HOW CAN I RECOVER POINTS OR MY LICENCE?

In both cases, a course at an officially appointed centre (about 200 driving schools nationally) is compulsory. Its cost must be covered by the driver and lessons are given by specialised personnel depending on the nature of the offence, e.g. driving with excess alcohol. There are no indications at this time of the schools where English is offered as a medium of instruction but there are such schools in the heavily populated expat's areas. The list of schools is on the Trafico web-site.

Partial recovery of points: the 12-hour awareness course can be carried out once every two years (once a year for professional drivers) and a maximum of four points can then be obtained if passed. It costs €170 at time of writing this advice.

Recovery of driving licence after losing all points: a 24-hour course costing €320 must be attended and a test taken at the Jefatura de Trafico.

The course includes common subjects regarding driving and safety regulations, encouraging group debates and reflection, and specific subjects that affect each driver individually depending on the offence committed.

SPECIAL MEASURES FOR PROFESSIONAL DRIVERS.

The law considers a professional (or vocational as described in the UK) driver anyone who, with the necessary driving licences, is employed to drive a transport vehicle, being either for passengers or goods as listed on page 82. The law establishes special benefits for these drivers, mainly reducing by half the licence recovery period as their livelihood is affected.

WHAT HAPPENS IF I LOSE POINTS?

You can partially recover a maximum of four points if you pass a special course that you can only take once every two years.

WHEN YOU LOSE POINTS:

2 POINTS

⇒ Stopping or parking on bends, brow of a hill, tunnels, under bridge cross-roads <u>or any other area</u> considered hazardous to traffic flow or pedestrians, e.g small roundabouts.

⇒ Stopping or parking on bus lanes or in areas where paint on the road designates no stopping or parking.

⇒ Using radar speed camera detectors (that sense radar beams), but not the GPS navigation systems that advise only the location of cameras.

⇒ Driving without lights when they are necessary in poor visibility or for example on a three lane road where the centre lane is used for overtaking.

⇒ Riding a motorbike or moped with a passenger under the age of twelve.

3 POINTS

⇒ Changing of direction of travel against traffic signs or road markings forbidding this action.

⇒ Driving and using a mobile phone manually, headphones, earphones (except deaf-aids) or any other device that could distract driving concentration.

⇒ Not maintaining a safe distance from the vehicle in front.

⇒ Driving without a seatbelt, riding a motorcycle without a helmet correctly fastened and/or other compulsory safety devices.

4 POINTS

⇒ Driving on motorways or highways with vehicles that are forbidden access.

⇒ Driving a vehicle with 50% or more passengers than the maximum allowed for its category, except buses and coaches.

⇒ Driving a vehicle without a driving licence for its category.

⇒ Throwing objects on the road or nearby areas that may cause a fire or accidents.

⇒ Negligent driving creating danger for other vehicles.

⇒ Exceeding speed limits by over 40kph providing it is not also 50% above the limit. If the excess is between 30 and 40kph, this will be punished with three points and two points if it is between 20 and 30kph.

⇒ Not respecting the right of way, ignoring a red traffic light or not stopping at a STOP sign. (Note the police regard a STOP where the wheels are stationary for at least four seconds.)

⇒ Breaking overtaking rules, being a hazard to oncoming vehicles or overtaking in low visibility areas or circumstances.

⇒ Endangering or blocking the way of cyclists when passing them.

⇒ Causing a hazard by illegal parking/waiting on a motorway or highway, including the hard shoulder if vehicle is not mechanically broken down.

⇒ Ignoring the signals or instructions of a traffic officer.

⇒ Accelerating or carrying out other manoeuvres that hinder overtaking vehicles. This includes

6 POINTS

⇒ Drink driving if the alcohol level found in breathalysing tests is above 0.50mg% (0.30mg% for new or professional drivers) If the level is between 0.25 and 0.50 (0.15 to 0.30 for professional or new drivers) the loss will be four points.

⇒ Driving under the influence of drugs, stimulants and similar substances.

⇒ Reckless driving, driving in the wrong lane or taking part in illegal races.

⇒ Refusing to undergo tests for alcohol, drugs, stimulants and other substances.

⇒ Driving at more than 50% over the maximum speed limit, providing this is at least 30kph above that limit.

⇒ Professional drivers who exceed by more than 50% the maximum permitted time at the wheel, or reduce the obligatory rest times by more than 50%.

A table as used by the police/Guardia Civil for the speeding penalties is on the next page.

WHY, IN MY OPINION, THE ACCIDENT RATES WILL NEVER REACH ZERO.

The targets set by accident prevention authorities in Western countries are always that there will be no accidents. But my opinion is that this will never be when human beings are in charge of driving vehicles. Why?

Human beings, as a group, have failings such as an inablity to accept that traffic laws are set as the result of accidents and therefore are a means of reducing them if not eliminating them. For example, in the last 18 months, I have had to take violent avoiding action three times to stop cars driving into me, twice through stop signs, because the drivers were concentrating on their mobile phones held to their ears, trying to change gear and brake and so on. Even when you are involved in an accident where you are totally not at fault, apart from the injury or even death aspects, it will cost you money to recover even with 100% fully comprehensive insurance. And your vehicle never feels the same again and often is not if the repairer is not first class. Having to share the roads with drivers who are either drunk or high on drugs is another major problem today. We try to avoid the famous Puerto Bañus near us at weekends because we know that many of the regular visitors there take drugs as others elsewhere drink beer. This was advised to me by a young friend who works there.

That is some of the reasons why we will never reach zero. And as the old saying goes, "There is nowt as daft as folk!" It still applies today.

THE FOLLOWING TABLE SHOWS THE OFFICIAL SPEEDING-PENALTY RATES IN SPAIN, AND IS A GUIDE AS USED BY THE POLICE/ *GUARDIA CIVIL* AND THE COURTS. UPDATED FROM 1 JULY 2006. NOTES: > = UP TO. "91-100" = 91 KPH TO 100 KPH. FINES: 3.500 KG + 9 PASSENGERS APPLIES TO MOST NON-COMMERCIAL VEHICLES. 9 PASSENGERS INCLUDES THE DRIVER.

Road Sign Speed >	30	40	50	60	70	80	90	100	110	120	>3.500kg & 9 + passengers	Remainder of vehicles
Speed without fine or points.	>40	>50	>60	>70	>80	>90	>100	>110	>121	>132	No Court case	No Court case
Without points but with fine option.	41-60	51-70	61-80	71-90	81-100	91-100	101-120	111-130	122-141	133-152	€120	€120
2 points	61-70	71-80	81-90	91-100	101-110	101-110	121-130	131-140	142-151	153-162	€150	€140
3 points				101-105	111-120	121-130	131-140	141-150	152-161	163-172	€220	€200
4 points							141-150	151-165	162-181	173-198	€300	€300
6 points	71-77	81-87	91-97	106-112	121-128	136-143	151-158	166-174	182-190	199-208	€450	€380
6 points	78-84	88-94	98-104	113-119	129-136	144-151	159-166	159-166	191-199	209-218	€520	€450
6 points	85 +	95 +	105 +	120 +	137 +	137 +	167 +	167 +	200 +	219 +	€600	€520

MORE NOTES ON OFFENCE S IN ADDITION TO THE PENALTY POINTS.

The authorities have a plethora of penalties to choose from to inflict upon those of us who are unable to follow the safety rules. In addition to these there are penalty points and jail -time.

⇒ **Alcohol and drugs**, driving under the influence. Penalties include, a jail sentence of up to four years, and / or a fine, and / or community service for 31 to 90 days, and licence confiscation. The police may keep the driver's licence at the scene of the offence if serious enough.

⇒ **Junior Driver Education.** Regional / local authorities now include road safety as a subject for school students from 12 to 16 years of age. When/if they pass, a certificate will be issued and this will be taken into account when they apply for a driving licence. This is a plus, not a penalty.

⇒ **Motorcycles** may be asked to pass the ITV (MOT?) mechanical safety test if stopped at any time. (Currently, ITV only after 5 years, unless it is a rental or commercial machine).

⇒ **New drivers.** Any driver who commits three serious or two very serious offences in the first two years of after obtaining the driving licence, he / she will have the licence revoked and be unable to have another for at least one year, and must attend retraining courses before the licence is reinstated after another driving test. All to be paid for by the offender.

⇒ **Re-offenders.** A driver will be considered a re-offender with three serious offences in a period of two years, and can be heavily fined with loss of licence. The loss can be avoided if the three are committed in more than one year (the minimum period) and if the offender agrees and satisfactorily attends the specified re-education courses.

⇒ **Moped/scooter (> 49cc) licences.** Holders who commit two serious offences, or one very serious offence in a two year period, will have their licence revoked.

⇒ **EU Approved Safety-jackets.** These are now compulsory and must be worn when outside of the vehicle (but not motorcycles) BY ALL during a break-down or an emergency situation at any time outside of an urban area (not just in poor visibility). You are expected to carry them inside the car (not in the boot). Sensible moto-riders have them as part of their riding clothes for normal riding.

ALL MUST BE ABLE TO PUT THE JACKET ON BEFORE LEAVING THE VEHICLE.

⇒ Driving without insurance. The vehicle may be impounded until proof of insurance currently paid is shown, and any fine is paid for not carrying the proof.

⇒ The use of video, DVD or Internet screens BY THE DRIVER is forbidden in the car while it is on the highway, including SatNav systems. Yes, even on a hard-shoulder. That is why they are designed to "talk" to the driver. Drivers must leave the road completely to adjust these devices so the car will not cause a hazard to others. Excepted are special screens used to give rear views instead of wing mirrors, as on some new cars such as supercars, and on large trucks and vehicle remote camera reversing systems.

⇒ Mobile phones. Only true hands-free phones, where the speaker (headphone) is NOT attached to the driver's ear / s, are allowed. This also includes music players. Only deaf aids are allowed to be inserted in a driver's ear/s. Note that as cyclists and pedestrians are road-users, they can be fined as well if they cause an accident through having their ears "blocked" with music or any such sounds, or if they are involved in one because they were "deaf". Also, can the employers of van drivers who supply or knowingly let their staff use a mobile while on the road and while working. After all, by not having a company supplied hands-free kit in the vehicle, they must also be culpable.

⇒ Cyclists may ride closely, two abreast on the right hand side of the highways as long as they do not cause a hazard to other road-users. They must wear approved safety helmets and approved reflective clothing outside of urban areas. Other vehicle drivers must give way to cyclists at all times especially on roundabouts and junctions. Colliding with a cyclist by a vehicle driver is very difficult to defend.

⇒ Heavy penalties for drivers who use a radar signal speed checking device to warn of such official speed traps. This includes all foreign cars.

⇒ While many may be annoyed at the many Laws, most are for good reasons based on actual accidents. Spain has had one of the highest death rates on the roads in the EU. Officially conducted polls show that about 60% of children are not strapped into a car seat, and those under three, or up to 150 cm (4ft: 9ins), of course, are not big enough to safely use the normal seat belts. The Police Forces, especially the *Guardia Civil*, have been motivated to apply these and existing road safety laws, to reduce the high death and injury rates in Spain, so please be warned and be aware. However, recent changes to the laws and the dedicated checking of them by the GC and policias are working, and the deaths for 2007 are down overall compared with 2006, except for the summer holiday period where they were up. The problem appears to be the apparent inability of many drivers to obey laws that have been made as the result of actual accidents, such as using a mobile phone at the wheel, drinking and driving, not wearing a seat belt or a helmet on a moto and speeding in the wrong places and most important, taking much needed rests on long journeys.

SAVING LIVES AND INJURIES IS THE OBJECTIVE - AND **IT IS WORKING.**

SO YOU HAVE BEEN BANNED FROM DRIVING?

Many drivers that are banned from driving seem to ignore the ban and carry on as before. We are told that this is common in the UK, but recently Trafico advised that they estimate that 2-million drivers drive here without a current driving licence which also means no insurance, so it seems to be universal. If they live in a small community, they are often soon caught and suffer the penalty of even jail if they have had an accident and have hurt someone. But what happens if you are banned and have the assets to negate the effects? The law in the EU at this time is that if you are banned in one EU State, if you are moving to another, even for a short period of time, you can drive there as long as you have your original driving licence. In Spain this means that your driving licence is handed to the police for safe keeping until the banning period is finished and then it can be collected, but if you can prove that you are going to go to, for example, the UK, as long as you do not drive a vehicle in Spain, you can collect your DL and travel (fly) to the UK and drive there. This is being changed though via Brussels.

The EU has been discussing this problem for some years and the last paper on it, called the Explanatory Report on the Convention on Driving Disqualifications, 1999/C 211/01, dated (approved) 24 June 1999, states that the question has not been settled yet. I have also telephoned the DVLA and they confirm this and that is why such people as the "inflated Jordan" who was last year (2006) in the UK was banned for a year and fined £5.000 (€7.000) for drunken driving (again) was seen a few days later according to the Press, driving a rental car in Ibiza .

So there it is. However, of course, you must inform your insurance company of the ban and the possibility exists that you may find it very difficult to obtain cover, especially for a drinking / drugging and driving ban.

However, make sure that you understand the instructions on how any ban works and avoid the error that a reader in the Gran Canarias made where he was stopped for speeding at 100 kph in a 60 zone in 2005 (before penalty points started), was fined and told he was banned for a month. He later wrote to me, (for sympathy?) to tell me that he went home and did not drive his car for a month. At the end of the month the policia local (who had trapped him and issued the penalty) called and asked him to bring his licence to the station. This was because he had 15 days to let the authorities know that he was either going to legally dispute the charge or not. He did not, and after that "admission of guilt", the ban started. So he was inadvertently and effectively banned for two months in all.

MOST TRAFFIC LAWS ARE MADE TO SAVE LIVES.

DRIVING IN THE SPANISH TOWNS/CITIES.

The advice here applies to most cities, towns and villages.

All the major cities are beautiful, especially in the old centres, some of which are restored or are being restored as traffic-free tourist areas. The buildings and old palaces (*palacios)* are well worth visiting and many tourists miss a lot by sticking to the beaches and the bars while on holiday. The rental car business in Spain is very competitive, so in summer when they are very busy and in September and October as well, always book well ahead. Make sure it is air-conditioned in the summer: from December to May, you do not usually need air-conditioning in the car. There are no charges for the daily mileage but refer to the advice in this book on renting vehicles in Spain. If possible book directly with a rental company, even over the Internet, to save money.

The author's advice on driving in Madrid is, if possible, don't! The traffic is very dense, the streets often narrow, especially the older back-streets, and parking almost impossible. The best way to see Madrid is by underground (*metro* - clean and fast), taxi, bus, or an organised tour. Barcelona and other cities all suffer from similar problems but have the same excellent solutions. Stay outside of town and travel in by public transport; safer and cheaper especially if you have a drink.

The new AVE high speed trains have now reached Malaga, and they are unique compared with say the British ones in that they are clean, very fast and relatively inexpensive. Also if they are more than five minutes late according to the published schedule, you can apply and get your fare back. And I know where this has happened but 99% of the time, the trains are on time. Why is Britain so far behind? The train was invented in the UK.

Malaga City, in the Province of Malaga is on the south coast on the Costa Del Sol, was not really a tourist city due to the bulk of the suitably prepared tourist destinations being along the coast from Nerja to Gibraltar. However it is now well worth a visit if you appreciate some of the attractions such as the recently opened excellent Picasso Museum, the old cathedral and Gilbafaro Castle. The great tour liner-ships are now stopping off there. But as ever, beware of pick-pockets and other con-people.

There are some points to note with driving in Malaga, as in many other older Spanish cities. These are (to name a few): -

Road name plates in many cities, especially Malaga, may be a series of pretty but impractical ceramic plates placed high on a building where, unless you have a pair of binoculars, you cannot easily read them especially when driving by in traffic. They are also very few in number, possibly only one at a complex intersection, or only on one side of the road in the whole street. If you can, use a SatNav or have a manp reading passenger with a good street map.

Direct left turns are often forbidden to keep the traffic flowing and avoid rear-enders, but watch out for a road junction where a large "divided island" is built into it. I have drawn a plan of how they work with more information on Page 110. Sorry it is a bit basic. If a solid white line in the centre of the road has a dotted section at a junction where you wish to turn left, you may do so with extreme care, but look to see if there is a time restriction sign (only at certain times?).

This forbidding of making direct left turns applies on many two-way roads on the open road as well, and they are well sign-posted, especially where there is a single or double central solid white line (yellow at road works). Refer to the Signs Pages for details. Usually you only have a short distance to go to reach a roundabout or junction where turning left or returning back the way you have come is easy without causing a traffic-jam or accident, but if you cheat and disobey the sign, you may hear the piercing sound of a policeman's football whistle telling you that you are "off-side", and then be involved in a discussion on your misdemeanour, with the usual paperwork, possibly getting a "red-card" *(multa* or fine*)*.

REAR VIEW MIRROR ADVICE.   It is a good idea when parking in the narrow streets, to fold your door/wing mirrors back if it is very narrow. It is not uncommon to see these mirrors hanging down broken after they have been hit by a truck or another car.

ROADS WITHOUT FOOTPATHS. Where there are no footpaths in a residential area, the speed limit is automatically 20 kph (12 mph) unless signed otherwise. It could be as low as 10 kph for the whole urbanisation or district where the roads are narrow and this will be on a sign at the entrance. You must also legally give pedestrians a clearance of at least 1-1/2 metres (4-feet) and this is worth remembering if you hit one and have to go to Court. Some village roads where pavements are very narrow have white lines painted in the gutter. No part of your vehicle is not allowed to be over these lines, including wing mirrors, etc as they are intended to ensure that pedestrians have enough room on the path without being hit by, for example, a door mirror.

I personally have had a few "arguments" with a few drivers who speed at ridiculous rates in our residential areas and they seem to think that a "50" speed sign means 50 mph, not 30 mph. We have a cat and there are always children and other pets about. It starts off with a polite from me, "Please do not drive too fast as we have children and pets around here...." and often ends up with, from the driver, "I was not driving too fast, mind your own business, etc." All the usual from those who should not really be driving at all when you smell their alcoholic breath. One in 2007 despite his nice and polite female companion unsuccessfuly telling him to stay cool as I was being polite (perhaps that was the reason - he may have thought I was a pushover), insisted on being obnoxious and then called my wife a rude name. Before I had got to him to demand an apology my wife had run up to him and torn his shirt and he was so surprised he walked away muttering leaving me laughing. No one messes with my wife. The few Spanish who do it though are usually bemused and usually say "vale" (OK) with a smile. Is that why there are so many camera traps in the UK? I hope not.

INFORMATION ON TYRES AND OTHER CAR SYSTEMS.

HOW INFLATION AFFECTS TREAD-TO-ROAD CONTACT

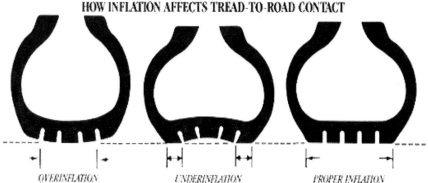

OVERINFLATION   UNDERINFLATION   PROPER INFLATION

Both overinflation and underinflation reduce tread contact with the road. Proper inflation assures maximum contact.

Why it is important to ensure tyre pressures are correct, especially if you carry a heavy load over a long distance. Correct inflation keeps the most tread in contact with the road, ensures a longer tyre life, better fuel consumption and less chance of an accident.

All wheel alignment: OK, we know it costs about €30 (£20) to have it done, but it not only greatly extends tyre life but makes the car much more pleasant to drive and lowers fuel consumption again.

LOW ASPECT RATIO TYRES. These are where the height of the tyre is much less than normal giving a more rigid sidewall. While making steering response better in fast driving, but in practice most drivers are unable to take advantage of this on the roads as it can be too dangerous. There are four disadvantages with the "extreme" types of these tyres (below 45%):

1. They are much more expensive than the commoner types.
2. They can be difficult to find in an emergency, especially when touring in a "different" country. I had one BMW owner/reader wait two days in rural Spain for the delivery of the special size. He also had different sizes front and rear and no spare the correct size.
3. They provide less protection for the rims, which are usually expensive special ones, on rough stony dirt roads.
4. They are less comfortable than tyres with greater height.
5. Only a very experienced driver can take advantage of them on public roads at speeds which could be described as dangerous.

RADIAL PLY TYRES that are now standard on just about all vehicles, except some heavy duty slow ones have been with us for many years and for good reason. They keep the tread on the road even and under heavy cornering, supply more comfort as the sidewalls are flexible, and also have steel belting under the tread to stop most punctures. They also have less rolling resistance and so give better fuel consumption. But it is important that they are checked preferably weekly for pressures and for damage after hitting bad bumps or rubbish in the road.

TYRE TREAD DEPTH

The law in Spain about minimum worn tyre tread depths is that the tyre must have a miniumum of 1,6 mm all round and across the tyre rolling surface. In the event of an accident, an insurance accident assessor will check this and if lower on any tyre may disallow any claim on your part.

But with a tread depth of even 2 mm, in heavy rain, speeds have to be kept low (not more than 80 kph–50 mph) to avoid sliding or "aquaplaning" in even a moderately hard braking situation. ABS (Anti-lock Brake System) braking systems will not stop you "floating" (aquaplaning) on the rain-water covered roads, nor will they allow you to stop more quickly except in certain circumstances. They just eliminate the panic, foot hard down on brake pedal action, "help, I am going faster, out of control" that many inexperienced drivers do when in an emergency stopping situation. The depth of the tread and tyre pressures are the most important factors in stopping quickly in these conditions and on all cars it is best to have the best tyres on the front end (steering and weight transfer while braking.

UK magazine Auto Express took three cars, a Renault Clio 1, 4 litre, a Ford Focus 1, 8 litre and an Audi A4, 2 litre. They tested the cars at a test track where the speeds and distances can be accurately measured, and the road could be sprayed uniformly with water to provide similar conditions as on an autovia or motorway. The starting speed for each vehicle with an independent measuring device (not the car's speedo) was 113 kph (70 mph) which in the UK is the maximum limit. Here we are allowed to go at 120 kph or 75 mph, so the stopping distances are greater if you are crazy enough to drive at these speeds on a very wet road.

Test Car, braking from 113 kph (1)	Stopping Distance with 3 mm tread (2)	Stopping Distance with 1, 8 mm tread (3)	Difference in Stopping Distances (4)	Speed of 1, 8 mm car when 3 mm car had stopped. (5)
Renault Clio 1,4	113 metres	151 metres	38 metres	80 kph
Ford Focus 1,8	91 meters	135 metres	44 metres	80 kph
Toyota RAV4 1,8	118 metres	155 metres	37metres	80 kph
Audi A4 2.0	97 meters	127 metres	30metres	65 kph

⇒ Column 2 shows the stopping distance with 3 mm tread tyres, accurately measured and prepared for the test. It is interesting to note that the 4 x 4 Toyota RAV4 stops 27 metres further on than the Focus, which could be due to its higher centre of gravity as this vehicle is supplied with wide treads. It could mean that the water cannot be dispersed quickly enough by the tyre treads and so should never be driven in similar conditions at speeds greater than say 80 - 90 kph. One would think that the Renault being lower and lighter than the Focus and the Audi would stop well under 100 metres, but it did not. The Focus and the Audi are shown as the safer cars in these conditions, but it also shows that all cars, especially those with very wide tyres, should not be driven more than say 90 - 100 kph in heavy rain to avoid aquaplaning.

⇒ <u>Column 3</u> shows the same cars with the wheels changed to the same make and type of tyres with only 1, 8 mm of tread.

⇒ <u>Column 4</u> shows the difference in stopping distance between the two differently equipped but otherwise identical vehicles in each row, and as you can see the difference for the Ford Focus was a massive 44 metres more which is just over 140 feet. This represents more or less 10 car lengths, the difference between stopping and having a nasty accident where usually the driver of the car at the rear is judged to be at fault depending on the circumstances.

⇒ <u>Column 5</u> shows the speeds of the 1, 8 mm tyred vehicles as they "pass" the just stopped 3 mm cars. The differences show the choice between a nasty collision and safety depending on your tyre tread depth, although, of course, if the vehicle behind yours has 1, 8 mm tyres, it could after you have stopped with your good tyres, crash into your rear end at a speed as much as 80 kph if on the highway in similar conditions. A frightening thought and an important thing to note after a road accident when looking at the other driver's vehicle with your camera ready.

While mentioning ABS (BRAKING) SYSTEMS, many drivers think that they can allow you to brake in a shorter distance. This is not strictly true, except on a very wet, icy or greasy road where a driver's lack of skill may mean that in a panic, the brake pedal is just stood on causing a locked-wheel skid. The main design advantage of ABS is that you can <u>maintain steering control</u> while braking heavily, even on a mixed road surface, e.g. one side of the car wheels on the tar, the other on the dirt at the road side. On a slippery road, especially after it rains after a long dry period and the road is very slippery (body repair shops work overtime for a few weeks), instead of sliding out of control off the road, you can still steer the car hopefully away from other traffic while braking, but with this system, the tyres ability to better grip the road and stop you in a shorter distance is mostly a fallacy.

For those who do not know what ABS brakes are, they are devices fitted to vehicles, even motorcycles, that ensure the wheels do not lock and skid when braking. Just as the individual wheel is about to lock up, the system automatically releases the braking oil pressure to that wheel's brake.

Another device is (various names by different makers) <u>ESP or Electronic Stabilisation Programme</u>, this one being the VW name. This is where if a vehicle is going too fast for say a bend, the system (if switched on by the driver) takes over, lifts the accelerator and the system automatically brakes gently on individual road wheels to hopefully bring the vehicle under control again. To experienced and skilled drivers, this system may seem to take the fun out of driving (that is why you can switch it off) but I am sure you would agree that there are many whose skills are never developed beyond those of just getting from A to B, and if the system in an emergency saves lives, it has to be good.

The EU is considering making ESP which currently, except on the very pricey vehicles, is an option, as well as ABS, compulsory on all vehicles in the near future.

XENON Lighting. For the last 30 years or so, halogen headlights have been the standard on all motor vehicles. They are very reliable and give an excellent white light. EU regulations state that headlights must not have a higher wattage (or brightness factor) than 60 for main beam and 55 for dipped. XENON lighting uses xenon gas instead of halogen gas in the bulbs or lamps and is purported to give a much higher brightness without going over the 60 watts legal limit. (Don't ask, it must be magic!) Also the bulbs last the life of the vehicle (if not smashed). But as the Xenon systems (they need other control units) are listed as an option that can cost as much as a €1.000 extra, or more if an expensive German car, and halogen bulbs last 5 years usually, with excellent lighting, so personally I cannot really see the point. Unless you are night-blind anyway of course and need a lot of help. But then perhaps you should not drive at night for your own self preservation and comfort. My wife hates driving at night.

BRITISH VEHICLE REGISTRATION FORMS.

The old V5 motor registration documents issued prior to January 2004 are now obsolete. This means that from July 2005, the Form V5C is the only legal registration document that will be generally accepted by the authorities especially in Spain and on the Continent.

Now you may say, how does that affect me here with my UK plated vehicle? Well, the whole purpose of the newer Form V5C, like the driving licences, is standardisation in Europe so a policeman reading your V5C elswhere, knows what details should be in a particular block regardless of the language of the document. What it also means is that unless you have the newer document, you could be issued with a fine if stopped at the side of the road if the policeman is having a blitz day and knows the laws. Also, selling the car can become a problem, because the older document may not be accepted in Spain without an official translation into Spanish, or at least it may cause a delay in any transaction. Fortunately though, not everyone in Spain keeps up to date with the changes, but on a planned blitz day on the roads, they usually have a lecture by the experts before they leave the station.

Please note that it is illegal to sell a foreign plated car in Spain unless it is being transferred to Spanish plates as part of the sale. This applies throughout the EU. But it happens. Also, if you are buying and taking a UK-plated car back to the UK, check before you buy that it is free of any taxes and fines owed, or worse still, it has been reported stolen. It can be checked through the DVLA web-site.

Please go to the DVLA web site at this address for more detailed information:
http://www.dvla.gov.uk/

TYRE PRESSURE TABLE

Bars	Psi	Kpa
1	15	100
1,1	16	110
1,2	17	120
1,3	19	130
1,4	20	140
1,5	22	150
1,6	23	160
1,7	25	170
1,8	26	180
1,9	28	190
2	29	200
2,2	32	220
2,4	35	240
2,6	38	260
2,8	41	280
3	44	300
3,2	46	320
3,4	49	340
3,6	52	360
3,8	55	380
4	58	400
5	73	500
6	87	600

Correct tyre pressures are very important for safety and the long life of tyres, and for driving pleasure. A soft tyre can cause skidding or even a blow-out with disastrous consequences. Rental cars especially need checking on acceptance or soon after.

Also, in the event of an accident, the investigator will check the tyres to see if they are a possible cause.

For those confused by the three ways of measuring tyre pressures, the table here will tell you what the local gauges at the service stations show if you are used to PSI or pounds per square inch.

Most gauges here have "Bars" or barometric pressures and Kpa, or Kilopascals. The figures are the same with the decimal point moved, but many garages also have a "psi" or pounds per square inch scale on the gauge.

The valve caps on the inflation points on the wheels are very important to keep out dust which is very prevalent here, especially in the summer. I always make sure mine are fitted.

The figures are rounded off, as the average pressure gauge will not measure tenths of a unit.

As a guide, the average car used locally should have about 200 - 220 Kpa. Laden for a journey, could mean 30 to 50 Kpa more. Check your operator book or if it is there, a sticker usually found in the doorway of your car to be sure.

TYRE CODE TABLE FOR WEIGHTS AND SPEEDS

Code on Tyre	Max. load. Kg	Code on Tyre	Max. load. Kg
62	265	82	475
63	272	83	487
64	280	84	500
65	290	85	515
66	300	86	530
67	307	87	545
68	315	88	560
69	325	89	580
70	335	90	600
71	345	91	615
72	355	92	630
73	365	93	650
74	375	94	670
75	387	95	690
76	400	96	710
77	412	97	730
78	425	98	750
79	437	99	775
80	450	100	800
81	462		

Why are wheel sizes still rated in inches instead of a metric measure?

The modern pneumatic tyres and wheel sizes were first designed by British and American designers who specified inches in their drawings. It is far too expensive to change the designs now for the wheel diameters to be in centimetres although tyres have long been converted to metric.

Codes on tyres

Date of manufacture:

Code starts with an "E" that denotes EU homolgamation.

Codigo xxxx xxxx 3407

3407 = week 34 in 2007.

Some tyres have arrows to denote correct direction of rotation direction when fitted.

THE MAXIMUM LOAD TABLE above shows that most weight per tyre that it is designed to carry when inflated to the pressure as recommended by the manufacturer. Even tyres of the same physical size can have different loads due to the construction of the tyre.

The maximum speed table on the right shows the maximum continuous speed that a tyre is designed to run at. The sizes for any approved EU vehicle are shown in the *Tarjeta de InspeccionTecnica de Vehiculos*. Only the sizes listed on the card may be legally fitted to that vehicle.

Example tyre size. 195/65R16 96V

195	= nominal width of tyre in mm.
60	= percentage of tyre wall depth e.g. 60% of 195mm.
R	= Radial Ply construction.
16	= Diameter of wheel in inches, e.g. 16 inches.
96	= maximum static load = 710 kg (per tyre).
V	= 240 kph maximum continuous speed.

See also coding above right.

Code	Speed
M	130
N	140
P	150
Q	160
R	170
S	180
T	190
H	210
V	240
W	270
Y	300
VR	>210
ZR	>240

MORE GENERAL NOTES ON DRIVING IN SPAIN.

Some of the following also apply "at home", but should be emphasised due to the importance of observance in Spain to avoid spoiling your holiday, or worse.

⇒   Road-junctions, remember to give way to vehicles coming from <u>your left</u> (you may be used to right) if you are on the minor road.   The <u>only time</u> you give way to traffic coming <u>from your right</u> is when road-sign markings (no priority signs) dictate, and this can be, for example, on a roundabout or a "blind" T-junction. The other common road sign is a <u>give way</u>, "*ceda el paso*" (white background, inverted triangular sign with a red border). Also there may (should be, if not worn away or covered in tyre rubber and oil in the summer months) a give-way sign, an inverted white triangle, painted ON the road. See also the (confusing) sign on page 262 which is a give-way to the right.

⇒   Priority roads. These are main roads and are marked with a yellow diamond on a white background for the priority traffic to follow, with a black diagonal line through the diamond when the priority ends. You have right of way.

⇒   Emergency vehicles: all have priority, including virtually anything with a siren, flashing roof lights or a bell. Safely pull over and stop or visibly slow down so the driver knows he/she can safely pass. It is an offence (and silly) not to not do so.

⇒   Wearing of seat belts, if fitted, by <u>all persons</u> in the car, is mandatory in Spain, and the <u>driver can be fined</u> for anyone in the car not obeying this Law. Being caught <u>without a seat belt</u>, even in the rear seats, can cost you as the driver two penalty points, and you and any adult passengers up to €300 each at this time.

⇒   It is illegal to have a child aged <u>under twelve</u> in the front seats. Also, you may not have a child seat in the front due to possible injury from airbag inflation. Also, if in an accident where personal injury occurs, the insurance company concerned may refuse, or attempt to, in part or in full, to compensate the injured offender.

⇒   Headlamps must be used when driving after dusk/dark or in poor visibility, and this includes when other vehicle drivers may have problems in <u>seeing you</u>, and while the reader may think this point is the same everywhere, offenders abound and cause accidents.

⇒   Make sure your headlamps are <u>converted</u> to driving on the right side of the road. Refer to your car's handbook. Penalty points are lost by offenders.

⇒   You must use your dipped headlights in tunnels, not just parking lights.

⇒   Most tunnels have speed limits, but some where there are wide hard-shoulders allow the limit posted on the road before the tunnel to continue.

⇒   Keep a good distance from the vehicle in front as the official laid down figures are specified as 4 seconds or 100 metres for a MAM under 3.500 kg vehicles and 6 seconds or 150 metres for over a MAM of 3.500 kg.

⇒ Flashing headlights behind a driver in the fast lane will normally cause him/ her to move over into the right lane if there is no traffic in front of that driver. Spanish drivers are usually very good at pulling over without this indication from the driver behind. Most offenders who stay in the outer lanes are usually foreigners or the younger, "macho" *señors* from major Spanish cities. You may also use your flashing headlights to prevent an accident, but for no other reason legally such as allowing a driver to exit a side street or especially to warn of a speed trap. You are not allowed to have headlights on at all when parked.

⇒ Toll roads. When approaching a set of payment booths, slow down well in advance. Have the cash ready to save time. Note the cash booths with a green arrow light over the lane: these are open. There is more on Toll roads in this book.

⇒ Traffic lights. Spain has saved millions by only having full-sized traffic lights installed, in most cases, at the point where the driver has to stop: that is not on the other side of the junction as well. This would have placed the first driver in line in a difficult position as the driver cannot see the traffic lights without peering forward and up so to overcome this problem, there are miniature red and green lights on the post holding the main lights at driver eye-level and you can use these to check when you can go if you are at the front of the queue.

⇒ A vehicle travelling on a tarred road has priority over any vehicle at junction that is emerging from an untarred road. Priority is also always given to vehicles on rails (trains & trams).

⇒ At a road junction where there are no signs, and the road are equal in status, you must give way to a vehicle coming from your right.

THE SEQUENCES FOR TRAFFIC SIGNAL LIGHTS ARE:

RED for STOP.

FLASHING AMBER. CAUTION warning at the junction. If safe to, PROCEED SLOWLY. A flashing amber light always means caution even when not at a road junction. Many accidents happen in Spain due to drivers accelerating on the amber light. If at a pedestrian crossing, you may go if there are no people crossing.

GREEN — GO, if safe to do so. Check for traffic light "hoppers from usually the left".

AMBER after GREEN, STOP if you have not passed the stop line or keep going if by stopping quickly may cause an accident (rear-ender). Police may be watching at these points and usually have a partner down the road to stop you if you do not obey this safety rule. This offence can also add penalty points on your licence.

⇒ When going through junctions with a yellow stripes painted on the crossin area, make sure you can exit that area BEFORE entering. If the traffic lights change and you are stuck there due to the traffic in your direction not moving, you can receive a fine and lose penalty points. On busy days, there are usually local police on duty for this and other reasons and a blast from a football type whistle is not a good sound to hear then.

⇒ <u>Flashing red lights</u> on a post at the side of the road are used to warn of traffic lights or another hazard such as a roundabout on a fast (80 kph or 50 mph?) road ahead, or you are entering / in a restricted speed area.

⇒ When driving in heavy traffic on a dual carriageway (*autopista, autovia, carretera*, etc.) If the traffic ahead is stalled especially in your lane, you must by Law, switch on your four-way flashers/hazard lights to warn the vehicles behind.

⇒ It is a very necessary habit to be aware of drivers following too closely in Spain, and the author's car has been badly rammed from behind by a "dozy" (foreign) driver on the autovia who was not looking ahead, seeing and taking action to avoid a road jam 200 metres ahead. I stopped in good time but he hit our car with all four wheels locked and that incident has since caused my wife to be very apprehensive whenever I brake even very moderately on the autovias.

⇒ <u>Slow driving</u> is one of the main causes of accidents in Spain according to Trafico reports. It is significant that many of the older Spanish drivers did not get a car until late in life due to Spain's economic position under Franco and in the thirty-odd years since, so many "rode a donkey" or only a moped for many years. They are therefore not used to driving at speeds that many foreigners have grown up with, — but do tend to live a longer stress-free life.

⇒ <u>Horns</u>. You are NOT ALLOWED to sound your horn <u>at night</u> in town especially residential areas and a fine will be the result if caught. Horns must only be used <u>in an emergency</u> as a warning to prevent an accident, which can include on a narrow road with sharp blind bends, or when overtaking.

⇒ Do not drive in <u>bus-lanes</u> except in an emergency, which must be then proven.

⇒ <u>White lines.</u> A single or double white line in the middle of the road, usually accompanied by the requisite signs, means no overtaking and the fines are very heavy, with penalty points or licence suspension for offenders. You may only cross a single white line to turn left if there is a short broken line section at the turn. Otherwise go on to usually a roundabout and come back and turn right.

⇒ It is illegal to "undertake" (pass on the right) on a multi-lane highway (*autopista*, carretera, etc.) unless you are in a signed lane going off to another road.

⇒ Do not practice "road rage" as in an argument with the police, you will lose and they are allowed to "restrain you" using force and will do if necessary. Forget about claiming for assault by a policeman unless you are visibly injured by more than a "clipped ear", especially if you are young. The Spanish still respect sensible sober "senior citizens". If you are not used to driving on the Continent, this problem should not apply to you, of course, as you will be extra careful due to being unfamiliar with the roads, especially when driving on the right.

⇒ Motor scooters and mopeds. It would appear that at least 50% of young moped and scooter riders are suicidal, ignore all road laws, especially red lights and Stop street signs, and their high accident rates tend to prove this perception. Do not get upset with them unless they they actually hit your vehicle or put your life in danger. (We were all young once and we survived.) Many do have accidents and they can often be seen riding their only means of transport (scooter) with a leg in plaster, often with crutches strapped on the back, and it is the opinion of the author that the police and parents do not take enough action (discipline) to help them save themselves, although the police do have occasional "blitzes".

⇒ Driving school instruction is given for riders of up to 49cc machines, and the test questions are on the Trafico web-site as explained in this book. Despite frequent warnings, far too many moto-riders ride without crash helmets and other protective clothing. They say it is too hot, even in winter and as a consequence, insurance for two-wheeled vehicles in Spain is consequently very high. There have been complaints in the motoring Press about it, but the author can see no solution without intensive training and more action by Trafico and the police to reduce the high accident rates. Always give scooter / moped riders a wide berth.

⇒ From late 2007, the moto rider licence classifications have changed (A1, A2 & A3) and these are explained in the relevant pages in this book.

⇒ You must have a nationality identification plate of your country fitted to the rear of your foreign vehicle, although with the new EU plates with this feature on them, this applies more to the older vehicles. I see some UK vehicles have a Union Flag instead of the GB in the ring of stars. If so, then those cars need a "GB" sticker as well to be legal in other EU countries.

⇒ Snow chains are compulsory on some (mountain?) roads when necessary, and road signs advise these areas. It is an offence to not drive with them fitted if the road is posted and the conditions are such that it is necessary because you may get stuck and block the road, or worse. You may also use studded tyres.

⇒ When in a three-lane road with the centre lane used for overtaking, you must have your headlights on dipped as a safety precaution so any vehicles approaching from the other direction, can see that you are coming towards them and pull back to the right. Sensible law, but hardly anyone obeys it.

⇒ We still see far too many people with a broken down vehicle outside of town, out of the vehicle and not wearing an approved reflective jacket. The police have been instructed to be very tough as there has been deaths and serious injuries as a result. The drivers whose vehicles has hit the other persons have reportably said, "I did not see him until it was too late." Hence this jacket Law.

⇒ Cars must not be overloaded, (with heavy roof luggage as well), although the French drivers going to and from North Africa do not seem aware of this Law. High gusty winds can cause such vehicles to be very "exciting" to drive, and also forces them to travel at very low speeds holding up normal traffic. You often see them with no rear suspension travel at all.

⇒ Pet animals must be restrained in a vehicle and not allowed to be free to romp around in the passenger section. This also applies to children; safety belts/chairs!

⇒ Anti-glare equipment (heavily-tinted glass, blinds, etc.) must not be fitted to the rear windows of vehicles unless two wing mirrors are fitted. See also tinted glass chapter in this book.

⇒ Reversing into side roads to effect a turn and three-point turns is not allowed in city/ village streets. U-turns (one sweep) may be made on wide main single-carriageway roads when safe to do so and the road signs and centre lines do not forbid the action. Remember to turn left, the opposite way to the UK and Ireland.

⇒ Beware of donkeys, sheep and goats on narrow country roads. Some minor roads are very narrow especially in mountainous areas, with hairpin bends and blind corners. You should use your horn here for safety's sake, and listen for any other driver doing the same from the other way. Keep well to the right side of the road and drive carefully. Many drivers seem to need a white line painting in the middle of the road to keep right.

⇒ It has been said before in this book, but bears repeating as it means an instant fine and penalty points if a driver is caught. You are not allowed to use a mobile phone without a proper hands-free kit fitted in the car with no ear-pieces. Some phones have bluetooth ear pieces which are not allowed at all while behind the wheel, even stopped on the road in Spain. This also includes the use of music equipment with ear phones. You are not allowed to even pull over to answer the mobile phone unless you are completely off the public road, and this includes the hard-shoulder which is part of the road. Those of us who are "good drivers" abhor the stupid habit of driving and talking into a handheld phone and despite driving expensive cars, many drivers seem to still be doing it. It is legal to use a proper hands-free system with separate speaker and microphone though, even though this in my opinion really is also a dangerous distraction. And we have a quality hands-free kit in our car. The police are instructed to be very tough on this offence.

<u>IT IS IMPORTANT TO NOTE</u> that , even in a rental car, you are expected to carry: -

⇒ Two EU APPROVED RED TRIANGLES which are to be placed at the side of the road, plainly visible to traffic, if you are forced to stop for any reason on or just off the road on the hard-shoulder. If on a narrow two-way road, one should be facing the opposing traffic flow on the other side of the road, the other behind your vehicle. If on a fast road, one about 100 metres behind your car (especially if there is a blind corner there) and the other about 30 metres behind. The spacing depends on the speed of the traffic on that road. Carry a torch to warn other traffic also if necessary. Many people have been killed or seriously injured in Spain while working on their car after a breakdown at the side of the road. You do not need these triangles on a motorcycle which can usually be moved out of the road lanes.

⇒ SPARE LAMPS OR BULBS for your headlights and rear lights. If you are stopped by the police and do not have spare lamps/bulbs, you may be fined, especially if you have a failed lamp. You must also have the tool/s to change them.

⇒ A reflective jacket (day and night) or vest *(chaleco)*, EU approved, for use while working on the vehicle or walking on the road after a breakdown, etc. anywhere outside of a lit town area, even in daylight.   Must be kept in the driver section of the car so it can be put on before exiting the car, and able to be seen from outside the car for police checks. Carry enough jackets for the main occupants.

⇒ If you wear spectacles for driving, you may be asked to show a spare pair if stopped by the police.   Drivers again have used as an excuse in the past that an accident was caused because they had mislaid or broke their spectacles and "I had to drive".

⇒ You may be asked for a cash deposit for the items below supplied by the rental company, who are bound by the law to make sure they are in the vehicle when it is delivered to the renter.

CHECK LIST FOR YOUR, OR THE RENTAL, VEHICLE.

◆ Approved reflective triangles.   2
◆ Spare set of lamps (bulbs), plus tool
   to fit them, if needed.   1 set
◆ Approved reflective jacket/vest.   1 (or more).
◆ Plus, your spare driving spectacles if worn.   1

You do not need to carry a first-aid kit or a fire extinguisher unless you are operating a PSV or HGV (taxis, buses and trucks), although they are recommended.

DRIVING A FOREIGN-PLATED VEHICLE IN SPAIN.

A. Foreigner—anyone who is not a citizen or permanent resident (has *residencia*) in Spain.

B. Foreign plated car—any vehicle not on Spanish registration plates.

As a tourist or visitor, you are not permitted to use your foreign passenger car or motorcycle in Spain for more than six months in any one calendar year. You may if you are an official student or officially working for a Spanish organisation who will organise the legality. This can effectively be extended to a year if from July of one year to June of the next. Commercial (working) vehicles are restricted to a one month but must be driven out of Spain and back (on business?) to qualify and they must not be used locally for deliveries or business, only for delivering from / to outside Spain, etc. It is essential in all cases that the driver / owner can prove that he / she is obeying the Law, and is not up to the police to prove that you are not, and it has been known where the police, during a roadside check, have charged drivers (usually commercials) where the car is only suspected of being operated illegally.

For private vehicles and as an EU citizen, you are classified as a tourist if you stay less than six months in Spain. If you intend to stay for more than six months especially if you have a property here, you will have to register for an NIE (*numero de identification de extranjero*, or foreigner's identification number). This will make it easy for you to buy a Spanish plated vehicle for use in Spain. There is no charge for this and it is a simple task, if you like queuing. You do not under EU regulations have to carry your passport with you (especially with the extremely high cost of British passports). I carry a photocopy of my passport and have had it accepted with no exceptions, as well as having a Spanish driving licence, but a foreign EU licence with a photo on it will be OK. Longer than six months, then you must register (*residencia):* a small charge is made for this to cover the cost of the administration and now it is an A4 certificate (since March 2007), not a card, although the cards are still legal until they expire. Again carry a photcopy with you which can be backed up with your driving licence with a photo on it. Spain is then classified as your main place of residence and then you pay taxes here, etc. When you take out *residencia, if you have a foreign-plated vehicle,* you then have 30 days to re-register it onto Spanish plates, but you do not need to change your foreign EU driving licence as long as it is current. You can keep your foreign EU licence, but the Spanish one is OK and can have benefits as explained in the Driving Licence pages in this book.

However, when your foreign EU licence expires at say age 70 (60 for vocational classes), you will have to obtain a new Spanish licence if you are resident here, and if you do not have the medicals as the Spanish do, your DL will have expired legally regardless of the actual date of expiry on the DL itself. I know this is repeated but most people who do not buy this book or take any interest in being legal are placing themselves at risk, especially if they have a serious traffic accident.

However, you should protect yourself from unnecessary Spanish police charges such as using your foreign-plated vehicle here while being also resident. The police, especially the *Guardia Civil* are patrolling the main roads looking for drug dealers so they randomly stop vehicles, and they may choose you and if you cannot prove that you are not resident here (for less than six months per year, and consequently using the car within the six month rule), they will charge you and it is up to you to prove that you are innocent, even if you have been here only a month remembering that, if you an EU citizen, your passport will not be stamped to prove this. If you are not resident here, carry copies of documents to prove this such as airplane, boat or train tickets, etc. If you are caught and proven to be resident here, you will also be forced to register the car in Spain within 30 days, with the taxes to pay, and still be fined, or have the car impounded, or at least have to employ a lawyer to sort out the problem.

Many foreigners use their cars for sometimes years without paying Spanish or their home country's taxes and, especially if it is an old vehicle, with it being un-roadworthy and a potential danger to all. Also, the insurance company will not usually pay out more than the minimum dictated by law if you have an accident. Another problem is that if you have not followed the 30-day rule, you will not be able to avoid the import duties on the vehicles however long you have owned them. The new duties from January 2008 are based on the CO_2 grammes per kilometre official figures, and if you vehicle is an older model, this figure will be measured at the ITV Station and could attract the higher tax levels regardless of the engine size.

were not driving within the Law and their policy rules. The author has heard of people driving without insurance at all because they discovered that they could not get insurance locally, especially if the vehicle is over ten years old, and their company in the foreign country would probably not cover the risk if they knew that was being driven mainly or totally in Spain without their knowledge.

Spanish insurance companies (not an insurance broker who can do it through, for example, Gibraltar) are not allowed to insure a foreign car in Spain except in special circumstances such as for a few months before exporting it, although you may be able to do it through the Spanish Branch of a UK company (in Gibraltar?), remembering that a car that is not roadworthy (no MOT/ITV) is generally not insured according to many of the insurance companies' rules. Please study the policy small print and ask your broker/agent.

It is not unknown for the police to note when a vehicle is being driven consistently for more than the six months (outside the local school is a favourite place), and to take action against you, and the author personally knows of "victims". You may apply to the local Customs officials (*aduanas*) for your vehicle to be "sealed" (*precintado*) and "unsealed" when you are not using it, so that you have proof that you are obeying the Law. The a*duana* will notify the local *Guardia Civil* who will actually carry out the sealing, which is usually merely placing a special "seal" tape across the steering wheel on a car, and the handlebars on a motorcycle. The process is not expensive but fines are quite heavy for those who are caught breaking these Laws. Also, make sure that you have a safe place to park the vehicle, certainly off the public roads. Apart from vandalism problems, the vehicle may be towed away and scrapped by the police as "*abandonado*" - abandoned.

YOUR FOREIGN PLATED VEHICLE.

If you take out residence Spain is your main place of residence - 183 plus days a year, then you have to put your owned foreign-plated vehicle onto Spanish plates within 30-days from when *residencia* is granted. Not many people know this but the officers of the *Guardia Civil* do, and the author has a copy of an actual *Guardia Civil* charge sheet with a stiff fine for this offence, issued to an English driver. You cannot buy a Spanish-plated vehicle without at least an NIE.

If you take up full residence in Spain, it is better to buy a vehicle with Spanish registration to use in Spain. You can have your vehicle transferred to Spanish plates.

However, due to the procedures, cost of transfer, resale price and the (minor) problem of a left-hand drive (steering wheel on the right) vehicle in Spain and the EU, unless the vehicle is a valuable classic, etc., it is better to buy a Spanish-plated vehicle.

IMPORTING A VEHICLE TO SPAIN FOR OFFICIAL RESIDENCE.

If you wish to import a vehicle into Spain as you intend to live here for more than the six months but intend to return with it to your own country, the following notes apply, but it is advised that for your specific need, you place it in the hands of a Spanish advisor (*gestor*) or lawyer (*abogado*) as they will know the latest rules as far as Spain is concerned, and how to smooth the paperwork through the system. Check with the local Consulate for your country of origin or where you wish to return to with the vehicle for the rules in that eventual destination.

EU CITIZENS. Vehicles owned by the EU citizen & sales taxes paid in country of origin. The importation will be exempt from import duties and registration taxes, but not fees to carry out the registration procedure, plus the cost of using an advisor (*gestor*). The conditions are: -

⇒   You must have owned the vehicle for at least three months.

⇒   The procedure applies to caravans and trailers, but vehicles with engines of up to 49 cc are not classified for this purpose as a "motor vehicle" and may be imported as personal belongings.

⇒   It must have originated in an EU country (see below, homologation, non-EU citizens).

⇒   You must have paid VAT (*IVA*) or sales tax in the country of origin, and have proof of this. If not, then you will have to pay VAT at the 16% rate based on the local value of the vehicle as laid down in the tax authorities tables.)

⇒   You must obtain a certificate of non-residence (*baja de residencia*) for the period concerned from the country you are leaving. This certificate can be obtained usually from the local town hall of the country you are leaving, OR it can be a declaration made to the Spanish Consulate in the country you are leaving, OR, it can be made at your local Consulate e.g. British - very expensive now, soon (one month?) after you arrive here.

⇒   The vehicle, depending on type of use, see pages 96 - 98 , will have to pass the ITV and be checked for the correct EU homolgation as explained in this book.

⇒ You must also be able to prove residence with your local property deeds (the full *nota simple, not just the first pages*) or a current rental contract for more than three months.

The issued certificate may then be attached to your vehicle importation papers. It should be noted that these procedures must be started within one month of the issue of your Residence Certificate (*residencia*) application (not issue) date. I know, it is repeated in this book, but many people who have lived here for years do not know this when questioned by myself. It is recommended that, if your Spanish language skill is weak, you should use an expert advisor (*gestor*), as this is not a common procedure. See pages 287 - 288.

NON-EU CITIZENS.

The same rule applies as above, as far as using a vehicle without Spanish registration, that is, no more than six months in any one calendar year. As a Non-EU person, if you are visiting here for any length of time, you may buy a vehicle and register it on tourist plates (*matricula turista*) if you intend to export it back to your original country at some time in the future. However, you must pay local road tax and it must comply with local Laws. This saves you paying Spanish VAT (or any EU) taxes other than the road tax, if it is intended to export it back to your own country and if the regulations there allow this to be done. You will need to clarify these details in your original country or at the local embassy/consulate. As far as buying the vehicle and registering it on a tourist plan, use a local main dealer who is familiar with the procedure, or a *gestor*, who will carry out the procedure for you. It is not done very often. See pages 287 - 288.

PERMANENTLY IMPORTING VEHICLES OWNED BY A NON-EU CITIZEN.

The importation of personally owned vehicles (only one or two unless an acknowleged collection of historic interest, etc?) will be subject to import duties and registration taxes, and fees to carry out the registration and the costs if using an advisor (*gestor*). The conditions are: -

The vehicle must be standard to EU specifications for that vehicle, known as homolgation (*homolgomación*). To ensure that it does, a certificate called a *ficha reducida,* must be issued by the manufacturer and this can be organised through the local main official distributor for the make of vehicle, assuming it is imported into the EU. It will cost from about €140 to €500, depending on the size and type of vehicle (much less for motorcycles), and can take sometimes a couple of weeks or more to complete.

⇒ This applies to any motor vehicle imported into Spain whether it is owned by an EU citizen or not. That is, if it was not manufactured or previously licensed in the EU. So an owner bringing in a vehicle from a non-EU country will have to have it homolgated (approved officially).

⇒ The procedure applies to caravans and trailers, and even scooters and mopeds, light cars and quadricycles.

⇒ You will have to pay VAT (IVA) based on 16% of the local value of the car depending on its age.

⇒ You must obtain a certificate of non-residence (*baja de residencia*) from the country you are leaving. This certificate can be obtained usually from the local town hall of the country you are leaving, OR it can be a declaration made to the Spanish Consulate in the country you are leaving, OR, it can be made at your local Consulate (e.g. British if you are British - but very expensive to have done now) within the 30 days after you arrive here.

⇒ The vehicle will have to pass the local roadworthy test (ITV) and cannot be driven on Spanish roads until this has been done, and you will be issued with temporary plates to allow you to complete only this action during the application procedure which usually takes about a week.

There is a lot involved, and it is recommended for the newcomer to Spain, that you place this work in the hands of a *gestor* who is not only legally qualified to offer these services, but is also up to date with any new changes in the Laws. Get a quote (not an estimate) first though! See pages 287 - 288.

HOWEVER, UNLESS THE VEHICLE IS A "CLASSIC" OR YOU REALLY WANT TO KEEP IT HERE I RECOMMEND THAT YOU ,

DO NOT BOTHER.

It is more trouble than it is worth.

EU ITV/MOT VEHICLE TESTING.

This table shows, at this time, the safety inspection for roadworthiness testing standards for private vehicles throughout the EU. The test is known in the UK as the "MOT", or Ministry of Transport Test. The years are noted from the date of first registration. "Free" means no test needed in this period. The other countries are listed for your convenience, and more countries joined in May 2004. Unfortunately I do not yet have the periods for the new countries.

Austria.	Annually.
Belgium.	Annually from four free years after registration.
Denmark.	Four years free and then every two years.
Finland.	Annually from three free years.
France.	Every two years.
Germany.	Three free years, and then every two years.
Greece.	Every three years.
Ireland	Four free years, then every two years
Italy.	Four free years then every two years.
Luxembourg.	Three and a half years free than annually.
Netherlands	Three free years, then annually.
Portugal.	Four years free, then every two years.
Spain.	See table on next page for full details.
Sweden.	Two free years, then two more years, then annually from 5th year.
Switzerland.	Four free years, then three years, and then every two years.
UK	Three free years, then annually.

Vehicles	Frequency of ITV Inspections.			
	Exempt	Two years	Annually	6 months
1. Cars for private use. 2. Special vehicles used in works and services and self-propelled machinery, except those that cannot reach 26 kph due to their construction.	Until 4 years	From 4 to 10 years	More than 10 years	
Vehicles and a set of vehicles used to transport goods with a MAM of up to 3.000 kg.	Until 2 years	From 2 to 6 years	From 6 to 10 years	More than 10 years
1. Rental cars and motos with or without drivers. Small vehicles with windows based on vans but registered for commercial use. 2. Cars and motorcycles used for driving instruction.	Until 2 years		From 2 to 5 years	More than 5 years
1. Adaptable mixed vehicles. 2. Housing (camping vehicles, caravans)	The frequency is the most restrictive applicable, depending on the transport being of goods or people. Please check at the ITV station for your particular vehicle.			
1. Agricultural tractors. 2. Self-propelled agricultural machinery. 3. Agricultural tows. 4. Other special agricultural vehicles except cultivators & similar.	Until 8 years	From 8 to 16 years	More than 16 years	
Towed caravans with a MAM exceeding 750 kg	Until 6 years	More than 6 years		
Motorcycles, private use.	Until 5 years	More than 6 years		

1. Vehicles used to transport goods with a MAM exceeding 3.500 kg 2. Independent tractors for HGV.			Until 10 years	More than 10 years
1. Ambulances 2. Cars for public use including school transport service wit or without a taxi-meter. 4. Buses, including school transport and transport of children			Until 5 years	More than 5 years.

ITV INSPECTIONS.   Readers need to be aware that when they buy some used vehicles where the same model types are used as commercials and passenger vehicles, the ITV may well be classed as a commercial and require attending to as such. Check the permiso de circulacion. If in doubt, check with Trafico using a TASA 3.050. It is €8 - 9 well invested. For example, a normal passenger car not used as a taxi or a driving school vehicle, usually has the first ITV after 4 years, whereas the equivalant van based on the same body is classed as a commercial and has only two "free" years before the ITV is due. And the frequencies are shorter all through the van's life as the table shows. The used vehicle's "*Tarjeta de Inspeccion Tecnica de Vehiculos*" will show this when you are buying it. Also, white cars may have been taxis. The problem is that most will be high mileage, although I personally sometimes find that a high mileage vehicle that has been driven well and serviced correctly is often better than one that has been abused with a low mileage. Also be aware that there are people who can "clock" the odometers to lower the mileage readings. Occasionally, they advertise in the English Press here in Spain and yes it is a criminal offence here too.

TRUST NOBODY

Please note that as a visitor in your own car, your car does not have to conform to the Spanish testing standards, unless, of course, it is on Spanish plates. It must, however, conform to the owner's/registering country's standards, including a current certificate of road-worthiness which must be carried in the car. The law in Spain is that you must always carry the original or notarised documents as well as your driving licence. No documents and the vehicle may be impounded at the roadside. This includes the documents for your foreign vehicle.

GIBRALTAR MOTs. A question sometimes asked by residents who still have their cars on British registration plates is can I take my car to Gibraltar for the MOT? The answer is NO, as only cars with GBZ (Gibraltar plates) are accepted by the Gibraltar testing authority.

Your car must be taken back to the UK for this test, or put on Spanish plates.

Repeated here as it is not generally known: if you take out residencia, you must put your foreign plated car onto Spanish plates within 30 days. *Residencia* means that you intend to live here as your main place of residence and that automatically means over six months per year. The author has a copy of a charge sheet issued by the Guardia Civil for just this offence, committed by an English resident (name blanked out) here who did not take this action within the 30-days allowed and was caught in a road-block check.
You can buy a Spanish plated car when you live here for as your main place of residence. In other words, you have only an NIE.

Please do not forget that updates to this book are to be found on my

web site at: -

www.spainvia.com/motoringinspain.htm

THE ITV TEST.

You must phone for an appointment at the local ITV station before going and the one in the big city may not be the best allowing for traffic and their busy schedules. The days of just turning up ended in mid-2007. There is a national phone number for making appointments and it is 902 575 757 but the phone numbers and addresses for all the ITV stations in Spain are in the Trafico web site at:

http://www.dgt.es/tramites/itv/itv.htm

There will be a reception office where you must check in and pay and you are then given a form to carry with you while you drive through the testing points. As is usual, the steering, suspension, brakes, oil leaks and lighting are all checked, as well as the exhaust for excessive emissions and noise. This is going to be a worry for older cars with catalyctic converters where they are not functioning correctly. Our Ford Focus diesel which had completed 130.000 km, passed OK with a Gm/Km reading of 153, which is well within the specifications for a 2001 model. Another check is that the vehicle is not "falling apart" due to corrosion.

If your vehicle fails anything, you have two weeks to bring it back with the fault fixed for a retest the cost of which is covered in the original payment. But only one "free" check is allowed.

CAUTION. If you are going through a check for re-registration purposes, if you need, for example, new headlamps that dip right as the originals dip left and the vehicle fails because you have not changed them before the test, you must bring it back within the two weeks allowed with the correct headlights as the vehicle is not deemed roadworthy. One reader was told that a €300 fine would result if he did not. Also, if your vehicle is failed on serious safety grounds, make sure you take it back ready to pass, as Trafico and the policing authorities work very closely together and if the vehicle is not scrapped quickly or officially taken off the road (Trafico advised), it is a possibilty that the registration number may be "flagged" and advised to the police for stopping.

There is a few Euros to pay for the exhaust emission like a tax, and it was interesting to see that someone I waited with who had an old BMW M5 was charged half of what our Focus cost which was €6. His car is petrol but being old and with a 3, 5 litre engine, pumps out much more CO_2 compared to our modern diesel with a much smaller engine which is much more efficient. I believe this disparity will be changed in the near future with all the current anti-pollution actions.

The ITV Station also usually has the office where imported vehicles, including trailers, are checked as part of the process of changing to Spanish plates.

SPEEDING AND DETECTION METHODS.

In Spain, drivers are forbidden to use any method of detecting that there is a legally used speed trap ahead, especially radar detection equipment. Unlike France, where you are forbidden to even have a detection device in the vehicle, a nuisance if you are driving from the UK or Germany where they are legal to have and use, Spanish Law states that you may have one, but is must be disconnected while in Spain. No mention is made of the use of special paints that are on sale in the UK and elsewhere, these being claimed to stop speed cameras being able to photograph your registration plates. Perhaps there needs to be a test case, and does it work? I must find out.

It is also forbidden to warn by any method e.g. flashing your lights at oncoming traffic, that there is a speed trap ahead for the other driver / s. You can be fined for this offence.

From 2005, the Spanish government has been increasing the numbers of speed cameras to 500 nationally. Many are fixed, others are to be in small vans. Also, in Malaga, "blue and white" cars take pictures of offences such as bad parking, overtaking on the left illegally, and other offences. My web site will detail the permanent traps when possible.

As I cynically commented at the time, the camera salesmen have arrived. I personally have no problem with speed traps where there is a need for them due to there being an accident "black spot" (can I say that now, or would I be accused of racism?), but in the UK, it is regrettable that many drivers who are professionals and have had many years of no accidents or even fines, are now finding that their licences are in danger of being taken away after falling foul of these devices. There is no substitute for the police patrolling the roads and stopping dangerous drivers, especially since many are reported to have no insurance and/or a driving licence.

DVD AND SCREEN DEVICES IN THE CAR.

It is forbidden for the driver to use a screen device while driving or on the highway, including the hard shoulder. The only exception to this rule is where the device is a rear view mirror as in some of the more sporting cars such as Ferrari, or it is a reversing aid as in heavy goods vehicles. I agree with this rule as it seems ridiculous that a driver quite rightly is not allowed to have a map book on his/her steering wheel while moving, and a DVD screen is just that, where you must take your eyes and attention from the road ahead.

PEDESTRIAN'S RESPONSIBILITIES.

The chance of at least one UK or Irish pedestrian visitor per year in Spain being killed is high because he / she stepped into the road after <u>looking the wrong way</u>. Many more are injured. Far too many of those killed in road accidents in the Province of Malaga and the Costa Blanca holiday resorts, are pedestrians for often this reason. The dreaded N340 coastal road (reputed to be the most dangerous road in Spain) has camping sites north of the A7/N340 on the Costa Del Sol, and often in holiday times, pedestrians are seen to be crossing this very fast and busy 4-lane road by climbing over the barriers to get to the beaches even though many specially built footbridges are available. In addition to the pedestrians' deaths, motorists are sometimes killed or injured in the collisions.

Paso de Peatones or Travesias– Pedestrian Crossings.

UK visitors are used to "Zebra Crossings", where the pedestrian is deemed "never to be at fault". In Spain, the pedestrian is not always automatically in the right. Most car drivers will stop if it is safe for them to do so. Scooters / mopeds often do not.

There are basically three similar types of crossings in Spain and some are marked with alternate black and white OR red blocks painted on the road. They are: -

a)   At a road junction, controlled by the same traffic lights as for the vehicles.

b)   Controlled by a push-button on the posts at the crossing. ("*Espera*" means wait) Legally, you should not cross if the "green man" is not lit. Do not cross when the green man is flashing, and hurry if already on the crossing if it is flashing.

c)   Uncontrolled, with no lights. The traffic is supposed to stop when you step onto the crossing and you clearly and positively by, for example, showing drivers the raised palm of your hand. Do not assume they will though, especially in the major cities, and do not try to "stop" a fast driver with your hand.

d)   In some locations, the crossings are red and white, not black and white. This can denote that there is a built-up speed hump (*Travesia elevado*) where the crossing is located and it must be signed accordingly before each side. But in other towns, the same crossings are black & white so now one really seems to know.

IN ALL CASES, WAIT UNTIL TRAFFIC IS STOPPED BEFORE CROSSING AND MOST IMPORTANT WHERE YOU ARE CROSSING A DUAL PLUS LANE ROAD BEHIND A LARGE VEHICLE SUCH AS A BUS, KEEP LOOKING LEFT EVEN ON THE CROSSING.

Sadly, in early 2005, two Irish visitors were killed on a "pedestrian crossing" as they stepped past an autobus that had stopped at the crossing on the two lane road, into the path of a car that did not stop in the outer lane left hand lane. A tragic way to end a holiday! In the villages (*pueblos*) and old the parts of some cities, some streets are closed to through traffic, and are classed as pedestrian streets (*zonas peatonales*).

An interesting and excellent idea are the new light-controlled crossings in some towns where there is a large, about 8 inches or 20 cm square digital sign which counts down the seconds to when the pedestrian GO green will come on. The idea is to give impatient pedestrians who would normally try to cross on a red advice on how long they have to wait.

Pedestrians are not allowed to walk alongside major highways, (defined as autovias / autopistas) except in an emergency such as their vehicle breaking down, in which case it is safer to use a mobile phone, and then they must also wear a reflective jacket <u>put on before</u> they get out of the vehicle. Motorists will also be fined for stopping to pick up hitchhikers, who will also be fined, on these roads.

SAFETY TIP

After dark on unlit roads, always carry a <u>good torch</u> to shine on the road or your legs so the drivers know you are there at the earliest opportunity, and <u>always face the oncoming traffic,</u> as in any other country. Many may think you are a policeman waving them down, and most will be cautious because of your torch light. Some of the old mountain roads, especially in the South, are narrow, have no footpaths, and have many blind corners and it is advisable, and legally recommended to use your horn on the slower, blind ones. Driving in the mountains in the Gran Canarias is quite an experience in this respect.

Picture of a combination pedestrian crossing and speed hump in Calahonda on the Costa del Sol. It has red and white blocks painted on the road instead of black and white ones. Note there is a warning sign of the crossing but no indication of a speed hump.

PLEASE USE COMMON SENSE - AND BE SAFE.

PARKING.

Parking in the old parts of Spanish towns and villages is often very difficult, especially at holiday times, and especially if you have a large vehicle. Many of the coastal towns are building vast underground car parks to cope with the increasing numbers of visitors using cars. Parking out of town at a railway station where there is usually free parking, or even, if possible, somewhere close to your accommodation and taking a train or a bus, both usually airconditioned, into the middle of the town, is far more preferable. Fares are very cheap compared with parking and fines, and your car may also be saved from "accidental bump damage".

NOTES ON PARKING ARE: -

⇒ Car parks, open or underground, or multi-storey. The covered areas offer cool parking for your car in summer, and the peace of mind that you do not have to rush back because you can pay when you leave. If a right-hand drive car, a passenger is useful here to operate the machines, which are on the left hand side of the car when entering and exiting.

⇒ Pre-paid street parking, three types.

⇒ Blue Zone (*zona azul*), where the parking bay road markings are in dark blue, and you pay for the ticket at a pay-machine <u>before</u> walking away from the car. The <u>pay machine</u> is on the pavement and covers several bays and it is usually signed with a blue background, with a white "P", on the top. <u>Place the ticket on your dashboard</u> where it can be seen by the attendants. These bays are only in operation at certain times so read the payment details which, in tourist areas, are often in English also. If you do overstay and receive a fine (*multa*), on some machines, you may be able to clear it easily and quickly by paying about €3 (£2) into the parking meter and pressing the correct button to receive a receipt. Place the receipt with the fine ticket in the slot at the top of the machine. Do not do as some do by attaching the cash to the fine ticket and force that into the slot. This is far cheaper than being chased through the post or maybe the car rental agency debiting your credit card.

⇒ White painted road marking bays. These are usually free, but in tourist areas, there may be an attendant who will sell you a ticket for usually a €1. There is no time limit, or if there is, no one usually bothers, including the attendants, who are known as *guardacoches*, and are usually handicapped or retired people sanctioned by the local council and so earning a living, and will have badges and printed receipt books if you want a record. Beware of beggars posing as attendants.

⇒ Some towns have an hourly system (*Hora Zona*), and sell you a coloured ticket denoting 30 min. etc. These can be bought at nearby tobacconists (*estancos* or *tabacs*), and you indicate on the ticket what time you left the car. Do not try to "steal time" as the fines are as if you have overstayed anyway.

⇒ You may also see a sign indicating limited waiting allowed with a time stated. The driver is expected to be "honest" and use it for up to 10 minutes. You may be fined by a wandering "meter-maid" if you overstay.

⇒ Some larger towns operate a monthly "season ticket" system at a fixed rate.

⇒ You may find an alternating side of the street, parking system, where a blue & red sign (see sign pages) shows 1 – 15 on one side, for the first 15 days of the month, and 16–31 on the other side for the second 15 days. The days are when you cannot park that side. Look out for these as foreign visitors are often overjoyed to find an empty spot, not wondering why there are no cars on that side already.

⇒ You may find that some on-street parking bays are "reserved" by a local resident, who has paid the ayuntamiento for it long term. These are usually marked by black bands on a street post or wall with the car registration on it, the payment No. and the parked car will have a card with the same number displayed on the dashboard. Do not park here as it can mean a "towaway" if the owner arrives to use his parking area.

⇒ A No Parking Area sign (*Estacionamiento Prohibido*), where no on-street parking or waiting is allowed. It is indicated by a circular sign, blue background, red border, with red diagonal crossed lines through it. The sign may have a white arrow painted next to the diagonal, indicating no parking in that direction, and there may also be times shown (24-hour clock type) if the parking is restricted to certain hours.

⇒ As in the UK, yellow lines painted on the curb or the road near the curb, also indicate no parking or waiting. Double yellow lines = double trouble if you park.

⇒ In some villages, the line is painted white to indicate the area on the road allowed for pedestrians, often necessary due to the narrow pavements. On the highways (not *autopistas* & *autovias)*, these white lines also indicate pedestrian walkways (in an emergency) or where to stop your car in an emergency out of the traffic lanes.

⇒ If there is a symbol of a tow-truck on the sign, your parked vehicle may be towed away.

⇒ The access driveways to garages or residential properties may be reserved by the owner, organising this with the local council (*ayuntamiento*), usually for a fee, and there will be a standard sign affixed to the gate or door at the entrance. An example of this sign is illustrated here and in the signs pages. Watch out for these as the owners get very upset if you block their access, and your car will be towed or clamped (or worse by the resident) and a fine will also apply.

⇒ Spaniards, like many other nationalities are always in a hurry (except when you are) in the big cities, and if they cannot park very near their destination, some will anyway and risk a fine if it is for a limited period, such as visiting a shop. The author has witnessed a woman stopping and blocking a busy narrow street while she quickly went and bought a loaf of bread.   The police are getting very strict about this offence now with lost penalty points for all types of parking offences.

⇒ If you come back to find yourself blocked in your legal parking bay by another car, you may (illegally) blow your horn until the other driver returns. He / she will usually be listening for such a sound.

⇒ Bogus parking attendants (they "stand out") may approach you for a fee, and you have the choice of telling them to politely "depart", or paying them a small fee to possibly avoid having your paintwork scratched.

⇒ Loading and other reserved bays.   You will see empty parking bays with zig-zag yellow lines painted in the bay and a sign. These bays are for commercial loading at specified times (see the times on the sign-post) or for taxis, ambulances, etc. Parking in these will attract a fine and / or towing away. Also, you may see the zig-zag lines painted in the road adjacent to a parking area. This also means definitely NO PARKING, especially double.

⇒ Road sections where the road area is painted with white stripes. These indicate no parking as a vehicle will block the view of other drivers.

STICKERS YOU HOPEFULLY WILL NOT SEE ON YOUR VEHICLE.

Advice sticker left on pavement where a car was illegally parked. It advises that the car (Reg. No. written on the sticker in waterproof felt tip) can be found at the municipal car pound (or elsewhere) and the local telephone number to call. Usually has a bright red or orange background to attract your attention.

<u>Abandoned vehicle sticker</u>. Left usually on cars that appear to have been abandoned as indicated by the condition and amount of dirt covering it. Often left with the sticker for 4 to 6 weeks before towing away to be scrapped but the writer has seen cars left for over a year before being taken away by the authorities.

RESERVED PRIVATE PARKING ON PUBLIC ROADS

Some of the larger towns have in residential areas, individual reserved parking spaces where individual persons can pay an annual rent to the local ayuntamiento and they then may officially reserve a parking spot, usually outside their home which only they are allowed to use. The area can be painted with a border and must have a proper permanent small plate affixed to a wall or post where it can easily be seen by anyone thinking of parking there. If anyone does, the owner has the right to call the local police who will organise a GRUA to take the vehicle to the council vehicle pound where the costs will have to be paid before the vehicle is returned. However, the notice must contain the registration number on the plate with the wording "aparcamiento reservado" or similar as used by the particular ayuntamiento, along with an official receipt or licence number, otherwise anyone can just put a plate up and reserve a place: until they get caught.

PARKING METERS

There are various types of automatic parking payment machines in use is Spain and the one in the photo is typical of a later model although they are all similar. It also has the benefit of the overstayed parker to pay the usually modest fine imposed at the machine. However, many new tourists make the mistake of trying to force the cash amount of the fine into the slot on the machine instead of paying it into the normal "cash in" slot and then placing the receipt into the slot provided. Here is how it works.

Look at the display panel for how long you want to stay and place the necessary coins in the slot for that time. Press the large button near the receipt slot and you will receive a ticket which is to be left on the dash board of your vehicle where it can be seen by the attendant.

If you overstay, you will receive a fine (multa) slip left under your windscreen wiper. Pay the amount advised, which could be about €3 - 5, into the cash in slot as before and press the small lower blue button (might be different on other machines but it has a park-meter symbol on it showing the meter "blacked" off) and obtain the receipt. Fold the receipt and the fine paper together and place in the slot at the top of the parking meter. Sometimes this slot is damaged where kids have been trying to get at expected cash forced in by ignorant drivers.

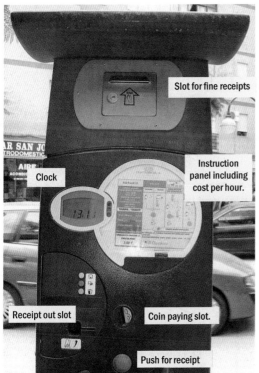

Slot for fine receipts

Instruction panel including cost per hour.

Clock

Receipt out slot

Coin paying slot.

Push for receipt

These machines are usually placed in zonas azul or blue zones where the parking spaces are painted with a blue border. They are usually in busy commercial shopping areas. If the bays are painted white, unless there is another sign with certain stated restrictions on it, parking may be free.

Also, look at the display panel as many are not in operation (although you may still put cash in) on weekends and national/local holidays, or during siesta times.

The machines are placed to cover about 20 parking-bays so you may have to walk a few paces to get to the one nearest your vehicle. It does not matter which machine you obtain your receipt from.

NEGOTIATING A "DIVIDED ISLAND".

As mentioned elsewhere in this book, Spain has what is referred to as divided islands by the Spanish, with traffic lights that are clever (if you are) in that they speed traffic through from secondary to main roads.

Looking at the sketch below, imagine that you are in your vehicle coming from the South/bottom of the page, and you wish to turn left. You have two options, you can either turn left on the A path, the main road, or carry on round and follow the B path as if it was a full roundabout. It is all a question of timing. If you are in the first three to four rows of cars at the traffic lights, and the people are not asleep, the lights are timed to allow you more than enough time to take path B. If not, then take path A if the centre highway in the roundabout if it is not too full, remembering that it is an offence (penalty points now) to block a road junction. The traffic lights are sure to be in your favour soon.

The above may seem a bit obvious if you have lived here and travel into the big city often, but for newcomers, it is a bit confusing. And that is what this book is about: to help drivers avoid confusion.

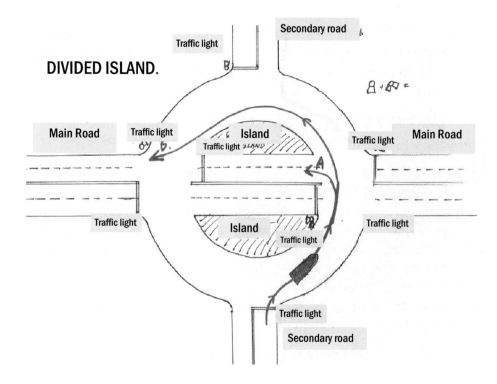

ROUNDABOUTS (*Glorietas or Rotondas*) - A GENERAL DISCUSSION.

The following has been included due to continual requests by readers of my newspaper articles for an explanation of the laws on these types of junctions.   As the new penalty points law includes not giving way on a roundabout, the information here is very important.

Many drivers do not fully understand the rules in negotiating what are called in the UK, roundabouts, in Spain, *glorietas* or *rotondas*.   As all drivers who can remember their driving tests if they were not too long ago (my first - for a motorcycle- was in 1959), the main purpose of a *glorieta* is to ensure that at a moderately busy intersection, and especially where there is enough road space to allow two lanes of vehicles, the *glorieta* or roundabout, compared with traffic lights/ *semaforas* provides an inexpensive, faster and much safer solution to allow vehicles to smoothly negociate the intersection hopefully without colliding with each other, simultaneously automatically and safely slowing the traffic speed in the junction.   A vehicle jumping a red traffic light on an ordinary cross-roads junction can cause fatalities whereas an accident in a glorieta is usually a fender-bender.   The problem is that many drivers in Spain (and elsewhere for that matter) drive with the idea that you must always give way to traffic coming from your left so that even when you are already in a *glorieta*, the madman who is still racing to the intersection from your left thinks that you must give way to him, BUT, IF THAT DRIVER HAS NOT YET ENTERED THE ROUNDABOUT, DRIVERS ALREADY ON THE ROUNDABOUT LEGALLY HAVE RIGHT OF WAY.

THE ONLY VEHICLES THAT HAVE RIGHT OF WAY BEFORE THEY ENTER THE ROUNDABOUT ARE AMBULANCES, POLICE CARS, ETC, WITH SIRENS IN ACTION.

The diagrams on the next page shows the signs and what they mean.   Vehicles entering the roundabout must exit according to which lane they enter, but in heavy traffic where someone who is trapped in the RH lane wants to exit left, allowances must be made by the other drivers so that vehicle can safely do so without any abuse.   Cyclists always have right of way in a glorieta and if you hit one, you have a 99, 9% chance of losing any case brought as a result.   But normally the law is that drivers entering in the RH lane are to exit right or straight on in the RH lane.   Drivers in the LH lane are to either go straight on keeping in the LH lane or to exit right out of the glorieta. See diagram.   Drivers must always give way to heavy goods vehicles with articulated trailers that may use more than one lane to negotiate the roundabout.

USE PATIENCE, COURTESY AND SAFETY.

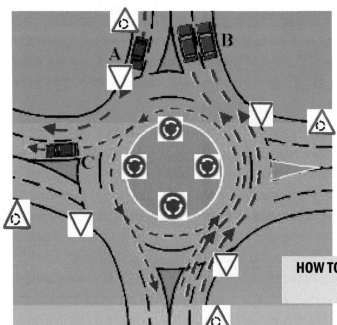

PLEASE NOTE.
It is better to avoid a collision than to argue about it afterwards when the other driver is in the wrong, but your vehicle is damaged.

HOW TO SURVIVE A SPANISH GLORIETA.

Warning sign on approach that a roundabout is ahead, and a reminder of the direction of travel. Usually situated <u>about 50 metres</u> before the entrance to the roundabout depending on the speed limit of the roads. There may even be two signs with subsequent lower speeds to give adequate warning. You must follow the indicated direction of travel and slow to at least 30 kph (not mph).

At entrance to roundabout. The sign "Give Way /*Cedo el paso*" (may also have a rectangular sign stating this on same post) also with the sign <u>painted on road</u> with " dotted white wait line". If traffic is already on the roundabout and blocking your path, you must wait at the give way marking on the road or next to the sign, and filter in when you can safely.

"Advice" sign on the roundabout facing entrances to remind drivers that they must follow the indicating arrows direction of travel i.e. anticlockwise. The Law is for drivers to "give and take"; act sensibly and with courtesy. Do not hit any cyclists: you may win on the roundabout but you will lose in Court.

See the next page for more rules of survival.

WHY ROUNDABOUTS (OR GLORIETAS)?

HISTORY

The first roundabout, or as it is called in Spanish, glorieta or rotonda, was installed in Paris in 1901 around the Arc de Triomphe. The first one in the UK was in Letchworth Garden City in 1910.

WHY HAVE THEM?

$\Rightarrow$ They are much cheaper to install and maintain than traffic lights.

$\Rightarrow$ The traffic through-put is as much as ten times higher that using traffic lights.

$\Rightarrow$ They are much safer as an accident is usually just a fender bender, whereas a vehicle jumping traffic lights often causes fatalities.

$\Rightarrow$ They slow traffic down to a safe speed at busy or even in residential area road junctions. Vehicles cannot "jump" the junction as they can a traffic light or a stop street.

$\Rightarrow$ They save fuel as traffic is not always standing waiting for a green light.

$\Rightarrow$ Mini-roundabouts in residential areas can be painted on the roads or with a small asphalt dome in the middle. The dome can be driven over in an emergency but normally this is not allowed. They again obviate the need for traffic lights or stop streets and so moves traffic smoothly through the junctions, again saving fuel as well as slowing speeders.

$\Rightarrow$ Remember that the right of way rule (give way to vehicles coming from your left) only applies ONCE YOU HAVE ENTERED the roundabout. Anyone "racing" to get through the junction quickly (because he is a bully or an idiot) has no right of way over any vehicle already in the roundabout and must wait at the give-way sign at the entrances. Unfortunately, many drivers are not aware of this rule but do not feel bad if one shouts at you because he/ she (usually "he") because he does not know how to drive. Thinking that thought will make you feel the skilled driver you want to be.

$\Rightarrow$ Remember that if a large articulated vehicle is negotiating the roundabout and needs to go into more than one lane to do so, give way so they can continue safely. If you collide with such a vehicle, the insurance company and the police will normally judge in the larger vehicle's favour.

DRIVING LICENCES

As we all (should?) know, the purpose of a driving licence is to ensure that the holder has reached a minumum standard of ability to operate the vehicle/s for which he or she holds the licence classification. We are told at the time (but do not often think so, especially the men) that once we have passed the driving test, we are expert drivers, but the fact is that at that stage, as experienced drivers will confirm, you are only judged safe to go out and really learn to drive safely by gaining experience. The Spanish authorities recognise this and have structured the system here to ensure as far as possible, that new drivers are not the unwilling victims of an accident soon after they have qualified as often happens in other countries where the new driver is too confident. To reach the required standard is not easy and anyone who successfully passes the course and tests has a good reason to feel proud.

Personally, I learnt to operate a car in an afternoon after buying a 1934 Austin 7 saloon car in 1956 when the Suez crisis was on (petrol rationing), and learners could drive a car without a qualified driver in the other seat. Mind you, unlike today where family cars often have as much horsepower as a racing car in those days, my little "Seven" only had 17 bhp, and I often had to battle against headwinds. I was very lucky to survive, but the roads were quite empty then.

IF YOU HAVE AN EU DRIVING LICENCE (*Permiso de Conduccion*)

From the beginning of 2005, due to Spain losing a case at the European Court of Justice in September 2004, anyone who resides or visits here can use their foreign EU licence as long as: -

⇒ As a tourist, you can use your foreign EU licence as it is. Carry the Form D740 with you though, as well as your passport (and your other vehicle documents if it is your car).

⇒ As a resident, that is you spend more than 183 days a year here, you may use your standard foreign EU licence but could register it at Trafico, although it is not a legal requirement according to the EU Directive. Readers have advised that the Trafico in some Provinces are not bothered, so perhaps they have been "swamped" and cannot cope. However if you have a professional driver's licence (HGV, buses, etc) it is best that you register it and take along your DVLA Form D740.   But the EU Directive on the subject states that you do not have to and cannot be punished for not doing so.

SUMMARY OF THE LAWS ON FOREIGN EU DRIVING LICENCES.

The following is contained in the book's text, but is clarified here so there is no misunderstanding.

1. A driver may use a vehicle in Spain as a resident (or a visitor) using a current foreign current EU driving licence (DL).
2. There is no legal need to change it for a Spanish DL.
3. Drivers may easily change it if for a Spanish DL you wish, but cannot be punished if it is not done as long as the foreign DL remains current.   The fee is less than €20 at time of printing.
4. It is very important that:
⇒   The date of expiry as printed on the DL has not been passed.
⇒   The periodical medicals have been satisfied as for Spanish drivers. If not, then the DL will be deemed to have expired, which means the driver has no valid insurance.
5. When the foreign EU DL has expired as shown on the date on it, if the driver is resident in Spain it must be changed for a Spanish licence.
6. The medicals may be taken at the specified periods as noted in this book and the record certificate kept as proof that the driver is satisfying the law in Spain.
7. The driver may register a foreign EU DL at Trafico, BUT DOES NOT HAVE TO, even vocational (HGV, buses, etc) and DLs. THE DRIVER CANNOT BE PUNISHED FOR NOT DOING SO.
8. When registered, the driver should receive the *avisos* (advice letters) with temporary 3-month licences from Trafico when a medical is due, or if the foreign EU DL is about to expire if it has been registered at Trafico. But DO NOT DEPEND ON IT. As with the expiry date e.g. UK DL at age 70 (60 yrs. for vocational DLs), KEEP A DIARY.
9. REPEATED AGAIN, legally, if a driver has not taken the required medicals, THE FOREIGN EU DL HAS LEGALLY EXPIRED IN SPAIN. Very serious if a Court case is pending.
10. If stopped at the roadside for an offence for which a charge results, where the police can prove or be reasonably suspicious that you reside in Spain, the driver is subject to the same laws as are the Spanish licence holders, that is, if the offence is *muy grave* (very serious), depending on the arresting officer's decision, the DL may be impounded. If not so serious, the DL details will be noted and the facts recorded at Trafico along with any fines.
11. If a future offence occurs, the previous offence will be taken into consideration especially as far as the DL being withdrawn is concerned. In Spain that means it is confiscated.
12. It is expected that from 2010 the standardisation throughout the EU of DLs will start and be fully implemented where all have an EU DL by 2032. However, drivers with current DLs will not have to renew them until they expire, hence the 2032 date. This will mean that, for example, if a driver is banned from driving in one EU country, it can be picked up electronically in all countries, even at the road side.

PLEASE READ AND OBSERVE, ESPECIALLY REGARDING THE MEDICAL CHECK NEEDS.

In the UK, the same applies for HGV and PSV drivers with foreign EU licences only, but there are no periodic medicals in the UK yet for ordinary licence holders but the system is being discussed there. This may be changed there as well.

⇒ The foreign licence should be an EU type with the "ring of stars" on it but not necessarily so. These are designed to be understood in all EU countries by officials, in other words, "multilingual", otherwise you need an official translation into Spanish.

IF YOU HAVE A NON-EU DRIVING LICENCE.

You must have an International Driving Licence (IDL) which can be issued in your home country, except for certain countries where there is an agreement with Spain, which is usually valid for only for one year. However, with the IDL, you must always carry your original driving licence which must be kept valid. That is, if the original is out of date, the IDL is not legal. There is more information on IDLs in my web-site and in this Book.

THE DIFFERENCES BETWEEN A FOREIGN EU AND A SPANISH LICENCE?

There are different classifications which are given in detail in this section, but one major difference as far as everyone is concerned is that, unlike some other EU countries e.g. the UK, you have to take a simple medical every ten years until age 45, then every five years until age 70, and then every two years. In the UK, this applies only to HGV and public service drivers such as buses, taxis, etc, but recent discussions in the UK could mean that the Spanish system could apply in the UK in the near future.

BENEFITS OF REGISTERING YOUR FOREIGN EU LICENCE.

⇒ Let us be plain. It is not a legal EU requirement to register your foreign EU licence at Trafico, but there are benefits.

⇒ You do not have to worry if stopped on the highway by the authorities, especially now the new (2007) PDA's or electronic communications with Traficos' records are being used and especially if you are involved in an accident followed by a Court case and your licence is not fully legal because you have not had a periodic medical.

⇒ You will be advised by post (hopefully) when your licence is expiring, that is, for example, when you need to have a medical to extend it, even if it is only for one classification. This comes in the form of an "*AVISO*" (example in this section) sent to your registered (with Trafico) address for the *Permiso de Conducción* (driving licence). It is important if you move to get the address changed and you have 10 days to do so. It can be done by post with a form TASA 2.23, *Solitud de duplicado de .... and is free.*

All *Trafico* forms can be downloaded off the Internet as explained in this chapter.

(NOT) REGISTERING YOUR FOREIGN EU DRIVING LICENCE.

Until late 2004, you could not drive a Spanish plated car that you owned without having a Spanish driving licence although the Spanish government was breaking an EU Directive. At the EU Court of Justice in September 2004, the Spanish government was ordered to obey the EU Directive where EU citizens did not have to change their licences for (in this case) a Spanish one and they could drive on it until it expired as on the licence date of expiry. But, in line with the same EU Directive is the fact that you must obey the laws of the country where you are a resident, so although your UK DL, for example, expires at age 70 years, the EU Directive also states that you must have the same medicals and obey the same DL laws as do Spanish drivers. So although the expiry date on your foreign DL may say, for example, 2030 if you do not have the periodical medicals as all drivers in Spain do (and it is being discussed that this will be standardised in the EU soon) your licence will have LEGALLY EXPIRED, even if the police are not aware of this at the side of the road. After all, it took them a year to be knowledgeable about the legality of driving a Spanish vehicle owned by a foreign EU driving licence holder. It is if you have an accident where it is found that you have not had the medicals where you can be in serious trouble because not only could the Court blame you - you should not have been driving as you DL was not legal- but your insurance will be declared invalid as well.

Part of the Laws insisted on by Trafico was that you have to register your foreign EU driving licence at Trafico. According to the EU Directive, this is not so, and you cannot be punished for not doing so. But there is a benefit for doing this and that is you have an automatic reminder in the post from Trafico when a medical is due, important if you have some classifications where the medical periods are only three years such as the BIP, C1, and so on as listed in this book in the DL pages.

If your licence is one issued before 1990, that is the non-EU "ring of stars", then you are still legally supposed to get an official translation of it. It is much easier to get a later EU credit card type of driving licence which the officials here can easily understand.

However, when you have to renew your licence here when it expires anyway at say age 70 years, (60 for a vocational one) as a resident here, it will have to be changed for a Spanish one and this is not a problem as it is valid in the UK and anywhere in the EU as well as elsewhere outside the EU with an International Driving Licence which costs currently at Trafico, less than €20.

As stated in the relevant pages on having a medical in this book, do not worry that the certificate supplied after the medical says that it is valid for three months only. This is the time given for the Spanish licence holders to renew their Spanish licence and the photo on the medical certificate is used for the new DL. That is why it is embossed or stamped so it cannot be changed for the photo of someone who cannot pass the medical, thus avoiding fraud. The certificate is still proof that you have had the required medical as per the Law.

The relevant EU Directive states that there is no need to register your foreign EU licence in another EU country where you have become resident, BUT, if Trafico have a record of your licence than they will send you the *avisos* (advice letters) to make sure you do not forget, for example, the necessary medicals. If you are reading this before you move to Spain, or even come here as a regular visitor, although it is not mandatory, I suggest you change your old driving licence for a new credit card type with the EU ring of stars on it. It makes it easier for most policemen to understand at the side of the road and gets you on your way quicker as it is standardised to be multilingual.

Other EU States and especially the UK are currently (at time of printing) discussing bringing in periodical medicals as is Spain.

_____

EU COUNTRIES WHERE YOUR EU DRIVING LICENCE IS 100% LEGAL.
The following countries are in the EU at time of printing:

Austria, Belgium, Bulgaria, Czech Republic, Republic of Cyprus, Denmark, Estonia, Finland, France, Germany, Greece, Hungary, Iceland, Ireland, Italy, Latvia, Liechtenstein, Lithuania, Luxembourg, Malta, Netherlands, Norway, Poland, Portugal, Romania, Slovenia, Slovakia, Spain, Sweden and the United Kingdom.

CHANGING YOUR FOREIGN EU LICENCE FOR A SPANISH ONE.

If for any reason you need to renew your foreign EU driving licence, such as losing it, damaging it beyond use, or it is just plain worn out, you can do it through the DVLA-UK, or authority in your home country, but if you are resident here as your principal home, you could be breaking the Law because your application will give a false address. It depends on the tax status. It is a simple matter to change it for a Spanish one which has all the benefits of the foreign one and the check list for doing this is at the back of the book. The DVLA information is on the www.dvla.gov.uk web site, including the forms that can be printed out.

YOU LIVE HERE AND ONLY HAVE A FOREIGN NON-EU LICENCE.

You have three choices: -

⇒ If you have no licence at all, you must take lessons and pass the Spanish driving test. Check with your local driving schools. In Marbella, Malaga, Fuengirola and Benalmadena lessons in English are available at selected *autoescuelas*. Refer to my web-site pages for some known schools.

⇒ If you have a valid non-EU licence, you can drive on an International Driving Licence (IDL) for up to one year while you take lessons and pass the test, even if this takes many months. The theory will be your main work. For the practical, you should already be experienced and only need one or two lessons. If you are stopped by the police at the side of the road, they will be satisfied with your foreign licence with the IDL, and there is much more information on this subject in my web-site.

The actual questions (in Spanish) for the driving test, with answers are at: -

www.dgt.es/aula/cuestionarios/cuestionarios.htm

There are three sets for up to 49 CC scooters or mopeds, motorcycles and 4-wheel vehicles. Also, my web site has addresses of driving schools that teach in English in selected areas where there are concentrations of expats. If you know of any where you are please let me know and I will add to the list. I make no recommendations as to the efficiency of noted schools. The schools have translated the questions into English to make it easy for "students". From 2007, the government is starting a scheme where young children can pay a Euro a week towards their driving lessons when they are old enough. It is quite expensive now to take a course making me glad that I learnt to ride and drive for next to nothing in the old days. But I have passed the British Advanced Motoring test since.

Non-EU visitors must have an International Driver's Licence (IDL) which can be issued by their country of normal residence. It will have the Spanish translation included. If you are in need of an International Driver's Licence, check with you home country for how to get one, as many countries state that the legals ones must be obtained from certain agencies, eg the USA from AAA: the UK the AA or DVLA. There is more info. in my web site at www.spainvia.com and select "INTERNATIONAL DRIVING LICENCES" in the menu on the Home Page. The IDL must be carried with your original driving licence.

One of the problems that former Commonwealth member citizens, as listed below in the table, who have moved to the UK, and have exchanged their foreign licence for a UK one is that when they come to Spain, the licence is not accepted for exchange for a Spanish one. This is because IF the licence offten where the driving test was taken, and although it is acceptable for the UK (although we should all have our doubts now as in many countries especially in Africa, rampant corruption means that driving licences can be easily bought), Spain refuses to accept any other than the countries where they have a reciprocal agreement for exchange such as Japan, South Korea, Andorra, Bulgaria, and Argentina (others pending). Drivers with such UK licences need to be aware of this at this time. Perhaps the law will be changed soon but for the reason given, I think it is unlikely.

DESIGNATED COUNTRIES FOR EXCHANGE OF DRIVING LICENCE FOR A UK ONE.

Australia, Barbados, British Virgin Islands, Canada, Falkland Islands, Faroe Islands, Gibraltar, Guernsey, Jersey, Hong Kong, Isle of Man, Japan, Monaco, New Zealand, Republic of Korea, South Africa, Switzerland, and Zimbabwe.

See: http://www.direct.gov.uk/en/Motoring/DriverLicensing/DrivingInGbOnAForeignLicence/ DG_4022559, for more details and restrictions. I have reported on the gross corruption in especially countries like South Africa where if you pay the relatively low price of a few pounds, it is possible for a blind man to obtain a driving licence. But still the UK allows DLs from there and other such countries to be exchanged for British one. It is frightening. If you cannot arrange a legal driving licence any other way, you will have to take the Spanish driving test and this consists of theory and practical with tests for each and they can only be done at a registered driving school. Fortunately, some Spanish driving schools in the expat. areas have someone who will give the training in English and ensure that you have the best chance of passing the test which is normally in Spanish. However, the the examiner makes allowances for any language difficulties, and a friend who gives such lessons here on the Costa Del Sol, says that the people who come to him who have already got foreign licences, need only concentrate on the theory as the practical (assuming the "student" is not already a bad driver) is relatively straightforward as long as the "student" is competent and experienced. Two practical lessons are usually enough.

The following applies: -

⇒ The practical can only be taught in specially adapted cars with dual foot control cars with a registered instructor. You are <u>not allowed</u> to practice with just any driver in any car, even in a public car parking lot which in Spain is classed as a "public place" as the road is, even if they have a full licence. In Spain, anywhere public is the same as being on the road. The theory is taught first and once the examination for this is passed, you can start the practical. The theory questions are available on the Trafico web-site at www.dgt.es - in Spanish, but selected schools have them in English. From the home page, select AULA on the top menu, and then the classification you need such as *coches* (cars). The questions are in Spanish with two or more answers, and you select the correct one. The test will give you a score, but not the answers.

⇒ (Please note if buying a used car. Watch out if you are offered one of these. Check the car documents for who has owned it before and ask the seller if the vehicle has been a rental, taxi or driving school car. If in any doubt at all, you can either forget it or apply to Trafico for a "vehicle history" for about €8. Take the registration and the VIN No. to enter on the application form TASA 3.050)

⇒ As stated before, some driving schools have the questions in English on their computers. There are some schools who have translated the questions into English and offer this facility at a cost in booklet form.

⇒ If you have driven before and already have a foreign licence, then you may only need one or two practical lessons before your instructor decides you are ready.

⇒ The test is in Spanish, but the examiners, depending on where you are taking the test (and it should be in the same town where you have been taught so you know the roads well) will allow for this, and your instructor will coach you with the terms such as *"cambio direccion a la derecha"* or "change direction to the right.

⇒ The instructor will take you around the driving test roads so you are familiar with them.

⇒ After passing the driving test, you, like all drivers, qualify for a "probationary B licence" and you have to display an "L" plate in the rear window (white with green background) with a maximum speed restriction of (80 kph) for one year. Then you can qualify for a full "B" licence if you have committed no offences during this period.

⇒ The minimum age for a "B" licence for a car (see the licence tables) is 18 to 65 years, but if you are over 65 when you pass the test for a Spanish licence, the B-licence year's probation procedure does not apply.

⇒ If you are <u>under 45</u>, the Spanish licence is <u>valid for ten years</u> then it expires. You must then re-apply to renew it after a simple medical. See the table in the driving licence chapter. If your foreign EU DL is registered with Trafico (not legally required but advisable) then you will receive in the mail an "Aviso" (advice letter) stating what you need to do to keep your licence legal. It is an excellent idea as you need not go to Trafico and you reciev a temporary 3-month licence so you can do it by post as described in this book.

⇒ MEDICALS FOR FOREIGN EU DL HOLDERS. Every 10 years, even for a foreign EU licence which is now legal in Spain and anywhere in the EU as a resident until it expires (age 70 for a UK one) you must take a medical until you are 45, then it has to be renewed every five years with a medical until age 70, unless you drive commercially, then it is to 60 years of age. Please see the table in the Driving Licence chapter in this book. This means that foreign licence holders, e.g. UK expats, must have the medical and retain the certificate in case of a need such as after an accident or an authority (police) wanting to see that you are indeed legal. From 70 years of age, it is renewed, after the brief and simple medical every two years. The possibility is that if you do not take the medicals and you are involved in an accident, a Court may declare that you did not have a valid driving licence at the time of the accident. The official letter stating this fact (in Spanish) is in my web-site:

www.spainvia.com/drivelicenceletteradsl.htm

⇒ Each renewal approval involves a simple medical check testing your eyesight and reaction times, and questions about your health such as having diabetes, etc. If you are fit, it is very easy. An example is in this book on page 144-146.

⇒ You will be refused renewal, or perhaps given maximum driving speed restrictions if you are medically unfit (but you can still drive). You may be medically checked at the *Trafico* office location or some local clinics where it is advertised *Centro de Reconcimiento Medico de Conductores*. See address list link below.

⇒ The medical is simple: and eye test; a coordination test where you have two handles to simultaneously "drive" two cars along a two winding roads without leaving the road, and a medical questionnaire about any problems. You can practice the test and it is simple.

⇒ The addresses and phone numbers for all Spain for all these *Centros* are in the Trafico web site at:

http://www.dgt.es/tramites/crc/crc.htm,

⇒ In Spain, there is no difference on the licence for an automatic transmission car (as you can have in other countries where you are then not allowed to drive a car with gears), but then, all the driving school cars have manual gears, and the number of automatic cars on the road in Spain is very small; reported to be less than 5%.

⇒ The newer credit card type of licence is now being issued in Spain after years of delay compared with the UK. Both types, the older and the new are illustrated in this book.

⇒ When you have your new licence, make a good photocopy as this will be useful you if you have to renew it after losing it. Also, if you wish you may carry a notarised by a gestor or at Trafico (both for for a fee) photo-copy.

⇒ You may change your foreign EU licence for a Spanish one, and in fact will have to if you lose or damage your existing one unless you have a genuine address in your "old" country that you may (illegally?) use.

If you go to Trafico, the licence can be issued on the same day as the application, but allow at least four hours in the offices. The *Trafico* offices are open (at time of publication) from Monday to Thursdays, 09H00 to 17H00, and Fridays 09H00 to 15H30 except *ferias* (holiday fairs) and other holidays, but phone yours to double check this before you go because the standard hours are 09H00 to 14H00. Beware though that the cash desk usually closes 30 minutes earlier so it pays to get there at opening time.

They are all listed in the Trafico web site at:

http://www.dgt.es/tramites/donde_realizar/donde.htm

Click on the Province for you "local" offices.

Warning for first time visitors. Get a "queue ticket" from the machine as soon as you enter the Trafico hall.

VALIDITY OF DRIVING LICENCES

All Driving Licences have a period of validity and this is shown on the licence as the expiry date. However, in Spain, as previously noted, there are also validity periods designed to ensure that drivers are fit physically to drive, and the table below shows these details.

This means that regardless of what legal driving licence you have in Spain, as a resident here (more than six months/183 days per year) you must follow the instructions as stated in the table even if you have a foreign EU driving licence. From the age of 70 there is no Trafico charges for renewing your licence in Spain. See the following pages for licence classes.

Classes \ Renew >	Every 10 yrs.	Every 5 yrs.	Every 3 yrs.	Every 2 years
LCC: LCM: LVA: A1: A: B: B+E	Until the holder reaches 45	From 45 to 70 yrs old		From 70 years old
BTP: C1: C!+E: C: C+E: D1 D1+E: D: D+E		Until the holder reaches 45 yrs	From 45 to 60 yrs	From 60 years old

To "renew" the licence, a very simple medical must be passed to test especially eyesight, physical reactions and general health as far as, for example, serious heart problems, -- anything that can be a danger on the road.

Clinics, called "*Centro de Reconocimiento Medico de Conductores*, where the medical may be taken are usually near the place where you renew your driving licence, eg *Trafico*, but also most towns have an approved clinic. Your Spanish neighbours will know. The medical usually costs about €25 - 30 which is a bit steep as, in my opinion and experience, the test officers appear not to need to be medically qualified and it takes only about ten minutes.

But remember that if you are stopped by the Guardia Civil, etc, and found to have an expired licence, you will not only be fined, but will have to find someone with a licence to drive the vehicle away, hopefully not a GRUA to the police/ *ayuntamiento* compound!

If you have a foreign EU licence, ignore the words on the medical certificate that it is valid for three months only. This is for the Spanish licence holder whose licence expires when a medical is due. Keep the certificate in a safe place and carry a photocopy in the glove compartment with the other vehicle documents.

DRIVING LICENCE CLASSIFICATIONS

The following pages give details of the various classifications with explanations.
(Only Trafico personnel can have committed them to memory?)

Driving licences for mopeds, Invalid vehicles and certain self-propelled vehicles.

The LCC and LCM licences are not needed when the holder obtains the Class A1 or A licence.

The LCC, LCM and LVA are not needed when the holder obtains a Class B licence.

In other words, the A1: A & B licences cover these classifications.

Terminology

MAM or Maximum Authorised Mass is the total weight of a vehicle, including a vehicle plus a legally loaded trailer if applicable, as allowed by the relevant Law.

TARE weight is the unladen weight (no load or passengers) of the vehicle with all fluids and equipment to allow it to operate correctly, including a full tank of fuel.

Symbols used in the tables: > = more than: < = less than.

Moto = motorcycle, with/without sidecar, or scooter.

Licence Class.	Vehicles and Notes	Minimum Age
LCC	Autocycles (mopeds and scooters with an engine up to 49 cc) with 2 or 3 wheels and light quadricycles (small cars). 16 yrs. minimum age if they transport a passenger and the machine is designed for it. These are noticeable on the road by their number plates with small letters & numbers. NOTE: It was announced almost two years ago that the minimum age was going to be changed to 16 years to ride a small moto or scooter. At the time of printing this edition, it has still not been actioned.	14
LCM	Vehicles for people with reduced mobility.	14
LVA	Special self-propelled agricultural machines and groups where the MAM or dimensions do not exceed the stated normal limits (not an oversized vehicle). MAXIMUM No. of persons inluding the driver = 5.	16

License Class	Authorised to drive these vehicles	Minimum Age (yrs)	Notes
A1	• Light motos without a sidecar and a maximum engine capacity of 125cc and maximum power of 11 Kw with a power / mass of not more than 0,11 kW/kg. • Mopeds/ scooters with 2 / 3 wheels and Light 4 wheelers (quads). For persons with mobility problems. Note, this classification with the others for motos, A1, A2, & A3 are announced at time of printing to be enforced from later 2007.	16	• May tow a trailer with a MAM of not more than 50% of the unladen weight of the tow vehicle. • Power/mass is the relationship between the engine power and the weight of the unladen vehicle. Example. For a vehicle weighing 100 kg unladen weight/mass, the maximum power allowed is 11 kW.

Engine Horsepower.

The methods used in Spain for measuring engine power are *CV (caballos de vapour)* and Kilowatts (kW). "bhp" (brake horse power) is the common UK and USA method of measurement, but the difference is very small between CV & bhp. Kilowatts is the commonest modern international form of measurement.

100 cv = 98,632 bhp = 73,55 kW

License Class	Authorised to drive these vehicles	Minimum Age (yrs)	Notes
A2	• Motos with an engine capacity up to 400 cc from age 18 before allowed to move to A3 after 2 years or age 24. • Autocycles with 2/3 wheels or light quads. • For persons with mobility problems. • Vehicles with 3 wheels and non-Light quads whose mass does not exceed 550 Kg designed to go at not more than 45 kph with an engine capacity higher than 50 cc. • Motos, with or without a sidecar, with a power rating of not more than 25 kW • Motos with or without a sidecar, with a power/mass of not more than 0,16 kW/kg	18	• Covers the classification of A1 as well. • May tow a trailer with a MAM of not more than 50% of the unladen weight of the tow vehicle. • Maximum engine power allowed is 25 kW. • Max. Power/mass is calcualted: - 25 kW: 0,16 kW/kg = 156,25 kg The maximum mass of moto unladen is 156,25 kg.

THE NEW MOTORCYCLE CLASSIFICATIONS, A1, A2 & A3, ARE FORECAST TO COME INTO EFFECT BY January 2008.

License Class	Authorised to drive these vehicles.	Minimum Age (yrs)	Notes
A 3	• Motos over 400 cc but after the licence holder has had an A2 DL for at least two years or is at age 24. • Motos with a power rating of more than 25 kW • Motos with or without a sidecar, with a power/mass of more than 0,16 kW/kg • These two classifications need a qualification of two years experience of riding before being issued.	24 Or 2 years with an A2 licence.	To qualify to ride this classification, the rider must have two year's experience of riding with a A2 licence or to have achieved the age of 24. The licence may then be upgraded / endorsed to show qualification. Also covers all motos in A1 & A2 classifications.
B	• Automobiles whose MAM is not more than 3.500 kg and where the number of seats does not exceed nine including the driver. A Light tow of not more than MAM 750 kg is allowed. • Vehicles with 3 wheels whose MAM does not exceed 3.500 kg. • A vehicle (car, etc) with a towed vehicle, where the MAM of both vehicles is not more than 3.500 kg and the MAM of the towed vehicle does not exceed the MAM (unladen mass) of the towing vehicle . • Mopeds/scooters with 2/3 wheels and Light Quads of not more than 49 cc capacity. • After three years, the holder may ride motos up to 125 cc capacity. • For persons with mobility problems. • Special self propelled agricultural vehicles including towing, —where the maximum masses and dimensions do not exceed the regulation limits. —whose MAM or dimensions do exceed the regulations or transport up to 9 persons including driver • Special non-agricultural vehicles or groups(towing) : - —Where the maximum allowed speed is not more than 40 kph. —that can transport up to 9 persons incl. driver..	18	• This licence does not allow operation of vehicles in license class A1 and A. • It does not allow operation of motos with two wheels of more than 125 cc engine capacity, or with a sidecar • If held for 3 yrs. plus, the "B" licence holder may drive a vehicle up to a MAM of 3.500 kg plus a trailer up to 750 kg = Total 4.250 kg <u>Example</u> Car with MAM up to 3.500 kg plus a tow of 750 kg giving a MAM of 4.250 kg These types of tows should carry the registration plates of both vehicles at the rear of the towed vehicle positioned for easy reading as in the regulations. PLEASE NOTE THAT WHERE NUMBERS OF SEATS OR PASSENGERS ARE MENTIONED IN A VEHICLE IN THESE PAGES, IT <u>INCLUDES THE DRIVER</u> UNLESS OTHERWISE STATED.

License Class	Authorised to drive these vehicles	Minimum Age (yrs)	Notes
BTP	To drive, having qualified for a Class B licence: - • High priority vehicles such as ambulances • School transport vehicles for pupils. • Public transportation vehicles of a similar type. • All vehicles with a MAM not more than 3.500 kg and up to 9 seats. Experience requirement At least one year with a Class B licence and passing the special test for the BTP licence.	18	The one year experience rule may be waived if special training is taken at a Driving Education Centre and then passing the final tests. If the driver has a Class B licence, and classes C1, C, D1 and D are passed, the driver can automatically qualify for a BTP licence.
B + E	• Pair of towing + towed vehicles where the tower needs a Class B licence and the trailer a MAM of more than 750 kg as long as they do not qualify to be driven with a Class B licence. Class B licence needed by the driver.	18	• Not allowed to drive classes A1 and A using this licence. Example. Car with MAM up to 3.500 kg + trailer with MAM of 751 + kg = 4.251 + MAM
C1	• Automobiles where the MAM exceeds 3.500 kg but not 7.500 kg, and where the number of seats does not exceed nine, including the driver. Light towing is authorised with this licence. Not allowed to ride a moto with 2 or 3 wheels, with or without a sidecar.	18	• Not allowed to use for class A1: A • Can be granted a BTP licence vehicles. • If transporting more than nine persons but not more than seventeen, this is allowed with this licence. • Licence D is needed for more than seventeen persons. Example. Car with MAM of 7.500 kg + light tow of MAM 750 kg = 8.250 kg

License Class	Authorised to drive these vehicles	Minimum Age (yrs)	Notes
C1 + E	• Towing where the automobile is as for a C1 licence, but with a non-light (>750 kg) trailer, as long as: - —the total MAM of the vehicles does not exceed 12.000 kg, and —the MAM of the trailer does not exceed the unladen mass of the towing vehicle. Not allowed to ride a moto with 2 or 3 wheels, with or without a sidecar.	**18**	• Also can drive classes B+E, D1+E, if the driver has a D1 licence. • Not allowed to drive A1 & A classes. <ins>Example</ins> Tower with MAM of >7.500 and unladen MAM (tare) of 4.500 kg = 12.000 kg of MAM for both.
C	• Automobiles where the MAM exceeds 3.500 kg and where the number of seats does not exceed nine. Light tow up to 750 kg. Will also need a class B licence. Not allowed to ride motos with or without a sidecar on this licence.	**18** with a skilled certificate for goods transport **21** without the certificate	• Allowed with class C1 and BTP licences. • Not allowed with A1 and A licences. If more than nine persons, up to seventeen, are to be carried, a class D1 licence is needed. A D licence is needed for more than seventeen.
C + E	• Towing vehicles with the automobile authorised to be driven with a class C license and a trailer with a MAM exceeding 750 kg • Need a valid C licence Not allowed to ride motos with or without a sidecar.	**18** with a skilled certificate for goods transport **21** without the certificate	• Must have classes B+E, C1+E, D1+E (if the holder has D) & D+E (if the holder has D) <ins>Example.</ins> Car with MAM up to 3.500 kg + trailer with MAM of 351 kg = 4.251 MAM

License Class	Authorised to drive these vehicles	Minimum Age (yrs)	Notes
D1	• Buses and trolley buses for short distances up to 50 km, where the number of seats exceeds nine but not more than seventeen. They can be joined to a Light tow not more than 750 kg. <u>Need a Class B license.</u> • Automobiles used to transport goods but for which up to seventeen people can be specially authorised. • Special non-agricultural vehicles or similar, that can carry up to seventeen persons. • Special self-propelled agricultuarl where the MAM or dimensions exceed the regulation limits or carry ten to seventeen persons.	21	• May not be used for classes A1, A, C1 and C • Must have the BTP class licence. To drive buses more than a 50 km range, the following is needed by Law: - • A professional driving skills certificate to transport passengers by road, or, • Completed one year of experience, with a minimum of driving goods vehicles of more than a MAM of 3.500 kg, or driving short distance buses. • Does not include the riding motorcycles with 2/3 wheels, with or without a sidecar.
D1 + E	As for D1 classes, for a trailer with a MAM that exceeds 750 kg as long as the total both vehicle's MAM is not more than 12.000kg, and the MAM of the trailer is not more than the unladen MAM (tare) of the towing vehicle. Need Class D1 licence and passengers are not allowed in the trailer.	21	• Must have classes B+E, & C1+E (if the holder has a C1 licence). • Not allowed to drive classes A1, A, C+E, even if the holder has a C class licence. • Not allowed to ride motos with or without a sidecar.

D	21	• Buses and trolley buses where the number of seats exceeds nine. Can be joined with a Light tow >750 kg Need a class B license • Automobiles normally used to transport goods, but can occasionally be for up to seventeen persons. • Special self-propelled agricultural vehicles or groups (towing) of th same, where the MAM exceeds the limits set by regulation or when transporting more than seventeen persons • Special agricultural vehicles or groups (towing) of same transporting more than seventeen poeple.	• Must have classes D1 and BTP licences • Does not cover classes A1, A, C+E, and a C licence • For long distance bus driving (50 km +), the driver must hold: - --A professional driving skills certificate to transport passengers by road, or, --Have a minimum of one year's experience driving vehicles used to transport goods of more than a MAM of 3.500 kg or driving short distance buses 50 km< This class does not cover motorcycles with or without a sidecar.
D+E	21	• A set of couple vehicles where the towing vehicle is to be driven only by a driver with a class D licence and a trailer with a MAM that exceeds 750 kg. Need a class D licence	• This licence covers vehicles in the classifications B+E, C1+E if the holder has a C1 licence. • Does not cover classifications A1 & A • Does not cover riding motorcycles with or without a sidecar

MORE NOTES ON DRIVING LICENCE TERMS. For the purposes of the information in this book: -

• A VEHICLE is a device that is capable of circulating through bot public and private roads and that are bound by the Motor Vehicles Circulation and Road Safety Laws

• An AUTOMOBILE is a powered device used to transport persons or things (goods), and for the towing of other vehicles (trailers). The towing vehicle can be called a "tractor", which must not be confused with a farm vehicle. Special vehicles are not included in this definition.

• A SPECIAL VEHICLE is a self-propelled or towed vehicle designed to carry out specified work or services and includes agricultural machinery, including agricultural trailers. Because of the work, they are exempted from complying with some of the legal technical specifications that apply to vehicles. This includes the normal dimensions and weights specified for automobiles.

• All road users are subject to the Laws, especially for safety reasons. This includes pedestrians, cyclists and animal powered equipment.

TOWING VEHICLES AND TRAILERS IN SPAIN.

These are treated differently in Spain to the UK and Ireland. In these countries, there is no need to have the trailer or caravan registered in its own right with an issued registration number. In Spain, the law is different for good reasons noted below.

Trailers up to 750 Kg MAM (Maximum Authorised Mass: the designed and accepted after testing by the homolgamation authority that this trailer is safe to use in the authorised and designed manner with a load that gives a maximum mass or weight as noted i.e. >750 Kg). You therefore can buy a trailer with a MAM of say 420 Kg or 350 Kg which is usually a box trailer designed to be towed by a car. However, the trailer must have a plate fixed, usually riveted, securely to the trailer where it can be easily seen at the roadside, and if you get stopped on the road, and have no plate, an offence is committed if you have a Spanish plated towing vehicle. The plate gives the MAM and date of manufacture etc. and the manufacturer. If you are importing such a trailer from the UK or Ireland, you will need to go to the COE office at usually the ITV station with the entire trailer's documents and yours to have the trailer inspected and they will fit a plate for you (if they consider it safe and not some backyard special) so you are legal. If the trailer is exported to Spain by a UK or Irish company, they may have these plates at the factory so you can organise the fitting before you go. They will obviously have to see the trailer, even if via photographs at their local dealer where you may have bought it, to make sure that it is the same as when it left the factory.

All Trailers over 750 Kg. In Spain these are registered as with a car, etc. and have a special number, with black lettering on a red back ground, prefixed "R" for *remolque*, Spanish for trailer. Obviously this includes most caravans as well as horse boxes, in fact anything that has a MAM of 750 KG plus. As such, they are treated as motor vehicles in that they have to be homologated, that is approved by the EU as submitted by the manufacturer with a specification list as with the motor vehicles. As on cars, etc, you have a list of the wheel sizes and tyres that must only be used and so on. Also, there must be a replica registration plate, in Spanish called a *marca* the same as the towing vehicle.

For a caravan or trailer that is being imported from the UK & Ireland etc. it is important that well before you leave, you contact the manufacturer and ask for a paper copy of the specifications for that trailer as issued for Spain.

The manufacturer will have this and will not only be able to make sure that your trailer is correctly specified for Spain but issue you with the correct plate or organise it with the Spanish distributor. This I have helped organise already for some readers, but do not get disheartened if you come up against "walls". Many locals (Spanish dealers) are not used to this procedure and may say it cannot be done. The secret is to organise it well before you come to Spain so the CEE/ITV inspection for the registration can go smoothly in one trip. Remember that officially you are supposed to start the procedure within 30 days of becoming registered as resident here. To leave it longer, certainly months down the line (as many do with their UK-plated cars) you may be expected to pay import duties as the Tax people may insist that you are importing it, not bringing it here as personal property.

If you are bringing here some months after registration as resident, keep all the proofs that you have owned it for X-months or years, as well as the ferry tickets, etc. Most important, of course, is the original invoice showing that IVT (VAT) has been paid.

The ITV inspection periods are covered in this book on page 96 to 99.

Do not forget to make sure your trailer is insured. Ask your broker for the details on how you wish to have it done and also specify which vehicle you will be using as the tow vehicle. It is not covered by your normal car insurance.

Category B Vehicles		EXAMPLES OF TOWING COMBINATIONS			
Unladen Mass Kg	MAM	Trailer MAM	Combination MAM	Required Driving Licence	Comments
1.025	1.450	850	2.300	B	Unladen mass of the towing vehicle > MAM trailer and MAM of combination < 3500 kg
890	1.375	925	2.300	B + E	Unladen mass of the towing vehicle < MAM trailer; MAM trailer > 750 kg
1.875	2.955	745	3.700	B	MAM trailer < 750 kg
1.875	2.850	850	3.700	B + E	MAM trailer > 750 kg and MAM of combination > 3500 kg

NOTES: MAM = Maximum Authorised Mass which is the maximum designed weight of the tow vehicle or trailer fully loaded. Symbols: > = greater than... : < = less than...

The **SAFEST COMBINATION** in all cases is where the tow vehicle mass weighs more than the trailer mass. The first two columns are the tow vehicle, unladen and fully laden. The third column is the trailer fully laden, and the fourth columns is the total maximum mass of the two vehicles if both are fully laden as designed. The fifth column is the driving licence (DL) classification you must have to operate that combination as in that row. The sixth column comments on the set ups in each row as applicable.

- Row 1 shows that in both cases the unladen and laden weight of the towing vehicle is more that the MAM of the trailer. The driver needs a normal "B" licence to drive this combination.

- Row 2 shows that the unladen weight of the tow is less than the MAM of the trailer. As the trailer is over 750 Kg, a B + E driving licence is needed.

- Row 3: the tow has an unladen mass and a MAM less than the trailer which has a MAM of lews than 750 Kg so a "B" driving licence is OK in this case.

- Row 4: Although te weight distribution is OK, the MAM of the combination is over 3.500 kg so the driver will need a B + E classification again.

Trafico announced at the time of printing that they intend to have special driving tests for those who wish to use certain tow combinations especially for the higher MAMs. The test will include general knowledge and reversing.

Please note that you are not allowed to tow, for example, a Spanish trailer with a foreign vehicle. If you have not transferred your foreign EU vehicle onto Spanish plates and you are stopped, the Spanish trailer, even below a MAM of 750 kg will have a plate fixed to it with the manufacturer's name etc, the MAM on it and it will be identified as Spanish. A trailer over 750 Kg will, of course, have the red and black Spanish own registration on it, prefixed with "R".

TOWING TIPS

40% of weight in rear **60%** of weight in front

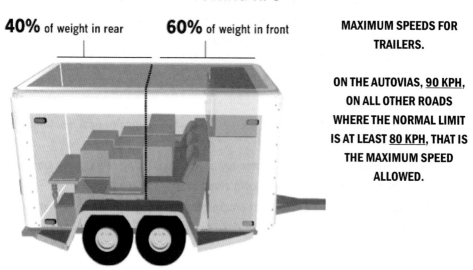

MAXIMUM SPEEDS FOR TRAILERS.

ON THE AUTOVIAS, <u>90 KPH</u>, ON ALL OTHER ROADS WHERE THE NORMAL LIMIT IS AT LEAST <u>80 KPH</u>, THAT IS THE MAXIMUM SPEED ALLOWED.

DO.

- Make sure the regulations as far as the weight of the tow and the towed vehicles are followed. See driving licence pages. It is forecast that special driving tests are to be introduced in Spain for towing with trailers over 750 kg MAM.
- Load the heaviest items in the front so the distribution is about 60% front to 40% rear, but do not put too much weight on the tow hook so the front of the tow vehicle is very light on the steering.
- Drive slowly, especially downhill. The maximum speeds anywhere are generally not more than 80 to 90 kph depending on the road type as in this book.

DO NOT.

- <u>Do not use your brakes</u> if the trailer starts to sway. This will worsen the sway.
- <u>Do not try to correct any sway by using the steering</u>. Hold the steering wheel steady straight ahead if possible until the swaying stops. To try and steer is likely to cause a "jack-knifing" of the vehicles.
- Avoid towing in windy, wet or icy conditions.

INTERNATIONAL DRIVING LICENCES (Dls) FOR SPANISH LICENCE HOLDERS AND THOSE WHO HAVE FOREIGN EU Dls AND ARE RESIDENT IN SPAIN.

For those who intend to drive outside of the EU, and have a Spanish driving licence OR are resident in Spain with a foreign EU driving licence, it is an easy matter to get the needed International Driving Licence from Trafico.   And it is relatively cheap; about €9 to €10 at time of printing.   Take all your documents to Trafico, complete the TASA form 2.3, "Conduccion Diverso" which can be downloaded from the Trafico web site, and join the queues.   Or send by post if you can spare your licence for about five weeks.   You must write under the heading "Motivo" on the form, "Permiso Internacional de Conducción".

You will need: -

⟹   The original and a good photocopy of your residencia or new residence certificate.

⟹   The original and a good photocopy of either your Spanish Driving Licence - *permiso de conducción or both sides of your foreign EU one..*

⟹   Two colour passport photographs the same size as your driving licence ones with plain white backgrounds. Get film ones: not printed on a computer inkjet unless you use a laser colour printer so the photo is waterproof. You can do this at most photo shops now when you take your own CD with the photos on it.

⟹   Post-office giro cheque for the correct fee amount.

⟹   An SAE for the return to you of the IDL.

If you are going in your vehicle to a country outside the EU, do not forget that you will also need a standard (old type) white sticker with "E" on it as the country identification on the EU number plate is not valid in most non-EU countries.

There is a lot of general information on IDLs in my web-site at

www.spainvia.com.

MORE ABOUT VEHICLE SPECIFICATIONS.

- Vehicles without an engine includes, Bicycles and bicycles with power assist (clip-on motor).
- The following are vehicles without a motor but are still legally vehicles. Trams, autocycles with two, three wheels, and Light quadricycles, and vehicles for persons with reduced mobility. Trailers with a hook tow or complete tow attachment, semi-towed and caravans. Special agricultural vehicles and trailers: special towed vehicles for works and services such as compressors and pumps, etc.

MOTORISED VEHICLES AND SPECIAL SERVICE MACHINES		
Automobiles	Special Self-propelled Vehicles	
	Special Agricultural	Special Works and Services
—Motorcycles (motos) with two wheels including those with a sidecar. —Vehicles with three wheels. —Quadricycles. —Cars —Bus or coach, including articulated ones.. —Trolley bus. —Double decker buses or coaches —Trucks. —Wagons / Vans —Tractor Truck (Towing unit) —Set of vehicles such as a truck and trailer, or a road train (with two or more trailers). —Special cars. —Adapted mixed use vehicles. —All-purpose vehicles	—Agricultural tractor. —Cultivator —Farm tractor —Farm vehicle. —Carrier (e.g. a sand trailer unit for use on icy roads).	—Work tractor. Earthmoving Equipment —Excavator / Digger —Loader. —Vibrating Roller. —Road Roller —Service tractor Road Service Machines —Mud scrapers —Snow ploughs —Road painting machines —Tourist trains.

Vehicles with a small white sign with "SP" on it in black lettering. This indicates "*Servicio Publico*", and shows that the vehicle is used for hire and transportation of paying customers or goods.

SPANISH NUMBER PLATES AND SIGNS ON VEHICLES.

Until 2000, the registration number plates could identify which Province and town/area where the vehicle was first registered. From 2000, a centralised computer data-base was started and the numbers consisted of four numbers and three letters (or vice-versa). However, as in most countries, there are special number plates for various reasons. They have a prefix followed by the registration number with different coloured backgrounds and numbers/letters. Trailer vehicles with a MAM of over 3.500 kg must carry the same tow vehicle registration plate <u>as well as</u> the trailer registration plate. When an older vehicle is sold/bought, it is given a new system number showing the latest registration layout, ie 1234 FTP instead of MA 1234 TF .

Code used below - W=white: R=red: G=green: Y=yellow: Bl=blue.

Example: R/W = red letters/white background

Prefix	Spanish Name	English translation	Letters & Background Colour.
CAT	Comisaría Abastec y Transportes	Police Supply & Transport	
CC	Cuerpo Consular	Consular Corps	W/G
CD	Cuerpo Diplomático	Diplomatic Corps	W/R
E	Vehiculos especiales	Special vehicles	R/W
EA	Ejercito del Aire	Air Force vehicle	
ET	Ejercito del Tierra .	Army vehicle	
FN	Fuerzas Navales	Naval Forces	
H	Vehiculo histórico	Historic vehicles	B/W
MOP	Ministerio de Obras Publicas	Mindsitry of Public Works	
OI	Organismos Internacionales	International Organisations	W/Blue
P	Matricular temporal particular	Temporary Private car license plate	W/G
PGC	Parque de la Guardia Civil	Guardia Civil Vehicle	
PMM	Parque Móvil de Ministerios	Ministerial Government vehicle	
PN	Policia Nacional	National Police vehicle	
R (etc)	Remolques y semi-remolques	Trailers and semi-trailers	B/R
S	Matricular Temporal Empresas	Trade plates unregistered vehicles	W/R
T	Matricular Turistica	Tourist Plate.	
TA	Technico administrativo	Technical & Admin. Staff	B/Y
V	Matricular Temporal Empresas	Trade plates for registered vehicles	W/R

Small yellow pltes with small numbering are for up to 49 cc scooters, etc and light cars.

THE OLDER EU (FLEXIBLE CARD) DRIVING LICENCE.

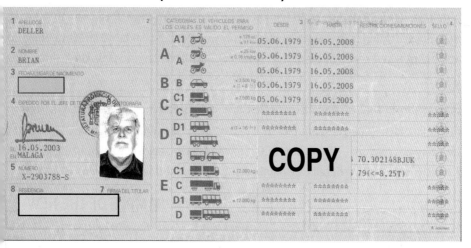

OBSOLETE NOW BUT SHOWN FOR HISTORICAL INTEREST.
WHAT THE TITLES MEAN.

SPANISH HEADING	ENGLISH TRANSLATION
1. Apellidos del titular.	Last Name / s.
2. Nombre.	First name.
3. Plaza y fecha de nacimiento	Country / Place and date of birth
4. Expedido por el jefe de trafico.	Place and date of licence issue with official signature of *Trafico* official.
5. Numero del permiso.	Licence number, usually the same as Spanish issued national identity number (NIE / NIF).
6. Foto de conductor.	Photograph and *Trafico* stamp.
7. Firma de Titular.	Signature of holder. (Do not forget to sign)
8. Residencia (not on later *permisos of this type*)	Holder's current home address.
The right hand side of the card shows what the driver is licensed to drive, with the column titled "*hasta*" (until) being the dates that the licence expires.	

THE "NEW" CREDIT CARD DRIVING LICENCE - *PERMISO DE CONDUCCION*

Introduced (at last) during 2005 but not issued until much later, this card replaces the more flimsy folding card shown on the previous page. It is similar in effect to other EU credit card type licence in the EU. It does not now have your address on it (from May 2007?).

Although it was supposed to be ready for issue, in June 2005, when I updated my licence after a medical, I was given another new folding card type, not one of these, but without the home address on it. But in May 2007, after another medical I was given the new type of card as below (some details are blanked out for "identity theft" reasons).

SAMPLE OF THE NEW *PERMISO DE CONDUCCION.*

< Front: your photo and other details but no address.

Rear below : with vehicle classifications and dates of expiry, using symbols for the vehicles to make it multilingual for Europe.

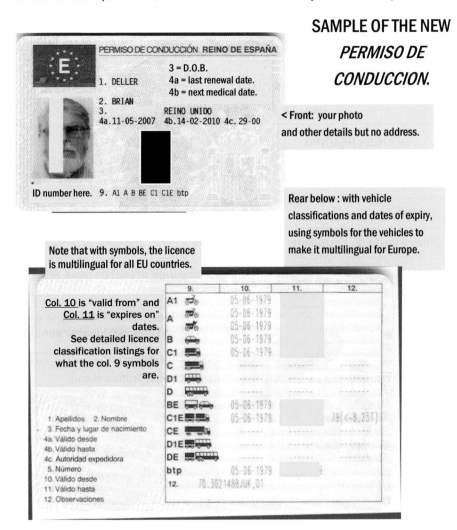

Note that with symbols, the licence is multilingual for all EU countries.

Col. 10 is "valid from" and Col. 11 is "expires on" dates.
See detailed licence classification listings for what the col. 9 symbols are.

DOWNLOADING FORMS FROM THE TRAFICO WEB SITE.

To save you time at *trafico*, or even better still, to obtain what you want and use the mail so you do not need to go at all, you can obtain the forms from the web sites and print them out. Here is how to do it for the DVLA in the UK and the *Direcion Generale de Trafico* in Spain. You will need Adobe Reader software, which is generally free. Obtain help from an "expert" if you have problems following the instructions below, or show this to an Internet cafe operator who will get you your forms printed out for a small fee.

Trafico in Spain.

Go to this web address, http://www.dgt.es/indices/dgtHtm_Impresos_es.html as follows:

⇒ Go to www.dgt.es

⇒ On the Home page that appears, click on "Conductores" under "Tramites" in the middle of the screen.

⇒ On the left side of the next screen click on "Modelos e Impresos".

⇒ You will be in the correct listing page. Click on the dot to the right of the TASA (rate) form you need as described in the book on page 142.

⇒ You can type in most of the information needed before you print it, or you can print the form out and fill in by hand. You receive two A5 printed forms on an A4 sheet of paper and both contain the same typed in info.

⇒ Send off with the correct payment which can be made at the post office. The PO clerk will know what to do.

⇒ Carry copies of the forms and documents sent along with the Correos receipt in case you get stopped on the road.

⇒ It normally takes 3 to 5 weeks to get the new document back from Trafico depending on how busy they are.

⇒ To get to the UK-DVLA web site: in the address bar of the Internet browser, write www.dvla.gov.net and then follow the instructions which are in English (of course).

More check lists are in the back of this book.

List of Trafico offices, addresses and telephone numbers.

A full list of addresses for Spain is on the Trafico web-site including opening times and telephone numbers. On the Internet, go to:

http://www.dgt.es/tramites/donde_realizar/donde.htm.

Click on the province you need and the address page will appear.

TABLE OF FORMS IN THE *TRAFICO* WEB SITE AT: -
http://www.dgt.es/indices/dgtHtm_Impresos_es.html

If you do not have access to a computer and the Internet where you can download the required form before you go and complete it with the help of a Spanish friend. If not, at Trafico go to the *Información* counter and ask for: -

Form No. (*TASA*)	*Impresos* (Printed forms) TITLE OF FORM TO APPLY FOR: -	
2.220/T	*Próroggo de la vigencia del permisso o licencia de conducción.*	In this first column on the web site, on the right of the titles, there are small buttons to click on with the mouse pointer to go to the form automatically in Adobe Reader. It will be in the language of Castelán which is correct unless you live in another area such as the Basque country or Cataluña, etc.
2.220/T	Extension of the validity of a driver's licence.	
2.23	*Duplicado del permiso de conducción o circulation.*	
2.23	Duplicate of a driving licence.	
2.28	*Licencia de conducción de ciclomotores.*	
2.28	Licence application for two wheelers up to 49 cc.	
2.40	*Canje del permiso de conducción.*	
2.40	Exchange of licence (including a foreign one)	
3.050	*Solicitud de cuestiones varias (conductores - vehiculos).*	Sorry, none in English.
3.050	Application for questions/answers for drivers and vehicles.	It is a simple matter to print out the form while in Adobe Reader.
9.03	*Solicitud de matriculación.*	
9.03	Application for registration of a vehicle.	
9.050	*Solicitud transmisión de vehiculos.*	
9.050	Application for transfer of a vehicle (By the buyer)	
9.060	*Solicitud de baja de vehiculo.*	
9.060	Application to scrap or de-register a vehicle.	
9.07/A	*Notificación de transmisión de vehiculos.*	
9.07/A	Notification of a vehicle transfer (by the seller)	

CHANGED YOUR ADDRESS - WHAT TO DO?

If you change your address, you will need to advise the various authorities so they know where you are, and to not do so can mean a fine being issued when they eventually find you. The step-by-step procedure is at the back of this book. You will need a set (two, one a copy) of the A5 form TASA 2.23, as in the list above(previous pages). Tick the square for the one/s you require.

As noted at the top of the form list, each form can be downloaded from the DGT web site, address at:

http://www.dgt.es/indices/dgtHtm_Impresos_es.html.

See page 141 for how to get there if you have problems.

Driving Licences.

Within <u>30 days</u> of your move, either send, or take if you wish, your licence to *Trafico* with the proof of your new address, namely a new *nota de empadronamiento.* This is the form issued by your *ayuntimiento* or town hall with your new address on it. There is no charge for the form (or there should not be as you are doing them a favour by registering), just a bit of queuing or waiting if by post. The new credit card type driving licences are now being issued but they do not have your address on them. I have updated my licence in July of this year 2007 and received (at last) the credit card type, for a picture. Again, the procedure check list is in the back of this book.

Permiso de Circulacion (Trafico)

This also will have to have the new address inserted and it is done by replacement and there is no charge for this service. However, there is a new permiso layout where the vehicle fuel type is noted so write in on the form the fuel, "*gasolina*" or "*gasoleo*".

The A*yuntamiento (council)* must be advised, even if the new address is in the same council area. They will need it for the annual tax, the *impuesto municipal sobre vehiculos de traccion mecanica* which is basically the same as the Road Fund tax. You will need to check in at your new *ayuntamiento* when making the next annual tax payment which for the current calendar year is always made at the *ayuntamiento* for the address on the *permiso de circulacion.* In other words, the payment is made to the ayuntamiento for the address on the *permiso de circulacion.* This can be made a stop order with your Bank is you wish and this is a very convenient way to pay often avoiding big queues.

<u>Your insurance company.</u> Remember that your circumstances may have changed where if, for example, if you are now parking off-road or in a lock-up garage, the premium may be less, but make sure that the insurer was not already under that impression from your first application for the old address.

The form shows the following visible text elements:

ESPAÑA FRANQUEO PAGADO Cartas

MINISTERIO DEL INTERIOR

DIRECCIÓN GENERAL DE TRÁFICO

AVISO

AVISO DE CADUCIDAD DEL PERMISO O LICENCIA DE CONDUCCIÓN

Temporary Licence Slip

AUTORIZACIÓN TEMPORAL PARA CONDUCIR

Clase de permiso o licencia
A+ -C1 -EC1

Fecha de caducidad de la vigencia del permiso o licencia de conducción
16-05-2006

DATOS DE/DE LA TITULAR

Payment details here

Período de prórroga	Bonificación	Importe a pagar (€)
5 o más años	0%	17,20
Hasta 4 años	20%	13,88
Hasta 3 años	40%	10,40
Hasta 2 años	60%	6,80
1 año o menos	80%	3,40

VALIDEZ 90 DÍAS

Firma del interesado.

Send this part back with photo, signature, licence, medical certificate & payment, as neccessary. If you have a new address, complete lower block with new details.

DIRECCIÓN GENERAL DE
JEFATURA DE TRÁFICO

Foto here. No Staples +

PEGAR FOTO AQUI
(O GRAPAR)

FIRMA (si

Sign here. Stay in borders

DNI/NIE:
FECHA DE NACIMIENTO:
PAÍS DE NACIMIENTO:
NOMBRE Y APELLIDOS:
FECHA DE CADUCIDAD:
NÚMERO Y FECHA DEL GIRO POSTAL:

RELLENAR EN CASO DE CAMBIO DE DOMICILIO O NO CONCORDAR ALGUNO DE LOS DAT...

DOMICILIO: (Calle o plaza)
LOCALIDAD:

New address details here.

Copy of an "*AVISO*" letter sent to remind you that your licence, etc. is DUE TO EXPIRE, in this case due to a medical being required. This only happens if you are registered through Trafico (with a foreign EU licence) or have a Spanish licence.

Note that you cut out the middle portion called the *AUTORIZACION TEMPORAL PARA CONDUCIR*, which is your temporary licence to carry as you must send/take your original licence with the application.

The lower portion you send in with a photo with a white background, held on with a dab of glue or Bluetac, no staples. Your signature (*firma*) ready to be scanned and copied onto the new card licence is written in the square tikled above it "*Firma, sin salirse del recuadro*". Keep within the lines. The marked table of costs show what is to be paid by Post Office Giro cheque if posted, cash if you go to Trafico offices, for how many years your current licence needs to be renewed before the next general medical falls due. For most drivers without HGV classifications, etc, it will be ten, five or two years depending on your age. If you have a new address, write it on the lower half of the form to be sent in with the other documents. Also see check lists at back of this book.

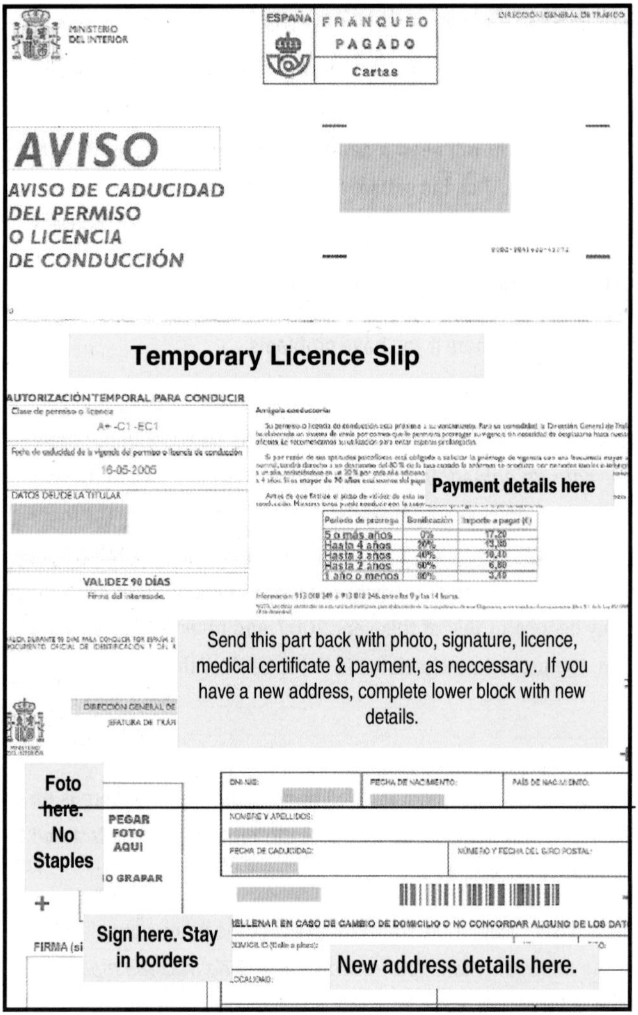

As the letter has a three month temporary driving licence for the classifications that are expiring (until the medical etc. has been satisfied) the benefit of this system is that you do not have to worry about driving without a driving licence while the new one is issued for whatever reason you need it changing. I did mine in 2007, through Trafico Malaga and it took five weeks using Correos. Carry copies of your old DL as well as the Correos postal receipt just to feel "safe" if you are stopped. Note that some of the blank out areas on the sample form are to hide personal details.

Receipt for a driving licence medical carried out at a local **CENTRO DE RECONOCIMIENTO MEDICO DE CONDUCTORES** or the Medical Centre for Examination of Drivers. They are situated in most towns, and the official list is in the Trafico web-site at :

http://www.dgt.es/tramites/crc/crc.htm

Click on your province for the list, telephone numbers and addresses. Remember that even with a foreign EU driving licence, the periodical medicals are mandatory and important in Spain.

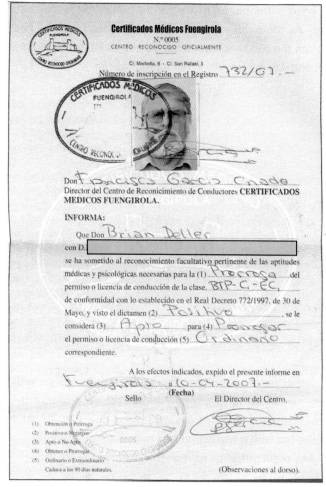

The medical report is ready to be sent to Trafico for issue of the new licence. On the reverse is either a list of reasons for rejection, or acceptance. The medical is simple and can be made at any of the registered clinics. It consists of:

1. A simple eye test.
2. A simple coordination test where two handles are each used simultaneously with both hands to keep two separate blocks on a computer screen within a winding "road". You can usually have a practice.
3. An oral questionnaire about any health problems, diabetes, heart, etc. If you have serious problems you may have restrictions such as only driving no more than 100 kph (A reader had this due to having only one eye.)

The medical takes about 10 to 20 minutes and please be calm if you are of a nervous disposition. They are very kind and will help you so it is nothing to worry about unless, of course, you should not be driving due to extreme health risk. Before you take the medical, look on the walls in the waiting room to see the tariffs.   If not there, ask to see a printed list as I have had reports of English speaking applicants being charged very high prices. The standard rate in 2007 is about € 35.

If over 70 years of age, there are no charges at Trafico for their paperwork and licence issues. One of the benefits of being a senior.

145

"DRIVING" THE CO-ORDINATION PC.

The señora in the photo is showing how to use the two independent handles which as they are turned, images on the PC monitor move thus testing the driver's co-ordination skills. It is easy for anyone who is fit to drive. There are several tests of which you are expected to do only one. One test is where there are two "winding roads" on the monitor with two blocks controlled by the two handles representing cars. As the roads move, you have to manipulate the two handles to keep the "cars" on the two winding roads. Do not panic as it is like an easy child's arcade game, and you are usually given a practice run.

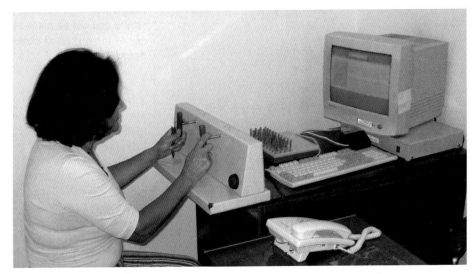

The other tests are for:

1.   Vision, and if you cannot read the bottom line with your glasses on with one eye blocked, you need new ones or really should not be driving, but I have had reports from readers who, for example, have only one eye and they have been passed but with a restriction to a maximum of 100 kph.

2.   Medical questions. Any problems such as diabetes, asthma, heart, etc.

As you sign for these the answers are basically a "sworn statement".

Also remember that although the medical certificate says that it is valid for three months, ignore this as Trafico has no set procedure at time of printing for recording us foreigner's medicals, so keep the certificate as a record that you have taken it and satisfied the law just in case of being stopped or having an accident where it would be said that your DL is not valid due to no periodical medicals having been taken.

Officina de Trafico - How to Navigate the "Sea of Faces".

A visit to most *Trafico* offices is an experience especially on a hot summer's day when the air-conditioning does not cope with the many hot bodies queuing for the various services, but the staff are very nice and helpful, even if your Spanish is not good, and if you have plenty of time, you can get to your objective. However, if you are in a hurry or cannot afford the day off work, use a *gestor* or go with a Spanish friend. There are people outside the offices looking for foreigners and others not familiar with the procedure to assist for a price, but their charges are such that you are better off using a *gestor* and letting him/her do the work, especially when you add your travel costs to the bill. Virtually none of the *Trafico* staff can speak English, and why should they?

You will/may need to use the *Oficina del Trafico* to: -

⇒ Obtain / change your driving licence, including if stolen. Do not forget the crime report number from the policia local.

⇒ As a new resident, register your foreign EU driving licence.

⇒ Register a change of ownership of a vehicle. If you have bought new or used from a Dealer, they will do this for you but make sure they have before you pay over all the cash unless it is a registered main dealer for a manufacturer. TRUST NOBODY.

⇒ Pay a fine (multa). This can be also be done by post or at the post office.

⇒ To obtain information on another vehicle or your own as on Trafico's system.

⇒ Register your change of address. Driving licence and *permiso de circulacion*.

⇒ To obtain duplicates (copies) of vehicle documents due to loss or theft.

⇒ Scrap (*baja*) a vehicle. Official scrap-yards (*desguaces or centros de recogida de vehiculos*) can also do this. An official list of all of Spain is at:
http://www.dgt.cs/tramites/cards/cards.htm

⇒ Obtain a new driving licence but in Spain, the driving schools will organise this for you when you have passed the test using their service.

⇒ Change your foreign DL for a Spanish one.

⇒ Obtain an International Driving Licence.

⇒ Moto and quadricycle driving licences are obtained locally at your ayuntamiento or policia local.

There are fees to pay, and they are listed in the Trafico web-site as they change each year. The fees are reasonable when compared with many other countries. If you are over the age of 70, a new driving licence is free, but sadly, not the cost of the medical.

Check lists are in the back of this book.

CARRYING DUPLICATES OF DOCUMENTS INCLUDING YOUR DRIVING LICENCE.

The loss of the original vehicle documents is not only a nuisance but will cost you time and money. Replacing them is a time consuming job, especially if you do not have photocopies. To avoid this, it is legal to carry CERTIFIED COPIES in the car. The certification may be done by: -

⇒   Trafico. Travelling and much queuing?

⇒   Your local *ayuntamiento*. If they object, carry a box of chocolates with you as a "bribe". It works for me! They will copy them and stamp them with a "*certificado*" stamp for the *ayuntamiento*.

⇒   Any other public (government) organisation.

⇒   Have them notarised by a gestor. However, this is the very expensive way.

Some *ayuntamientos* will initially refuse to do them as it gives them extra work, hence the box of chocolates bribe. And you are also paying their wages through local taxes.

Loss of especially the *permiso de circulación*, usually means a visit to the ITV for a physical check of the VIN number etc. to make sure that you are not trying to obtain documents for e.g. a stolen vehicle, so it makes sense.

LOST YOUR UK LICENCE?

If you live here as your main residence and have no address in the UK, if you lose your driving licence, you cannot get a new one from your last home where it was issued, as the address will be incorrect. However, you can apply to the authority, in the UK the Driving and Vehicle Licensing Authority (DVLA), for official confirmation of your licence and what it covered, and this can be used to easily obtain a Spanish one. The DVLA form is D737. More information is on the DVLA web site at: www.dvla.gov.uk.

Sorry still cannot find the equivalent for Ireland.

Author's Request.

If you find this book useful and worthwhile, please tell your friends. If you have any complaints or suggestions (not rude ones), please tell me. I can be contacted by E-mail at: -

bjdeller@spainvia.com: or by phone at (0034) 666-888-870.

Please make sure you put "Motoring in Spain" in the subject line, so I know it is not SPAM.

MUNICIPAL VEHICLE TAX (ROAD TAX?).

Owners of Spanish registered cars and motorcycles must pay a tax similar to the Road Fund Licence in the UK and many other countries, to the local Town Hall or *Ayuntamiento*. The amount varies slightly from town to town, that is, it is not nationally set at a fixed rate and a current sample (Malaga) list is usually in my web-site in the update pages around February each year. The costs vary from one area to another. There is no receipt to be displayed on your car's windscreen: however, you must keep a copy of it, usually in A4 paper form or on a slip of paper issued by the Bank, with the other documents in your glove compartment. As an example, for a car of the size of a Ford Focus 1750 cc, the tax is about €125 (2007) per year in Marbella, Malaga. Some are more, some less. The amounts vary according to the "fiscal" horsepower of the vehicle which is shown on the Tarjeta Inspeccion Tecnica de Vehiculos at the bottom of the right top column with the line heading of "Potencia fiscal/real CV/Kw". Our Focus is 12, 3/66 whicjh means that it is rated at 12, 3 fiscal or monetary power and an actual of 66 Kilowatts or 90 BHP.

The tax is called the

"*Impuesto municipal sobre vehículos de tracción mecanica*".

As a foreigner, you must also register with your local town hall, and to do this, you will need your NIE form or *residencia* card, and a copy of your proof of residence, such as a property rental contract for at least one year, or ownership of property paper copies (*escritura*), and present them at the desk at your local town-hall/ *ayuntamiento*. The *ayuntimiento* benefits from your registering and you will then be issued with the *Nota de Empadronamiento* confirming your residence in that area, and, the council will welcome your application as the registered population in their area helps their claims for cash from the government in grant form. This *nota* is re-issued each year, usually free of charge or for 50 *centimos* (you must collect it).

Payment of the local "road tax" is made before 1st May each year, and there can be a discount if you pay early or on time, and a "fine" if you pay late, usually 5% for the first month, then 20% for succeeding months. It must be paid to the *ayuntamiento* where the car was registered on January the 1st. So if you move or the car is sold to a new owner/address, the tax is still paid to the *ayuntamiento* as at January the first not the new one, until, of course, January the first next year. When you buy a used car, make sure that the tax has already been paid. Ask for the receipt.

If you move your address into another council area, you will need to advise the Ayuntamiento (as well as Trafico) *Trafico*. The transfer is noted each year in time (January 1st) for your vehicle to be on the new *ayuntamiento's* system. Another note is that some *ayuntamientos* no longer accept cash at their desks. You have to pay it into a special Bank account before you go to the *ayauntamiento's* offices. Please check in your area by asking a neighbour, etc. if this applies where you live. Some Banks for Andalucia are listed in my web-site.

CHECK LIST FOR PAYMENT OF THE AYUNTAMIENTO "ROAD TAX".

If for the first time.

⇒ NIE or *residencia* card or certificate (issued from March 2007).

⇒ *Nota Empadronamiento.* You will need to get this from the *ayuntamiento* using your property *escritura* or, if applicable, the rental contract for at least one year. (Crazy really as both do the same task.)

⇒ The *permiso de circulacion* for the vehicle with the local address on it.

⇒ The amount to pay in cash. If by post, a *Giro de Correos* (postal order, but check your office will accept this method). See above for Bank methods.

⇒ If not applying/paying in person, send a stamped self-addressed envelope.

You cannot sell or trade in your car without the latest *impuesto* receipt, fully paid up, being presented during the transfer of ownership.

If you go yourself for any changes, payments, or licence details at the *Trafico,* go to the information desk for the correct form first if you have not already downloaded it from the Trafico web site at : -

http://www.dgt.es/indices/dgtHtm_Impresos_es.html

Check lists for all the Trafico vehicle and driver procedures are at the back of this book.

EXAMPLES OF LOCAL "ROAD TAXES" FOR MOTOR VEHICLES.

Check with your local *ayuntamiento* for actual charges. These figures below show the fiscal hosepower used by the authorities to establish the annual charge for each class of vehicle. The actual costs may vary slighty for your local *ayuntamiento*.

VEHICLE TYPE & FISCAL HP. PASSENGER VEHICLES *(TURISMOS)* UP TO 3,500 KG.	Annual Tax Rate, Euros.(Check at your local offices. Will be be different each year)
Less than 8 HP	20
8 to 11,99	56
12 to 15,99	121
16 to 19,99	155
20 plus	199
AUTOBUSES.	
Less than 21 seats	136
21 to 50 seats	199
More than 50 seats	256
TRUCKS AND VANS.	
Less than 1 000 kg cargo rating.	69
1 000 to 2 999 cargo	140
2 999 to 9 999 cargo	205
More than 9 999	254
TRACTORS.	
Less than 16 HP	29
16 to 25 HP	47
More than 25 HP	144

TRAILERS AND SEMI-TRAILERS	Tax Rate €
750 kg to 999 cargo rating	29
1 000 to 2 999 cargo rating	47
More than 9 999 cargo rating	144
MOTORCYCLES.	
Mopeds	7
Up to 125 cc	7
125 to 250 cc	12
250 to 500 cc25	25
500 to 1 000 cc	52
1 000 cc plus	108

The above costs increase each year, supposedly in line with inflation. However, it is amazing how the costs vary at the different *ayuntamientos*. For the year 2007, the Ford Focus diesel was €126 in Benalmadena, and €107 in Marbella.

MOTORCYCLES – SOME OBSERVATIONS.

I love motorcycles, having owned and ridden them, including club racing and sprinting on tarmac, foot-ups and off-road long-distance enduros (some over 150 miles [242 km] in the USA), for over forty years.   Spain has an ideal climate for them, especially on the coasts where it is also hilly in many areas in the south, as Madrid gets cold in the winter and sometimes there is slight snow, but nothing like northern Europe. However, there are not that many large capacity motorcycles here possibly due to the high cost of purchase and insurance, but the towns are crowded with scooters  and mopeds, ridden in most cases by "kamikaze pilots", who swerve all over the road, jump or ignore traffic lights and Stop-street signs, and often add to the high accident rates amongst this class of rider. The sales of up to 125 cc motos doubled in 2005/6 due to fuel price increases, the crowded roads and the ability to ride a two-wheeler up to 125 cc on a normal car "B" licence. But accident rates have also increased.

Trafico has altered, or at the time of printing announced that it will be changing, the driving licence classifications so that riders can progess more slowly from the smallest to the largest, the new classes being A1, A2, and A3 as explained in the relevant pages in this book (pages 125 & 126).   As someone who learnt to ride on a 1939 Velocette 350 cc machine, with no rear suspension, and 6 volt candle lighting, motorcycles today develop so much power that some of the 600 cc machines can do almost 240 kph (150 mph), and the larger machines that can be bought over the counter if you have the cash, are so powerful, that they are capable of doing as much as 300 kph (190 mph), and still be quiet as well.   The new 300 kph Ducati 1046 costs nearly €67.000 (£42.000), but then there are many who can afford to pay as there are those who will pay a million for a supercar.

On the costas, especially in summer, many riding the smaller machines do not use crash helmets and often ride in "flip-flop" sandal shoes, no gloves, bare-chested (not the girls: well, not yet), and especially with no eye-protection.   Also, many modify the engines to give far more power (even illegally raising the engine capacity in some cases) as well as making the machine very noisy. As someone who has been a past volunteer instructor with the RAC / ACU Motorcycle Training Scheme in the UK, and with a similar organisation in South Africa where we taught even the local traffic police at one time, I feel very strongly that not only the authorities but parents must take urgent action to instil self-discipline in these, quite frankly, foolish youths.   After all, if you are involved in an accident with one, especially as a foreigner, your insurance, if you are covered, can be awarded high cost penalties / damages if it can be proved that you were at fault at all, and if your cover is not sufficient, you must pay out of your pocket. You also have to use a local lawyer; —more costs. Also, the rider may find "witnesses" to prove you were in the wrong as he / she lives in that district.

Occasionally when complaints reach a high level, the local police will have a "blitz", and organise roadblocks, confiscating machines until the fault, usually noise is corrected, a common complaint, or where riders do not have a crash helmet.   It is not unusual to see riders tearing around with their crash helmet hooked on their arm or on the back carrier. They say that it is too hot to wear them, even in winter!   Childish rebellion and do the Spanish really love their children to let them take such risks.

The few large machine riders you see often ride at high speeds (180 – 200 kph? Or 110 to 122 mph) along the four-lane *carreteras, autopistas* and *autovias,* and you often see a scooter rider still racing around with a leg in plaster, crutches strapped on the back.

Dipped headlights must be used at all times in the daytime by motorcyclists with engines over 49 cc although most machines now cannot be ridden without the lights on at all, although surveys have proved that many other road users still claim "to have not seen them".   Children must be at least seven years of age, to ride on a bike with a parent, and if with another adult (not the parent), written authorisation must be supplied by the parents, which the other adult must then carry and show to the police, etc. on demand.

You can rent motorcycles of all sizes in Spain, although it is not cheap, but for a day out on an automatic scooter to a Honda Goldwing, (a 1500 to 1800 cc six-cylinder moto) the cost can be justified on a holiday, - if you are confident about riding on the right side of the road.   The *caveats* when renting are the same as with a car. Make sure all prior damage is recorded, tyres are in very good condition and correctly inflated, and if you do not have a crash helmet, one will be provided.   Best to have your own as well as protective clothing.   Never ride a scooter / moto in "flip-flops, always wear sturdy shoes, and wear gloves. Even falling off at 5 kph can "spoil your week" with scraped skin. The rental insurance does not always include theft, so be careful and ask exactly what it does cover, because you may be asked to leave something of value such as your passport with the rental company, (although this is illegal) and if the bike is stolen, you will have great difficulty in getting it back until you pay the costs. And theft is a problem, although no worse than anywhere else in Europe. Bikes are usually supplied with security chains. Riders do not have to carry the same reflective jackets or triangles as motorists have to have, but their clothing should have this built in for safety's sake, especially when walking after a breakdown on the non-urban highways (anywhere over 50 kph limit usually or if the roads are unlit).

Foreigners are restricted to the ages stated on their driving licences. However, if you have a normal "B" car licence, this is sufficient to ride a moped or scooter, either with an engine capacity up to 49 cc, and if you have held that licence for three years plus, up to 125 cc. For all other machines over this size, a motor-cycle driving licence is needed as well as at least Third Party insurance, which can be expensive for reasons stated above. Many Spanish insurance companies are now unwilling to insure younger riders without expensive premiums because of the high accident rates.

Spain really needs a national incentive for road safety and skills training for young riders, and it needs to be insisted upon by the parents, as well as all the authorities. Loving Spain as I do, I have to admit that in many ways they have a way to go to catch up, as the accident rates prove, compared with, for example, the UK, where the excellent RAC / ACU Training Scheme was in operation some thirty to forty plus years ago.

As a point of interest, the generic word in Spanish for motorcycle and scooter is "moto", and when this word is used in other contexts, it also means "in a rush" and "to get really turned on sexually". No wonder the Spanish love their motos.

MODIFIED MOTOR-CYCLES (MOTOS).

As in other EU countries, it is illegal to modify your moto unless it is pre-approved by the manufacturer and the EU regulations, in other words homolgated. When you look around the Spanish cities at all the noisy scooters with modified exhausts, especially four-wheeled ATV's which are mainly intended to be used off-road, and many obviously with hotted-up engines, you wonder why the law is not enforced. Riders of quad bikes do not have to wear crash helmets, a crazy Law in my opinion, because your head is still exposed to the car bodywork or the lamp-post it can come into contact with kerb that you may hit in an accident. A likely event the way many seem to ride them.

New proposals are that motos are to be thoroughly checked for modifications to the engine and exhausts when they go for the ITV or MOT test.

However, as motos are not liable for this test until they are five years old, there is plenty of leeway in the meantime although another proposal is to reduce the number of years for this compulsory inspection.   What is does mean is that if you are buying a second-hand machine, it is important that you have it tested and accepted by the testing ITV authority before you pay over the cash, especially if it is a private sale, as you may have to buy a new expensive exhaust system and other parts to pass the test. Remember that ex-rental and commercially used machines are subjected to more frequent ITVs. Check on the *Permiso de Circulacion* and *Tarjeta de Inspeccion Tecnica de Vehiculos* before buying, or even at Trafico as described in this book. It is cheaper than finding out after the sale.

In practice, the larger modern sports motos are so close in performance to their racing counterparts used on the track, it is unnecessary to do much to improve them and most as sold new are quieter than small cars . After all, how fast do you want to go, when the larger sports motos already have 250 kph plus top speeds, with acceleration times that will leave Ferraris, etc. behind up to 160 plus kph?

SUMMARY
As can also be seen in the Driving Licence and other pages:
$\Rightarrow$ It was announced that from December 2005, no one under the age of 16 years can hold a moto licence. But we still see in many of the pueblos (villages) this being ignored.
$\Rightarrow$ Any passenger must be at least 12 years of age and the bike equipped from new to carry one.
$\Rightarrow$ No one under the age of 18 years can carry a passenger.
$\Rightarrow$ If you have a "B" car licence, you may ride a 49 cc moto or if the B-licence has been held for three plus years, up to a 125 cc moto with no further tests. But you will need specific insurance for it.
$\Rightarrow$ 16 year olds may ride machines up to 125 cc with the correct licence.
$\Rightarrow$ Riders do not need to carry breakdown triangles or a CE reflective jacket, but must wear bright clothing (with built-in reflective material recommended).
$\Rightarrow$ Dipped headlights must be on all the time while on the road.

⇒ You must wear a crash helmet at all times on the road: rider and passenger, and you should wear suitable protective clothing, especially footwear and gloves even when it is hot.

⇒ Carry safety spares such as light bulbs and corrective glasses, if worn.

⇒ You may not tow a trailer even if it is a three-wheeler unless it is as a visiting tourist with a vehicle legal as such in the country of registration.

⇒ May not ride without suitable eye protection. It is incredibly stupid to do this anyway even on a moped as it is so easy to lose an eye.

⇒ If you have a PROVISIONAL driving licence from your "home" country, it is not valid in Spain. This applies to all vehicles.

ROAD SIGNS IN SPAIN.

A comparison of the Spanish road-signage shows that there are many more than in say the British Highway Code book, perhaps as many as four times. No wonder it takes a long time to learn them all, and visitors from the UK and Ireland, where there are far fewer different signs, are at a loss to quickly understand when they see them for perhaps the first time. This can obviously be very dangerous for all drivers in the area.

Many of the road signs in Spain are common to adjoining countries on the Continent. Perhaps one day, the EU will be standardised in this matter, but until then it is vital that foreign drivers unused to the differences aquaint themselves with the Spanish signs to speed travelling by not having to dither at intersections but most important to avoid accidents and / or stiff fines for not obeying a sign.

While the Spanish police are understanding to a certain degree, it is no defence to state that you are a foreigner and do not know the signs. As in any other country, ignorance is no excuse. The author has questioned British (and some Spanish) drivers who have lived here years, and drive every day, on the meaning of some fairly common signs, and discovered that many had no clue as to what they meant! Perhaps the same the world over, especially for those who passed their driving test years ago. A few have even initially declined to buy this book because "I live here!", but some change their mind after a short oral "test". In fact, a UK-TV programme in May 2005, where several senior citizen drivers were tested extensively for their ability to drive and knowledge of the roads including signs in their own country, the UK, showed that most did not even know simple signs such at the beginning and end of a motorway or "no overtaking", etc. The best of the tested drivers was the oldest at 92 years of age (looked and acted 50 - 60 and sorry ladies, but he was a man) showing that age is not always the deciding factor.

The following pages show signs that are peculiar to Spain and some are universal on the Continent. It is obviously very important that you familiarise yourself with them. You may save a fine, - or far worse.

They cover: -

$\Rightarrow$ Priority signs, where you are told what to do for safety's sake.

$\Rightarrow$ Obligatory signs: you must obey them. (Cont. page ???)

SPECIAL WARNING ADVICE.

CAUTION. Example of a roundabout (*glorieta* or *rotunda*) with a "Give Way (*cedo el paso*)" on it to give preference to traffic coming OFF the *autovia* from the right. The road painting is almost worn away, but the sign is intact. The missing paint is no excuse in Spain if you have an accident in this case. Normally, traffic coming from your left ON the roundabout has priority, especially before you enter it.

Potential accident point for the unwary.

Readers are warned to be <u>especially careful of this feature</u> as many junctions in Spain have the road paint worn off the road and signs hidden away almost out of sight usually by over-grown plants. It would probably mean going to Court to prove the facts and innocence, or at least paying a lawyer to sort out the fault with the police/Guardia Civil and avoid a fine and/or loss of No Claims Bonuses for your insurance. If involved in an accident, take good photos on the spot and phone 112 for the Guardia Civil to witness why it occurred.

ROADSIDE SIGNS – DIFFERENT TYPES AND THEIR MEANINGS.

			EXCEPTIONS
DANGER & WARNINGS	Triangular with thick red border. White background with black symbols.		Traffic lights ahead warning, level crossings.
REGULATION EG. RIGHTS OF WAY.	These shapes are distinctive		Roads and bridges where the road is very narrow restricting passages in opposite directions
PROHIBITION & RESTRICTION SIGNS	Circular with thick red border. White background with usually black symbols.		All no stopping and parking signs.
OBLIGATORY SIGNS	Circular with blue background and usually white symbols.		Typical - turn on dipped lights when entering a tunnel or underpass.
END OF PROHIBITION OR RESTRICTION SIGNS.	Circular, white background with black cross stripes and grey symbols.		End of restriction area sign, end of minimum speed area. (Circular sign with blue background, white symbols)
INDICATION. GENERAL AND LANES.	Rectangular or square with blue background and usually white symbols/letters.		

160

SERVICES	Rectangular, blue background with black symbols on a white plate.	
INDICATION OF DESTINATIONS.	Rectangular, blue background on autovias/pistas & main roads; white background on expressways and normal highways; different background colours in towns.	

(Cont. from page 112)

⇒ General indication signs; e g "*Autovia* from this point"

⇒ Advice signs.

⇒ End of obligation area signs where you return to the previous rule.

⇒ Danger (*peligroso*) signs. Warning you of the need for caution ahead.

⇒ Prohibition signs. You "cannot do that here!"

⇒ General indication signs; e g "*Autovia* from this point"

⇒ Advice signs.

⇒ Vertical board signs are where temporary notices are placed to show the current state of the road ahead, especially in mountain areas where the weather can change quickly.

⇒ Officially approved (homulgamated) information signs.

⇒ Colour coding of various urban advice signs: what they mean.

⇒ Road works signs. These are the same as others but with a yellow background and as such, they are temporary until,the work is completed. Good place for a speed trap camera!

Please note that to save space on the sign descriptions, the author has abbreviated: - "Motorcycles" to the Spanish "motos" , and, "No Entry" to "N/E".

TUNNEL AND UNDERPASSES.

Especially in Andalucia, but anywhere there are road tunnels, extreme caution is needed especially when there is no run-off or stopping area at the side of the lanes inside the tunnel. At the entrances, there are: -

⇒ Signs advising the recommended speed to drive (note not faster, not slower unless you have a restricted speed vehicle).

⇒ Signs advising that the vehicles must drive on dipped headlights, with a similar sign with a diagonal at the end of the tunnel to advise switching the lights off.

⇒ In the tunnels there are overhead lit speed limit signs made up of lights in the same design as the normal speed limit signs (red circle, white background with black number). In the event of a vehicle stopped in the tunnel, this limit shown will be reduced or a cross shown instead indicating a blockage ahead.

⇒ Each lane at the entrance has an overhead sign with a green arrow facing down or a red diagonal cross. The arrow shows that the lane is open through the tunnel; the cross shows that the lane is closed for an accident or roadworks, etc. EXTREME CAUTION must be taken. A tunnel is a terrible place to have an accident.

⇒ Inside the tunnel, where safe, there are SOS phones whch must be used in case of an emergency. Mobile phones have a problem with no signal inside a tunnel.

⇒ Often the speed limit is the same as the road outside especially where tunnels have a lane for emergency stopping only. Where there is no such lane, there is usually an 80 kph speed limit. Sometimes speed traps are placed in tunnels with high accident rates.

⇒ There are often flashing amber lights on the walls at about 50 metre intervals that operate when the speed limit has been lowered in an emergency. Also if they are red, be ready to stop. Normally they are green.

⇒ In tunnels and underpasses, vehicles are, by law, to keep the following distances from the vehicle in front: -

| Up to a MAM of 3.500 kg | 100 metres or 4 seconds |
| Over a MAM of 3.500 kg | 150 metres or 6 seconds |

You will find that this law is largely ignored, but remember that in the event of an accident, you could be held liable if you were proven to be closer than the above distances and a possible cause of the accident. A tunnel blocked because of an accident is very serious, especially when fire breaks out, so extreme caution should always be exercised in these locations. There may also be signs to this effect. The normal distances at around 100 - 120 kph are 2 seconds in the dry and 3 - 4 in the wet on the normal roads.

UNDERSTANDING THE ROAD NUMBER SIGNS.

As elsewhere in the civilised world, roads are identified by numbers and colour backgrounds, usually with a letter code. Some common examples are shown here. Every main road has marker boards every kilometre, and these are often used in addresses for properties or turn-offs. By referring to a map, you can quickly locate where you are, or where you want to go.

 Indicates that this road is the Autovia (or if "AP", autopista) No. 68, at "Km marker board 275", that is, it is 275 Km from where the road starts.

The E-804 shows that it is also part of the European road system, and it may continue into the next European state. keeping the same E-number. An example is, "Careterra de Cadiz, Km 196".

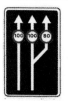
Lanes ahead showing speed limit for each one.

Single to two lanes with the outer (left) lane having a minimum speed of 70 kph.

Danger of fire warning. Do not throw "fire" out of the car. If you do and start a fire, it is a definite jail sentence in Spain.

The turn-off is here and 500 metres (1/2 Km) further ahead after the turn-off is a service area. (only). rodas

 Boundary entrance of the Pueblo (village) of Los Corrales...

Name of point of interest with height above sea level.

Boundary exit of the Pueblo (village) of Los Corrales...

Warning of a house of religion ahead with times of prayer. Make no noise and drive slowly at times noted.

Turn right for the N-120 to the village of Castañares, & then the next big town of Burgos.

 Exit 22 next (from autovia/pista).

 Exit 22 now (from autovia/pista).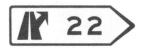

There is much more information on the following pages

SOME COMMON SIGNS.

 Speed limit sign showing the off-ramp or exit road speeds to be obeyed for safety reasons as there may be a curve ahead. Only affects those leaving the highway on the slip road as indicated by the arrow. Red circle, white background, black numbers.

 From this point, you must drive on dipped headlights or short range lights (non-dazzling).

 End of dipped headlights area. You are reminded to turn them off.

 From this point, you must not sound your horn or any loud acoustic device.

 End of horn sounding area.

Border to next country ahead

European network road. Most likely continues into next EU State.

Autovia (or Autopista if "AP" = Toll road.)

National road. Can be two way or 4-lane but not to autovia standard.

Autonomous Roads (maintained by the Province) 1st, 2nd, and 3rd levels.

 Minor road that can be used as an alternative (diversion or *desvio*) road to main route.

Please note that in many cases, a road can have two or even three numbers. For example, it can be an autovia as well as a European road, and a stretch of it can also be a local road section.

EXAMPLE PRIORITY SIGNS.

You have priority (right of way) to proceed.

End of your priority area.

Narrow road ahead. Do not enter if traffic is coming from other way. They have precedence

Indicates that ahead is a narrow road (bridge, etc?) and the other driver must give way to you.

Give Way. Can have symbol in triangle or text on a white rectangular sign below to qualify why.

Universal, must STOP sign. Road also painted if not worn away.

One way this direction. Several variations of this sign.

Cambio de Sentido. Change of direction. (over/under bridge?).

Beginning of road reserved only for automobiles (on the autovias?)

Start of lane reserved for saddled animals (horses, etc).

Walkway reserved for pedestrians. No other users.

All round signs with a blue background are "you must do" signs. Round and with blue or white background with a red border are "prohibition" signs.

Reserved for two wheeled motos.

Reserved for trucks. Usually with max. tonnage number.

For Bicycles only.

Reserved for horse-drawn carriages.

Minimum speed from this point.

Fit snow chains if needed. (Penalty fine if stuck).

Trucks of any type must use this road/lane, regardless of mass.

Reserved lane for trucks with all dangerous cargos.

Lane only for vehicles carrying 3.000 litres plus of dangerous liquids.

Lane only for for vehicles carrying explosive or inflammable cargos.

End of advised minimum speed limit area.

Use seatbelts (all, where fitted).

End of Prohibition Signs. Black on White backgrounds.

End of any prohibition area a previously signed.

End of speed restricted area, eg 60 kph.

End "no overtaking" area.

End of "no overtaking by trucks" area.

End of limited parking area.

GENERAL ADVICE SIGNS.

Start of
Autopista.

Start of
Autovia.

End of
Autopista.

End of
Autovia.

Sign on mountain
roads or where the
road can be blocked
by nature.
Temp. Boards are
placed to show
current status, abierto
(open) or cerrado
(closed), etc. and
reasons.

Road for
cars only.

End of road

Tunnel
ahead.

End of
tunnel.

Advised Max.
safe speed.

Advised speed
ends.

Area with advised speed range, start / finish.

One way
street.

All lanes one way. Can
be 2 or three plus.

Road ahead is one- way
to the right
(or left, etc, as
applicable).

Pedestrian crossing
ahead. Be ready to
STOP!

Pedestrian underpass ahead.

Pedestrian bridge ahead.

Advance warning of no through road.

No through road to left, (or ahead or right as applicable).

Public parking available here.

Taxi rank.

Bus or Tram stops ahead.

You may change direction (*Cambio de Sentido*) 300 m ahead, - on a single carriageway road.

End of dipped headlights area.

Emergency telephone on highway.

Exit slip roads signs to gauge slowing distances when leaving autovias and autopistas.

Entering / leaving a residencial area with hazard of children legally playing in street, etc. 20 kph (12 mph) maximum speed. Maybe no footpaths? Give way to pedestrians. Pedestrians must not obstruct traffic. Parking only where signed. Vehicles must give all pedestrians a minimum clearance of 1-1/2 metres (4 feet).

PROHIBITION SIGNS. (Note N/E = No Entry)

No vehicle traffic at all.

N/E, all vehicles.

N/E to cars & motos.

N/E , cars & trucks.

N/E to motos.

Maximum Speed limit.

No entry to agricultural vehicles.

N/E to mounted horses.

No vehicle more than 2 m (2 Yds) width allowed.

No trucks at all.

No trucks over shown weight.

No entry for trucks carrying dangerous products.

No entry to vehicles carrying explosive or inflammable substances incl. liquids.

No entry to carriers of 3.000 litres plus of polluting liquids.

N/E to vehicles with a towed trailer.

N/E animal drawn vehicles.

N/E to bicycles.

N/E to vehicles moved by hand.

N/E to pedestrians.

Limited height (in metres).

Note, for practical purposes a metre is equal to a yard.

Minimum following distance (in meters)

No entry to 2 & 3 wheel mopeds, and light quadricycles. Also handicapped vehicles

PROHIBITION SIGNS, CONTINUED.

Vehicles must stop here for reason given on another sign e.g. police post, etc.

Maximum all up weight limit.

Maximum weight limit per axle.

Maximum vehicle length.

Toll Road this way.

No entry to vehicles with trailers, except single axle trailers. Maximum tonnage shown on trailer sign.

No left (or right, if other way) turn.

No "U"-turn.

No overtaking.

No parking on this side of road on odd dates. (1st, 3rd, etc).

Trucks, 3.500 kg plus, not allowed to overtake.

No parking or stopping from sign to junction or next sign. Includes waiting with driver.

No parking this side of road.

No parking on this side of road on even dates (2nd,4th,6th,etc)

Limited time (shown?) waiting only zone. Driver must be in vehicle

No parking this side, 1st-15th of each month.	No parking 16th to 31st of each month.	Sample temporary signs seen at ROADWORKS. SIMILAR TO ALL OTHER TYPES BUT WITH YELLOW BACKGROUND.

DANGER WARNING SIGNS.

All these signs show that you have priority over the other road users exiting the minor junctions.

You must GIVE PRIORITY to vehicles coming from your RIGHT. (This is a rare but important sign to know).

Traffic lights ahead.

Roundabout/traffic circle ahead. Give way to your LEFT WHEN IN THE ROUNDABOUT.

Caution! "Opening" bridge ahead.

Tramway crossing ahead. They always have priority.

40

LOS CORRALES
DE BUELNA

Maximum speed throughout whole village/pueblo is on sign on or next to name of village.

DANGER SIGNS (Cont.).

Level crossing with gates ahead

Level crossing NO gates. Caution.

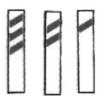

Distance markers (3, 2 & 1), on the RIGHT SIDE OF ROAD, to opening bridge or level crossing.

Distance markers (3, 2 & 1) on the LEFT SIDE OF ROAD, to opening bridge or level crossing.

1–track.

2–tracks.

Warning signs of immediate presence of a level crossing WITHOUT gates.

Aircraft fly low over road ahead.

Dangerous curve to right (or left).

Dangerous curves, both ways, ahead, as shown.

Road works ahead.

Steep hill ahead—DOWN.

These signs show uneven road surface ahead.

Steep hill ahead—UP.

Narrowing of road, as indicated.

Road can be slippery.

DANGER SIGNS. (Cont.).

Pedestrian
crossing ahead.
(Travesia)

Children in area

Bicycle crossing
area.

Caution, free ranging
domestic animals may
be on road.

Wild animals may
be on road.

Traffic runs in both directions
in lanes ahead. Often a
temporary sign on dual
carriageway after a serious
accident.

Obstacles(?) on road.

Road ends at
quayside.

Strong
cross
winds.

Loose gravel
chips on road.

Level drop on side of
road as indicated.

Poor visibility
ahead.

Usually traffic
congestion point
ahead.

Obstruction on
highway ahead.

Be aware of a certain
danger! No other sign
for it.

Road very
slippery when
snowing or icy.

GENERAL SPEED LIMITS IN SPAIN

Unless otherwise signposted.

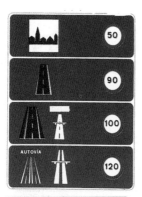

Urban areas—50 kph (30 mph)

Main two-way roads– 90 kph (55 mph).

Main 2-way with 100 kph limit or as posted. (62 mph)

Autovias and Autopistas– 120 kph (74 mph) mph).

On Auto-roads showing exit ahead with exit number.

You are at the exit 22 now. Usually shown with other information sign

Urban sign showing place of interest, in this case the beach, with distance in km.

Lane reserved for autobuses only.

PLEASE NOTE. SOME VEHICLES HAVE LOWER SPEED LIMITS. SEE THE TABLE ON PAGE 21.

Signs on Autopista/via showing Exit 223, with route to the N-623 to Santander.
Exit here at this point on slip road.

Diversion direction sign with number of minor road.

MORE SIGNS YOU WILL ALSO SEE.

Signs indicating you must not make a direct left turn 150 m ahead, but there is a turn right slip lane where you may then safely turn 150 metres (about 150 yards) ahead. You may also do a 180 degree turn there.

Serious fine if not obeyed.

SOS Telephones.
These are placed approximately 1–2 km apart on major highways. Press the button and ask for help. There is a recorded message in four languages. Leave your details and location and (eventually) you will be reached by a breakdown vehicle. Use if you have no service organised with your insurance

Road works. Maximum speed 40 kph (25 mph).

A SIGN WITH A <u>YELLOW</u> BACKGROUND INDICATES <u>TEMPORARY</u> ROADWORKS.

Sign placed on garage doors or gates (often at private residences) to advise road users <u>not to block access at any time</u>. Note this sign is only legal if it has the ayuntamiento details and a licence number on it.

Common Road Sign Types.

Description of Sign	Type
Triangle, white background, red border, black symbol/letters.	Warning!
Triangle inverted white background, red border and sometimes black symbol/letters.	Give way? You must note & obey!
Sign with yellow background, black border and symbol or letters. Different shapes and sizes.	Road works (*Obras*) Temporary signs similar to all other normal ones.
Circle, white background, red border, black symbol/letters.	You must note & obey!
Circle, blue background, red symbol	You must note & obey!
Circle, white background, black symbol/letters.	You must note & obey!
Rectangular sign, blue background with white letters	Advice on Autopista and Autovia roads
Vertical Boards. These are usually temporary advice signs with a white background- A loose board is attached to the backing board, often named "*Pajares*". The advice varies with the weather or special problems such as forest fires.	Mountainous areas, usually.

Lanes shown with minimum speeds in good conditions.

Lane reserved for buses only. You may cross over only at a road-junction.

These signs show closing/opening of lanes on a highway.

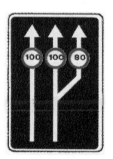 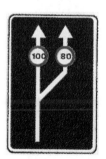

Must take direction in lane as shown.

Maximum speeds in lanes as shown.

HIGHWAY (AUTOPISTA, AUTOVIA,) SIGNS.
Rectangular, white symbols on blue background.
Circular, white background red border — maximum speed.
Circular, white letters on blue background — minimum speeds.

SERVICE SIGNS.

First Aid ahead.

Emergency telephone on highways.

Official vehicle test station. (UK, MOT test?)

Emergency treatment ahead with ambulance facility.

Repair facilities.

Fuel ahead, all types.

Public telephone.

Fuel ahead.

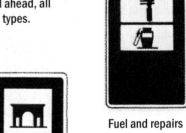

Fuel and repairs

National Monument

Pharmacy, often a lit flashing neon sign when open.

Camping, tents only.

Camping, caravans & tents.

Hotel or motel.

Restaurant.

Cafeteria or bar.

Land for caravan camping/parking.

Picnic area.

Departure point for hiking.

Rest area.

Youth hostel.

Tourist information.

Fishing reserve.

Train station with parking.

Underground train station with parking.

Other Services

Bus station with parking.

179

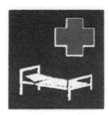

Hospital and/or Emergency medical station.

First Aid. Red Cross!

Post Office. (*Correos*)

Fire risk area. Take extreme care.

Parador. These are old buildings of some splendour that have been modernised by the Spanish government and used as at least 4-star hotels. Pensioners get a discount.

Parador de Turismo. As above but especially equipped and intended for tourists.

Albergue. A hotel/hostel usually in a remote area. Often similar to a youth hostel.

Do not panic. A common sign in South Africa now. Included here to show how lucky we are.

SIGNS INTRODUCED IN January 2004.

The signs and information on the next four pages were introduced by the Spanish Department of the Interior in 2003-04 as part of the ongoing campaign to improve road safety and reduce accidents in Spain.   Included in the changes are: -

⇒   The removal of the classification and signs for "Via Rapidas". These signs were with white symbols on a green background

⇒   Please note that the local police often have a football-type whistle to attract your attention.

⇒   It has also been advised in the Press that the police forces are buying more speed monitoring radar equipment, especially cameras. The locations of all fixed radar traps in Spain can be seen on the Trafico web site at:

http://www.dgt.es/trafico/radares/radares.htm

Police signal. With arm raised vertically, you must safely STOP until signalled to proceed in the direction indicated by the policeman on point duty. Usually the way you wish to go through the junction. Do not enter the road junction until signalled to by the officer.

Police signal. With arm, or both, arms held horizontally, all traffic is to STOP approaching the front and rear of the policeman.

Rocking a red or yellow hand held light. You must safely STOP and then move in the direction indicated by the policeman's arm and the light.

Continued >

SIGNALS FROM OFFICIAL VEHICLES.

 Red flag or light signal. Follow the police motor-cycle, or STOP if other signs indicate this action.

 Green flag or light signal. You may now safely pass the police motor-cycle as the road is now open and clear.

 Yellow flag or light signal. Take extreme caution in that area as there is a particular danger there (usually an accident or road works etc.).

 Left arm extended and moved up and down from the elbow. You must safely STOP on the right hand side of the road behind the police officer.

 Flashing red or yellow light. You must safely move to the right hand side of the road and STOP.

Continued >

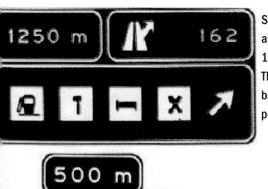

Sign on Autopista showing that 1 - 1/4 km ahead is an exit with a service area. It is exit 162 on that road.

The same sign with black letters on a white background shows that you are at the turn off point.

Sign on autopista showing that 500 metres ahead (about 500 yards) is an exit for a service area only unless another sign shows other reasons.

Sign showing that you have reached the turn off point form autovia and the services are another 500 metres distance.

On the autovias and autopistas, the advance warning turn-off roads are shown with blue background boards with white letters and symbols, and at the actual turn-off point, the boards are white with black letters and symbols.

Maximum speed 30 kph (18 mph) zone with pedestrians having priority.

Footpath/way ahead is OK for use by cycles. (Green background).

The author has had experiences of UK drivers thinking this means 30 mph, not 20 mph.

 Pedestrians in the area. They have precedence.

No entry for mopeds.

Turning left prohibited

 Bicycles only way.

Way reserved for mopeds (with pedals).

 End of reserved way for cyclists.

 Toll Road lane. Use if you have auto-pay system in your car.

Start of lane for cars.

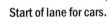

End of lane for cars only.

Bicycles must stay in right hand lane.

Service area with services available 500 m ahead.

Way/path/road suitable for cycling. Usually a scenic route. "5" shows 5 km in this case.

 senda ciclable 5

Cycle lane only. Painted on the road.

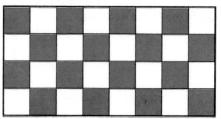

Chequered red and white sign painted on the road indicates an off-road emergency braking zone ahead (for heavy trucks?). No stopping or parking allowed from this point. Usually a sign at road side as well (on right).

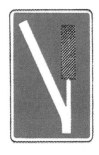

These "soft" bollards indicate: -
1. The presence of a temporary curve:
2. Road-works boundaries:
3. Other obstacles.

1.   2.   3.

A

B

Signs showing direction of driving at a *glorieta*/ roundabout. "A" on the *glorieta*, "B" warning before the *glorieta*.

Vertical board signs seen on mountainous and other hazardous roads.

ABIERTO	OPEN
PRUDENCIA	CAUTION
PRECAUCIÓN	EXTRA CAUTION
PELIGRO	DANGER
CERRADO	CLOSED

   Snow.

   Heavy rain damage.

   Flooding.

Sample boards for "*Pajares*" sign. These can be temporarily fixed if needed due to road conditions, etc.

Trucks, not allowed to overtake.

No trucks & 60 kph max. Speed.

Advice sign usually In mountain areas. Blocked roads; fallen rocks or snow , etc. Boards fitted temporarily as needed

Max. Weight 3,5 tonnes & chains may be needed for snow.

Maximum recommended speed for next zone, etc.

End of recommended speed zone.

Recommended speed range for zone ahead

End of recommended speed range zone

Sample of Disability certificate card. Valid anywhere in the EU, but if resident, get a local one when yours expires. Ask locally where. Usually at the ayuntamiento.

PROTRUDING LOADS ON GOODS VEHICLES.

These are classified as vehicles designed to carry loads. They are not motor cars or small vans, etc.

If a load cannot be split up to fit within the load area of the vehicle, than the load may protrude as follows: -

⇒ Where the vehicle is up to 5 metres in length: Up to <u>one third</u> of the length of the vehicle front and rear.

⇒ Where the vehicle is longer than 5 metres: not more than 2 metres at the front, and 3 metres at the rear.

In all cases the ends of the loads <u>must be protected</u> to prevent/limit damage to other vehicles and injury to other road users. The regulation boards and lights must be fitted.

Width Restrictions.

⇒ On vehicles exclusively designed and licensed to transport goods only, the load may protrude each side a distance up to 40 cm, as long as the total width does not exceed 2,55 metres.

⇒ If rectangular containers/boxes are carried, the longest sides must be in line with the length of the vehicle.

On vehicles less than 1 metre wide, the load should not protrude more than: -

⇒ Each side, 50 cm

⇒ At the rear, 25 cm.

⇒ On the front, not at all.

Special Loads.

⇒ Vehicles are to be considered as "Special Loads" when they exceed the MAM for all normal vehicles.

⇒ When they are greater than the maximum authorised dimensions.

⇒ The loads must be authorised using a special form, TASA 1.3.1 which must detail the transport times, the routes and confirming a pilot or escort vehicle/s will to be used.

⇒ The pilot vehicle must have an amber revolving light visible at 100 metres to warn other road users and to assist the special load driver/crew.

⇒ The pilot vehicle travels in front of the load vehicle on two-way roads, and behind on one way (*autovias*, etc.)

⇒ Pilot vehicles normally have a large roof sign with V22 for private and V23 for police on special duty along with an abnormal load sign.

OTHER COMMON SIGNS ON VEHICLES

Handicapped Driver

"B" licensed driver. Must be in car rear window on LH side. Used by drivers in the probationary year after the driving test.

"L" plate seen on vehicle with registered instructor teaching learner. Name of school at bottom. Has dual foot controls

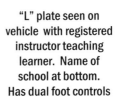

SCHOOL NAME

On rear of HGVs, etc. Vehicle restricted to maximum 80 kph (etc) at all times.

On rear of a vehicle. Cannot go faster than 40 kph due to design.

Test or research vehicle.

School Bus. Must be on front and rear and can be luminous.

 OR

Vehicle is longer than 12 metres. Plates fixed depending on vehicle fittings.

On front & rear, Public Service vehicle (taxi, etc). Must be illuminated at night.

Indicates the load protrudes from rear or front of vehicle. Sign min. size 50cm square. Can be two (see next page) if load is wide. The load must not protrude more than 1/3 rd of the vehicle's length where the vehicle is up to 5 metres long, and 3 metres where the vehicle is longer.

International Transport Sign. Needed when vehicle is used outside of the EU.

Protruding load signs where the load is wider than the vehicle. Must look as shown, fixed securely to the end of the load (front and/or rear) with a white light on the front, and a red one on the rear.

INCLUDES SIGNS PERTINENT TO COMMERCIAL VEHICLES.

Heavy Vehicle Load and Width Limits

⇒ Generally, the maximum width for a vehicle to have when on the highways is <u>2,55 metres</u>
⇒ For airconditioned (insulated walls) vehicles, and buses designed to transport prisoners, the maximum width is 2,60 metres.
⇒ The maximum authorised height is 4 metres, including the load.

Drivers of these vehicles must be aware of the road signs indicating where there is restricted width or height.

 Width warning ahead.

 Height warning ahead.

Max. vehicle length warning ahead

Weight Limitations

Due to the vehicle limitations or the road, maximum mass limitations are imposed on some roads. No vehicle may travel with a MAM or individual axle load more than set by the Law, or by the roads and vehicles.

 No entry for vehicles with a MAM > 5,5

Max allowed weight per axle.

Loaded or total MAM for any vehicle.

Translations of Common Notices seen on Signs.

Spanish	English	Advice
2 (?) m	Two (??) meters	Indicates distance. Just over two yards. 1m = about 3, 2 feet.
Abierto	Open.	
Acceso solo	Access only	Cannot get out of area here except same way as in.
Aeropuerto	Airport	
Aparcamiento	Parking	Also, *Estacionamiento.*
ATENCIÓN – USO MOTOR COMO FRENO.	Warning, Use engine as a brake.	Select a low gear to save brakes overheating. Usually before very steep and long inclines.
Autobus	Coach / Omnibus	
Autoservicio	Self-service	
Barrera e Seguridad	Security barrier	ARMCO or concrete, etc.
Bombero / s	Fireman / men	On a sign in a reserved parking area?
Cadenas para la Nieve.	Snow Chains needed?	(If needed) Sign shows tyre with chains fitted.
Calle de sentido.	One way street.	Usually on round sign, black horizontal line on white circle with red border.

Cambio de Sentido.	Change of Direction. Sign indicating where you go over or under the highway you are on to return back or take another route.	Where you may turn over / under a highway and go back the way you came. Signs are rectangular, Blue background, White lettering, giving warning of turn off ahead, and White background, Black lettering at turn-off point.
Camíon/es	Truck/s	
Carretera cerrado.	Road closed	
Cerrado.	Closed.	Used everywhere.
Coche / moto	Car / motorcycle or scooter.	
Completo	Full	Usually at the entrance to a car park.
Control de Coches con Camuflados	Traffic control with unmarked police vehicles	
Control de Galibo.	Police check point for vehicle condition and papers.	This is where you hope all is well with your vehicle and documents.
Contol de Velocidad	Official warning of a speed check ahead, now often a fixed radar camera.	Either a dangerous junction or a speed trap.
Curva/s Peligrosa/s.	Dangerous Curve / s.	Triangle, white background, red border and black symbol.
Desvío.	Detour or Diversion.	
........Desprendimientos	Loosening (of road surface) ahead.	Road has a (temporaray) bad surface.

Derecha.	Right	
Entrada	Entrance	
Fin (de zona, prohibition, etc)	End (of restriction zone, etc.)	
Firme deformado	Road surface badly deformed.	Slow down and be careful.
Furgón & furgoneta.	A van (or wagon) & a small van.	
Gasolinera	Petrol Station	
Glorieta / rotonda	Roundabout	
GRUA (Groo-uh)	Breakdown truck (or crane).	If needed, you can use this word when asking for help.
Guia (Guias sonoras)	Guide (Noise guides)	Raised parts of road to make tyre noise.
Izquierda	Left	
"L" plates in rear window of a car. (Driving school cars have a blue background, white L-plate usually on the roof of car).	Learner/probationer. "B" licence holder. Plates are white "L" on green background. Usually inside the rear window on the left.	After a driver has passed the test, there is a year "on probation" with certain restrictions e.g. 80 kph maximum speed limit.
No adelantar	No overtaking	
Peaje, Example "AP 7	Toll Road. "Autopista Peaje No. 7".	Often also has "Toll" in English as well on sign.
Playa	Beach	Indicates way to beach.
Poligono Industrial, or Zona Industrial.	Commercial District, usually factories and larger storage buildings.	Area where only businesses are situated.
Póngase en el carril.	Stay or get in (correct) lane.	

Puente bajo	Low bridge	
Puerta	Door	House, car, etc.
Puerto (de mar)	Sea Port.	
Recuerde	Remember	Usually the signed speed limit.
Red	Net (work)	As in Road network.
Ruta alternativo.	Alternative route.	
La primera quincena del mes.	The first two weeks of the month.	Often seen on parking signs for parking on different sides of a road.
La segunda quincena del mes.	The second two weeks of the month.	As above.
Libre.	Open to the public. (vacancies?).	Usually for a car park.
¡Recuerde!	Remember! Usually the speed limit.	
Salida de Camiones.	Exit (also entrance?) for heavy trucks.	Warning of a <u>construction site</u> access point.
Salida.	Exit.	
Semáforas.	Traffic lights.	
Semáforas cerrado a mas velocidad.	With a speed sign. Shows that the traffic lights are timed for this speed. Go faster and you will have a "red".	
SP, (Servicio Publico).	Public Service.	"SP" sign on back of taxis, etc.
Transporte escolar.	School bus.	
Travesía	Through road going through a small town.	Watch out for speed traps.

Via (de Servicios?).	Way (to toilets, etc).	
Via Rapida.	Fast Road ("fast way"). Not a motorway. Phased out in 2004. Noted here for information only.	A two- way single road, usually no centre barriers, wider than normal, good surface and intended to be for fast travel up to speeds of 90 - 100 kph or as was posted.
Zona de descansar	Rest Area Ahead	

Translation of Words Associated with Motoring –
Spanish to English & English to Spanish.

PLEASE NOTE.

In Spanish, as with all the Latin based languages, nouns are either male or female, so the item's definite article, "the" in Spanish is either; male-single "el": female-single "la", male-plural "los", female-plural "las". If there is a mixture of male and female, the word used is "los".   In this table, after each of the above Spanish nouns, the gender is identified as a help.   The pronunciation of the words is not covered here.   If this is a problem, show this book to the Spanish person to help you explain what you need.

SPANISH	ENGLISH
Acabado (adj)	Finish (paintwork, etc).
Aceite (el)	Oil
Acelarador (el)	Accelerator
Acero (el) – & adjective.	Steel, (as in llanta de acero—steel rim).
Acero inoxidable	Stainless steel
Aire / Agua	Air / water
Aleación (de ruedas)	Alloy (wheels)
Alimentación (la)	Fuel system. (Feed system)
Alineación	Alignment (wheels)
Altavoz	Speaker (radio)
Alternador (el)	Alternator
Amortiguador/es (el)	Shock absorber/s
Ancho (adj.)	Wide

SPANISH	ENGLISH
Anillo (el)	Ring
Antibloqueo	ABS (brakes)
Anticongelante (el)	Antifreeze
Anti-niebla (Faros)	Fog lights
Antirobbo	Anti-theft
Aparcamiento (el): Aparcar en doble fila	Car park: Double-parking
Arandela de Junta (la)	Washer, gasket, 'O'- ring
Arbol de levas (el)	Camshaft
Arbol de transmisión	Drive shaft
Arcén (el)	Hard shoulder
Asiento delantro/trasero	Seat front/rear
Averia (la)	Breakdown
Ayudas (la)	Assistance aids, ABS/ESB, etc.
Banda (la)	Tread (tyre)
Bares	Bars, of pressure. A bar is 15 psi.
Bastidor (el)	Chassis
Bateria (la)	Battery
Bicicleta de montaña (la)	Mountain bike
Biela (Bieletta) (la)	Connecting rod (small connecting rod)
Bisagra (la)	Hinge
Bloque y Culata	Block (engine) and head (cylinder).
Bobina (la)	(Ignition) coil
Bocina or Pito or Klaxon (el)	Horn
Bomba (la)	Pump
Botella para el agua (la)	Water bottle
Borne (el)	Terminal (Battery, etc)

SPANISH	ENGLISH
Bujía (la)	Spark plug
Cable (el)	Cable
Cadena (la)	Chain
Cadenas para la nieve.	Snow chains
Caja de cambios (la)	Gearbox
Calentador. (el)	Heater
Camara. (la)	Inner tube
Cambio automática. (el)	Automatic gearbox
Cambio de marcha (el)	Gear-change (stick).
Camión (el): Camionero	Truck: truck-driver
Capazco (el)	Carrycot for baby
Capó. (el)	Bonnet/Hood
Caravana. (la)	Caravan
Carburador. (el)	Carburettor
Cargador de bateria	Battery charger
Carnet de Conducir. (el)	Driving licence (also Permiso de Conducción)
Carril (el)	Lane or track
Carrocería	Bodywork
Carrocero/a (el/la)	Panel-beater
Cárter (de cigüeñal)	Housing (....crankcase, oil sump)
Casco (el)	Crash-helmet
Casco (el) de moto	Helmet, motorcycle.
Catafaras (el)	Reflector (car)
Catalizador (el)	Catalytic Converter
Cepillo (el)	Brush

SPANISH	ENGLISH
Ciclomoto (el)	Moped
Cierre centrolizado (el)	Central locking.
Cigüeñal	Crankshaft
Cilindrada	Capacity (Engine, cc)
Cinturón de seguridad (el)	Seat-belt
Coche (el): coche automatico	Car: Automatic (transmission) car
Cojinete (el) (de bolas) (de rodillos).	Bearing. (ball) (roller).
Columna de dirección (el)	Steering column
Combustible 95 or 98 Sin plomo gasolina 97 gasolina Gasoleo *or*diesel	**Fuel** 95 or 98 octane non-lead 97 Lead replacement petrol. Diesel.
Consumo (medio o mixto) (el)	Fuel consumption (average) (l/100km?)
Contrapeso	Balance weight (wheel)
Control de velocidad	Speed trap.
Correa del aircondicianado (la)	Air-con. drive belt
Correa de la distribución. (la)	Belt, drive, (toothed) for cylinder head valves.
Correa del servodirección (la)	Power-steering drive belt
Correa del ventilador (la)	Fan belt
Cotas	Figures (eg, bore and stroke)
Cremallera y piñón	Rack and pinion (Steering?)
Cuadro (el)	Frame
Cuatro tiempo	Four-stroke

SPANISH	ENGLISH
Cuentakilómetros (el)	Odometer (speedo distance recorder)
Cuero (el)	Leather
Culato	Cam cover
Delantera	Front (adjective)
Deportivo (el), coche	Sport (-car).
Deposito de liquido	Reservoir
Dirección , de giro (la)	Steering. (Turning circle, in metres)
Dirección asistida (la)	Power-steering.
Disco (el)	Disk e.g. Brake.
Distribuidor (el)	Distributor
Distribución ((la)	Delivery, usually type of cylinder head.
Doble árbol de levas por corea dentada	Double overhead camshaft with belt drive
Dos tiempo	Two-stroke
Eje (de rueda) (el)	Axle (wheel)
Elevalunas eléctrico (los)	Electric Windows (up/down).
Emisiones CO_2	Exhaust emissions CO_2 in Gr/Km.
Embotellamiento (el)	Traffic jam
Embrague (el)	Clutch
Encendido, Llave de (la)	Ignition, key
Enganche (el)	Hooking-up (for towing)
Escobilla (la)	Windscreen wiper
Escobilla/s (las)	Wiper (blade) Also brush.
Espejo (el): espejo retrovisor.	Mirror: Rear view mirror
Espejo lateral (el)	Wing mirror
Estárter (el)	Choke
Exéntrica (el)	Tappet

SPANISH	ENGLISH
Factura (la)	Invoice
Faro Antiniebla (el)	Fog light
Faros (los)	Headlights
Fecha (la)	Date
Filtro antipolen (el)	Anti-pollen filter
Filtro de aceite (el)	Oil filter
Filtro de aire (el)	Air Filter
Freno de mano (el)	Handbrake
Freno / s (el) - Frenos de antibloqueo	Brake / s - ABS Brakes
Funda (de coche)	Cover (car)
Fundición (la)	Cast Iron (engine-block, etc.)
Furgón *and* Furgoneta (la)	A large van and a small van.
Fusible (el)	Fuse
Fusibles (los)	Fuses
Gama (la)	Range (of choices)
Gamuza de piel (la)	Chamois leather
Gama (la)	Range (Range of models, etc.).
Gamuza de piel	Chamois leather
Gancho de remolque (el)	Tow bar.
Garaje (el)	Garage (for parking or at home)
Gasolina (la) (sin plomo)	Petrol. (unleaded).
Gasoleo (el)	Diesel fuel.
Gasolinera	Petrol (Fuel) Station
Gato carretilla (el)	Jack, trolley.
Giro (el)	Turn (as in steering turning circle).

SPANISH	ENGLISH
Glorieta	Roundabout or traffic circle.
Grua (la)	Breakdown truck or small crane
Guantes (los)	Gloves
Guanrera (la)	Glove compartment
Guardabarro (el)	Mudguard
Guarnición de freno	Brake lining
Indicador de la gasoline/gasoleo (el)	Fuel gauge
Indicador de nivel de aceite (el)	Oil gauge
Injector	Injector
Intermitentes (la)	Turn indicator7s
Juego (de)	Set (of)
Junta (el)	Gasket
Lampara y faro (la) – (el)	Lamp & bulb
Lavaparabrisas	Glass cleaner. (for windscreen reservoir?)
Leva	Cam
Limpialuneta	Headlight washer
Limpiaparabrisas (los)	Windscreen wipers
Liquido de Frenos (el)	Brake fluid
Liquido de Servidireccion (el)	Power Steering oil

SPANISH	ENGLISH
Liquido refrigerante (el)	Coolant (Engine)
Llantas de aleación (las)	Wheels, alloy.
Llave de contacto	Ignition key
Luz de freno (la)	Brake light
Luces de marchas atrás (las)	Reversing lights
Luces traseros (las)	Rear lights
Luz de advertencia (la)	Warning light
Maletero (el)	Boot (USA, - trunk)
Mando/s (el)	Control/s
Manillar	Handlebar
Manómetro (el)	Gauge (pressure)
Manos (la) (libre)	Hands (free, as in mobile phone kit)
Manguera del radiador (arriba/abajo) (la)	Radiator hose (top/bottom)
Matrícula (la)	License Plate/Number
Mecánico (el) or mecánica: female.	Mechanic
Mezcla	Two-stroke petrol mixture
Mitades	Split, as in folding rear seat on some cars.
Monovolúmen (Adj.)	People-carrier . (e.g. coche monovolumen)
Moto (la)	Motorcycle
Motor (el)	Engine
Motor de arranque (el)	Starter Motor
Muelle (el)	Spring (also pier or quay).

SPANISH	ENGLISH
Neumático (el): Llanta (la)	Tyre: wheel rim
Ordenador (el)	Computer.
Palanca de cambios (la)	Gear selection lever
Pantalla (la)	Screen (TV, etc).
Parabrisos (el)	Windscreen
Parachoque (el) (delantero/trasera)	Bumper (front/rear)
Par Maximo	Torque, Maximum (engine rating)
Pastillos de frenos (los)	Brake pads
Pedal (el)	Pedal
Pedal (el)	Pedal (bicycle)
Pedal de freno.	Brake pedal
Permiso de conducción	Driving licence
Peso (oficial) (el)	Weight (manufacturer's?)
Picaporte (el)	Door handle
Pie (el) *(Literally foot)*	Stand (support, motorcycle, etc).
Piel (la)	Skin & Leather
Piloto (el or la)	Driver
Pinchado (el)	Puncture
Pintura metalizada	Metallic paint.
Pistón	Piston
Potencia	Power, engine, eg, ? CV @ ? rpm
Presion (la)	Pressure
Presion de inflado	Tyre (inflation) pressure

SPANISH	ENGLISH
Protector de la cadena (el)	Chainguard
Pulgada / os (la)	Inch / es (Used for wheel diameter)
Radiador (el)	Radiator
Radio (la)	Spoke (wheel)
Ranchera (el)	Estate car, station-wagon (US)
Recibo (el)	Receipt (for goods/services)
Recto (adj.)	Straight line (Todo recto = straight on)
Rejilla (or colador)	Strainer (oil)
Remolque (el) (& caravana)	Trailer, semi-trailer or caravan.
Rendimientos (el)	Performance (figures)
Resorte helice (el)	Spring, Coil
Respaldo de asiento (el)	Seat back
Retrovisor (el)	Driving mirror
Rin de la rueda (el)	Wheel rim
Rotula ((la)	Ball & Socket joint
Rueda de repuesta (la)	Spare wheel
Ruedas (las) delantera / trasera (s)	Wheels, front/rear
Salpicadero (el)	Dashboard
Seguro (el)	Lock
Seguro a todo riesgo	Comprehensive insurance
Servo freno	Brake servo
Silla (la)	Seat
Silenciador (el)	Silencer
Suspensión	Suspension

SPANISH	ENGLISH
Taller (el)	Garage or workshop (for repairs)
Tambor de freno (el)	Brake drum
Tapacubos (el)	Hub caps/wheel trims
Tapicería (la)	Upholstery (seat covering, etc)
Tapa del depósito de gasolina/gasoleo (la)	Fuel tank cap or flap.
Techo solar (el)	Sun roof
Termostato	Thermostat
Testigo	Warning light
Timbre (el)	Bell
Tornillo (el)	Bolt, or screw
Todo terreno	4-wheel drive (all terrain)
Tracción (delantera o trasera)	Type of Drive (front or rear)
Traffic jam	Embotellamiento (el)
Transmisión (la)	Transmission
Trasero/s	Rear (adjective) / plural
Tratamiento	Treatment
Triángulos de emergencia	Emergency triangles
Travesia elevado	Pedestrian crossing ahead which is on a speed bump or raised part of the road.
Tubo de escape (el)	Exhaust system
Turismo (el)	Saloon or passenger car
Valvula (la)	Valve (tyre, engine, etc)
Válvula de admisión	Inlet valve
Válvula de escape	Exhaust valve

SPANISH	ENGLISH
Velocidad máximo	Maximum speed
Velocímetro (el)	Speedometer
Ventanilla (la)	Window, small and used to describe car windows.
Ventana (la)	Window, large as in a house, etc.
Ventilador (el)	Fan
Visor (el)	Visor
Volante (el)	Steering wheel

ENGLISH	SPANISH
Accelerator	Acelarador (el)
ABS (brakes)	Antibloqueo
Air Filter	Filtro de aire (el)
Air/water	Aire/Agua
Air-con. drive belt	Correa del aircondicianado (la)
Air-con. drive belt	Correa del aircondicianado (la)
Alignment (wheels)	Alineación
Alloy (wheels)	Aleación (de ruedas)
Alternator	Alternador (el)
Anti-polllen filter	Filtro antipolen (el)
Antifreeze.	Anticongelante (el)
Anti-theft.	Antirobbo.
Arcen (el)	Hard shoulder
Automatic gearbox.	Cambio automática
Axle (wheel)	Eje (de rueda) (el)
Balance weight (wheel)	Contrapeso
Ball & Socket joint	Rotula (la)
Battery	Bateria (la)
Ballery charger.	Cargador de bateria
Bearing. (ball) (roller)	Cojinete (el) (de bolas) (de rodillos).
Bell.	Timbre (el)
Belt, drive, (toothed) for cylinder-head valves.	Correa de la distribución o dentada. (la)
Block (engine) and head (cylinder).	Bloque y Culata.
Bodywork.	Carrocería.
Bonnet or Hood (USA).	Capó (el)
Boot or Trunk (USA).	Maletero (el)

ENGLISH	SPANISH
Bore and stroke, cylinder.	Cotas (las) Usually in the specifications!
Brake/s.	Freno/s. (los)
Brake disk.	Disco de freno. (el)
Brake drum.	Tambor de freno. (el)
Brake fluid.	Liquido de Freno. (el)
Brake light.	Luz de freno. (la)
Brake lining	Guarnición de freno
Brake pads	Pastillos de frenos (los)
Brake pedal (clutch)	Pedal de freno (el) (de embrague)
Brake servo	Servo freno (el)
Brake shoes	Zapatas de freno (la)
Breakdown	Averia (la)
Breakdown truck	Grua (la)
Brush	Cepillo (el)
Bumper	Parachoque (el)
Cable	Cable (el)
Cam	Leva (la)
Cam cover	Culato (el)
Camshaft	Arbol de levas (el)
Car	Coche (el)
Caravan	Caravana (la)
Cargador CD (la)	CD changer
Car park	Aparcamiento (el)
Carburettor	Carburador (el)
Carrycot for baby	Capazco (el)

ENGLISH	SPANISH
Cast iron, of (engine block, etc).	Fundición, de
Catalytic Converter	Catalizador (el)
CD Changer	Cargador CD
Central locking	Cierre centrolizado (el)
Chain	Cadena (la)
Chainguard.	Protector de la cadena (el)
Chains for snow	Cadenas para la nieve
Chamois leather	Gamuza de piel (la)
Coil Ignition	Bobina (la)
Comprehensive insurance	Seguro a todo riesgo
Connecting rod (engine)	Biela (bieletta, suspension?) (la)
Coolant (Engine)	Liquido refrigerante del motor (el)
Control/s	Mando/s (el)
Cover (car)	Funda (de coche)
Crankshaft	Cigüeñal (el)
Crash-helmet	Casco (el)
Dashboard	Salpicadero (el)
Diesel fuel	Gasoleo (el)
Distributor	Distribuidor (el)
Double overhead camshaft with belt drive	Doble árbol de levas por corea dentada
Door handle	Pictaporte (el)
Driver	Piloto (Feminine, pilota)
Driving licence	Permiso de conducción. (el)
Driving mirror	Retrovisor (el)
Drive-shaft	Arbol de transmisión (el)
Emergency triangles	Triángulos de emergencia (los)
Engine	Motor (el)
Engine capacity	Cilindrada

ENGLISH	SPANISH
Exhaust system	Tubo de escape (el)
Exhaust-valve	Válvula de escape.
Fan	Ventilador (el)
Fan-belt	Correa del ventilador (la)
Finish (paint-work)	Acabado
Fog light	Faro anti-niebla (el)
Four-stroke	Cuatro tiempo
Frame	Cuadro (el)
Front (adjective)	Delantara
Fuel 95 or 98 octane non-lead 97 Lead replacement petrol. Diesel: 1st quality and "Ultra" quality. Low quality diesel (cheaper)	**Combustible** 95 or 98 Sin plomo gasolina. 97 gasolina Gasoleo *or* diesel Gasoleo "B".
Fuel Consumption (average).	Consumo medio or mixto.
Fuel gauge	Indicador de la gasoline/gasoleo (el)
Fuel system	Alimentación (la)
Fuel tank	Depòsito del combustible. (el)
Fuel tank cap or flap.	Tapa del depósito de gasoline/gasoleo
Fuse, Fuses	Fusible (el) Fusibles (los)
Garage (for parking or at home)	Garaje (el)
Garage (for repairs, workshop)	Taller (el) (say tail-yer)
Gasket	Junta (el)
Gauge (pressure)	Manómetro (el)
Gear selection lever	Palanca de cambios (la)
Gearbox	Caja de cambios (la)
Glass cleaner. (for windscreen reservoir?)	Lava parabrisos
Gloves	Guantes (los)

ENGLISH	SPANISH
Glove Compartment	Guantera (la)
Hand (-free kit) For mobile phones.	(kit) manos de libres
Handbrake	Freno de mano (el)
Handlebar (Bike & Motorcycle, etc.).	Manillar
Handbrake	Freno de mano (el)
Handlebar (Bike & Motorcycle, etc.).	Manillar
Hard shoulder	Arcén (el)
Headlights	Faros (los)
Heater	Calentador (el)
Helmet, motorcycle.	Casco (el) de moto
Hinge	Bisagra (la)
Horn	Bocina *or* Pito *or* Klaxon (el)
Hub caps/wheel trims	Tapa cubos
Ignition key	Llave de contacto o Encendido, (la)
Inch (used for wheel diameter)	Pulgada (la)
Injector	Injector
Inlet valve	Válvula de admisión
Inner Tube	Camara (la)
Insurance	Seguro
Jack, trolley.	Gato carretilla (el)
Key	Llave (la) Say "lee-ar-vey"
Lamp & bulb	Lamparo y faro (la) – (el)
Lane or track	Carril (el)
Leather	Cuero (el)
License Plate/Number	Matrícula (la) (or placa)
Lock	Seguro (el) or cerradura
Maximum Speed	Velocidad máximo

ENGLISH	SPANISH
Mechanic	Mecánico (el) or mecánica: female.
Metallic paint.	Pintura metalizada.
Mirror	Espejo ((el)
Moped	Ciclomoto ((el)
Motorcycle	Moto (la)
Mountain bike	Bicicleta de montaña (la)
Mudguard	Guardabarro (el)
Odometer	Cuentakilómetras (el)
Oil, Oil-can.	Aceite (el) Acietera (la)
Oil filter.	Filtro de aceite (el)
Oil gauge	Indicador de nivel de aceite (el)
'O' - ring, seal, washer	Arandela de junta (la)
Panel beater	Carrocero / a (el or la)
Panel beater / body shop, also..	Chapa y Pintura. (sign outside)
People carrier	Coche monovolúmen.
Pedal (foot, also bicycle)	Pedal (el)
Performance	Rendimiento / s (el / los)
Petrol	Gasolino (la)
Petrol (Fuel) Station	Gasolinera
Piston	Pistón
Power, Engine.	Potencia
Power-steering	Dirección asistida (la)
Power Steer drive belt	Correa del servodireccion (la)
Power Steering oil	Liquido de Servidireccion (el)

ENGLISH	SPANISH
Pressure	Presion (la)
Pump	Bomba (la)
Puncture	Pinchado (el)
Rack and Pinion (Steering?)	Cremallera y piñón.
Radiator	Radiador (el)
Radiator hose (top/bottom)	Manquera del radiador (arriba/abajo) (la)
Range (of choices)	Gama (la)
Rear (adjective)	Trasero
Rear lights	Luces traseros (las)
Receipt (for goods/services)	Recibo (el)
Reflector (auto)	Catafaras (el)
Reservoir	Deposito de liquido
Reversing lights	Luces de marchas atrás (las)
Roof rack.	Baca (la)
Roundabout	Glorieta (la)
Saloon (or passenger) car	Turismo (el)
Screen (TV or navigation)	Pantalla. (la)
Screw, or bolt	Tornillo (el)
Sealing ring ('O'-ring)	Arandela de junta (la)
Seat front/rear	Asiento or silla delantro/trasero
Seat back	Respaldo de asiento. (el)
Seat belt	Cinturón de seguridad (el)
Set (of)	Juego (de)
Straight on (direction)	Todo recto

English	Spanish
Terminal (Battery, etc)	Borne (el)
Traffic Jam	Embotellamiento (el)
Torque, Maximum (engine rating)	Par Maximo.
Truck, Truck Driver	Camión (el) Camiónero
Turn, turning distance (steering)	Giro (el)
Turn indicators	Intermitentes (las)
Two-stroke	Dos tiempo
Two-stroke petrol	Mezcla
Tyre (inflation) pressure	Presion de inflato
Tyre: Wheel rim	Neumático (el): la Llanta
Upholstery	Tapicería (la)
Valve (tyre, engine, etc)	Valvula (la)
Van / wagon.	Furgón (el) or furgoneta (smaller-van) (la)
Visor	Visor (el)
Warning light	Luz de advertencia (la)
Warning light	Testigo
Washer (sealing joint)	Arandela de junta (la)
Water bottle	Botella para el agua (la)
Wheel rim	Rin de la rueda (el)
Wheel trim. (Plastic clip on?)	Tapàcubo (el)
Wheel - front/rear	Rueda (la) delantera/trasera
Wheel, steel.	Llanta de acero (la)
Wheels, alloy.	Llantas de aleación (las)
Window	Ventana (la)
Windows, electric .	Elevalunas eléctrico (los)
Windscreen	Parabrisos (el)
Windscreen wiper.	Escobilla (la)
Windscreen wipers.	Limpiaparabrisas or escobillos (los)
Wing mirror.	Espejo lateral (el)
Workshop.	Taller (el)

ENGLISH	SPANISH
Shock absorbers	Amortiguadores (los)
Silencer	Silenciador (el)
Spare wheel	Rueda de repuesta (la)
Spark plug	Bujía (la)
Speaker (radio)	Altavoz
Speedometer	Velocímetro (el)
Speed trap	Control de velocidad
Spoke (wheel)	Radio (la)
Sports car	Deportivo
Spring, general.	Muelle (el)
Spring, Coil	Resorte helice (el)
Stand (support, motorcycle, etc).	Pie (el) *(Literally foot)*
Starter Motor	Motor de arranque (el)
Steering	Dirección
Steering column	Columna de dirección (el)
Steering wheel	Volante (el)
Strainer (oil)	Rejilla (la)
Sump (Oil, bottom of engine)	Cárter
Sun roof	Techo solar (el)
Suspension	Suspensión
Tappet	Exéntrica (el)
Thermostat	Termostato (el)
Tow bar	Ganch de remolque (el)
Traffic jam.	Embotellamiento (el)
Trailer	Remolque (el)
Transmission	Transmisión (la)
Treatment	Tratamiento

ENGLISH TO SPANISH PHRASES USEFUL ON THE ROAD.

The following phrases can be used to ensure that the Spanish speaker supplying a service, etc., can quickly understand what you need.

At the Service Station (Fuel)/ *Gasolinera.*

English	Spanish	Phonetic Pronunciation
Fill it up, please	Lleno, por favor.	Lee-en-o, por fabor.
(?) litres of petrol/ diesel	(?) litros de gasolina / diesel, por favor.	(¿) litros deh gasoleena/deesel por fabor.
95 non-lead: 98 non lead super: 97 (leaded petrol) Diesel.	95 sin plomo: 98 sin plomo súper: 97 con plomo: Gasóleo o Diesel.	95 seen plomo 98 seen plomo sooper 97 con plomo Gasóleeo or Deesel
Where is the air and water?	¿Dónde esta el aire y agua?	Dondeh esta el ayreh ee agwa
Where is the next service station?	¿Dónde esta la próxima gasolinera?	Dondeh esta la prokseema gasoleenera

Parking/

Is there a car park nearby?	¿Hay un aparcamiento cerca?	Eye oon aparkameeyento terca?
Do you have some change for the parking meter?	¿Tienen cambio para el parquímetro?	Teeyenen kambeeyo para el parkeemetro
My car has been clamped Who do I call?	A mi coche le han puesto el cepo. ¿A quien llamo?	A mee coche leh an pwesto el thepo. A keeyen l-yamo.
What is the charge per hour/day/week?	¿Cuánto cobran por hora / dia / semana?	Kwanto kobran por ora/deeya/cemana

216

Breakdown/ *Averiarse.*

I have had a breakdown.	He tenido una avería	Eh teneedoh oona abereeya
Can you send a mechanic/breakdown truck?	¿Puede mandar a un mecánico / una grúa?	Puede mandar a oon mekaneeko / oona groowa
I belong to (?) rescue service.	Soy del servicio de grúa (?)	Soy del serbeetheeyo del groowa ...
Where is the nearest garage?	¿Dónde esta el taller más cercano?	Dondeh esta el tal-yer mas therkano
The car is a (make and colour) on the (road) near (km signpost or identifying sign)	El coche esta en (...) en la (.. autopista, etc) cerca (...)Or .. kilómetros de (SOS post, etc?).	El coche esta en la auto-peesta cerca...Or .. kilómetros deh ....
How long will you be?	¿Cuánto tiempo tardado?	Kwanto teeyempo tardara
I do not know what is wrong.	No se que le pasa	No seh kay le pasa.
I have locked the keys in the car.	Me ha dejado las llaves en le coche.	Meh eh dekhado las l-yabes en el kocheh.

Accidents. (Tel. 112, Emergency).

In the event of an accident (or a breakdown), if you are able, remember to place two triangles facing the traffic, one about 100 metres/yards away and the other about 10-20 metres/yards away, both facing the oncoming traffic. If the road is very narrow and two-way, place one facing the traffic behind about 75 to 100 metres away, and one on the opposite side of the road at a similar distance for safety. Give plenty of distance warning to allow adequate safe braking for the other traffic. Put your reflective jackets on.   Have your camera ready to take photos.

You must always call the local police or Guardia Civil if on a main road outside town if someone is injured, otherwise it is not necessary unless there is an altercation. Fill in an accident report but do not sign it unless you are fluent in Spanish and fully understand the wording. If police are called, obtain the police report number from the police station. Show your driver's licence and insurance certificate: complete an insurance accident form with the other driver if possible.   Do not admit to any fault regardless of what happened, and do not sign a statement other than the insurance report if you agree with it (or your lawyer agrees later). Note the safety condition of the other vehicle including tyres and for evidence of drink or drugs used by the other driver.

There has been an accident!	Ha habido un accidente	A abeedo oon actheedente
Can you help me please?	¿Puede ayudarme, por favor?	Puede ayoodarmeh, por fabor
It is ..... (location)	Ha ocurrido	A okooreedo
.. on the motorway	En la autopista	En la aootopeesta
.. on the bypass (around or through a town.	.. en la carretera	En la carreterra
Near	Cerca de	Therca deh
Where is the nearest telephone? (SOS on autopista)	¿Dónde está el teléfono más cercano / SOS?	Dondeh esta el telefono mas therkano
Call	Llame a	Le-ameh a
... the police	La policia	La poleethia
... ambulance	Una ambulancia	Oona amboolantheea
... a doctor	Un medico	Oon medeeko
... the fire brigade	El cuerpo del bomberos	El kwerpo deh bomberos
There are people injured.	Hay gente herida	Eye khente hereda
He / she is seriously injured.	Esta gravemente herido/a	Esta grabamenteh ereedo/a
He / she is unconscious.	Esta sangrando / a	Esta sangrando/a
Do not move him/her.	No le mueva	No le mueva

Repairs.

Do you do repairs?	¿Hacen reparaciones?	athen reparatheeyones
The (part) is not working	El / la (part) no funciona	El/la ... no funchiona
Can you repair it? (temporarily)	¿Puede hacerle una reparación? (provisional)	Puede atherle oona reparatheeyon? (probeeseeyanol).
Please make only essential repairs.	Por favor, hágale reparaciones básicas solamente	Por fabor, hágale reparatheeyones baseekas solomentah

Can I wait for it?	¿Puedo espera?	Pwedeh esperar
Can you repair it for today?	¿Puede arreglarlo hoy?	Puede arreglarlo oy
When will it be ready?	¿Cuándo estará listo?	Kwando estara leesto
How much?	¿El cuánto?	El kwanto
That is too expensive!	¡Es muy, muy caro!	Es moy moy karo
May I have the receipt (for my insurance), please?	Pueden darme un recibo (para el seguro), por favor?	Pueden darme un retheebo (para el segooro) por fabor.

Possible Answers. Show the Spanish mechanic this table.

No tenga las piezas necesarias.	I do not have the parts needed.
Solo pueda reparo provisionalmente.	I can only do a temporary repair.
Tendré que mandar a pedir las piezas.	I will have to order the parts.
Mas o menos, ... horas / días / semanas.	More or less ..... Hours/days/weeks.
Su coche / camino no tiene arreglo.	Your car / truck is not repairable.
Estará listo (tiempo y fecha).	It will be ready (time and date). Ask mechanic to write details.
Hoy mismo.	Later today.
A la mañana.	Tomorrow.

Insurance Matters.

I would like an interpreter, please.	Quiero un interprete, por favor.	Keeyero unn eenterpreteh, por fabor.
What is your name and address?	¿Cuál es su nombre y su dirección?	Kwal es soo nombrey ee soo deereektheeyon
Your insurance, please.	Su seguro, por favor.	Soo segooro, por fabor
The car / motorcycle ran into me!	El coche / moto choco conmigo	El kochey / moto choko konmeego
He / she saw it happen.	El / ella lo vio	El / e-yah lo beeyo

I had right of way!	¡Yo tenia derecha de paso!	Yo teneeya derecho deh paso
(He / she) was driving too fast!	¡Conducía demasiado / a rápida!	Condoothia demasiado/a rapeedo
(He / she) was driving too close!	¡Conducía demasiado / a cerca!	Condoothia demasiado/a terca

Show the other (Spanish) driver, etc. to see what is needed.

¿Puedo ver su ..., por favor.?.... (1) permiso de conducir... (2) certificado del seguro... (3) documento del regristo o "permiso de circulación" del vehículo.	Can I see your .... , please? ...(1) driver's licence. ...(2) insurance card/certificate. ...(3) vehicle registration papers.
¿A que hora ocurrió?	When did it happen?
¿Dónde ocurrió?	Where did it happen?
¿Hubo alguien más involucrado?	Was anyone else involved?
¿Hay testigos?	Any witnesses?
¿Se paso el limite de velocidad?	Were you speeding?
¡Sus faros no funcionan!	Your lights are not working (or on)!
¡Tendrá que pagar una multa!	You will have to pay a fine (on the spot).
Tenemos que tomar su declaración en la comisaría.	You will have to make a statement the police station
¿Por favor, una grúa?	Please call a breakdown truck?

ACCIDENTS AND BREAKDOWNS. (Tel. 112, Emergency or use SOS telephones).

PUT YOUR REFLECTIVE JACKETS ON. In the event of an accident or a breakdown, if you are physically able, place the two triangles you must carry by law facing the traffic with one about 100 metres/yards away and the other about 10-20 metres/yards away, both facing the oncoming traffic. This is very important and the distance should allow for another driver or drivers, perhaps speeding, to be able to stop or slow down safely especially if on wet roads. It could save your life or at least prevent your vehicle being hit. So the speed limit on the road can determine the distances.

If the road is very narrow and two-way, place one facing the traffic behind about 75 to 100 metres away, and one facing the other direction traffic on the opposite side of the road at a similar distance especially after dark. Give plenty of distance warning to allow adequate safe braking for the other traffic. Have your camera ready to take photos if an accident has occurred. If you do not carry a good camera (mobile phones are generally limited especially as far as being able to enlarge the picture clearly and using a flash in poor light conditions, then do what I have always done, carry a throw-away film cameras with a built-in flash. They cost about €6 to 10 and can be kept in the car.

You must always call the local police or Guardia Civil if on a main road outside town if someone is injured: otherwise it is not necessary unless there is an altercation. However, if the other driver/s are Spanish, you will find that they usually do call the police/GC as it solves for them any language problem. But beware of their actions, take their names and numbers and point out any evidence in your favour. This is where photos of skid marks, road signs and so on are very important. Fill in an accident report but do not sign it unless you are fluent in Spanish and fully understand the wording. See Anatomy of an Accident chapter in this book. If the police/GC are called, remember to obtain their report number from their office if they do not give you one on the spot. Show your driver's licence and insurance certificate. Do not admit to any fault regardless of what happened. Note the safety condition of the other vehicle/s including tyres and for evidence of drink or drugs used by the other driver/s. Do not be bullied by the other drivers who will often adopt this attitude if they know they are in the wrong. Most important, do not get aggressive even if the other driver does. Stay cool especially if there are witnesses around and if the other man starts to look as if he is going to hit you, hold up your hands with palms open to protect yourselkf but most impornatly to show that you do not want to fight.

VEHICLE & DRIVER INSURANCE NEEDS IN SPAIN.

Driving in Spain is often a pleasant experience, -- except in the rush hours in the major cities, and especially at holiday times. The country roads are relatively empty and the majority of Spanish drivers polite and courteous, well, in Andalucia. The author has driven from Madrid to Malaga on the main road in early June, in mid-week, and been pleasantly surprised at the very low volume of traffic on that major trunk road. However, in the holiday areas especially in July and August, the roads (and beaches) are crowded with holiday-makers, many Spanish taking their holiday breaks as well as other Europeans, etc. and then driving is no pleasure and can be very dangerous due to the few who are just plain bad drivers or who are incompetent. Driving too close to the vehicle in front is still a major problem in Spain but not as bad as a few years ago.

A (usually) French vehicle on its way to or from Morocco can often be identified by the number plate and a large amount of luggage on the roof, so much that the suspension on the "bump stops", or in other words grossly overloaded. They also often have trailers and I cannot understand why they are not stopped by the police and made to reduce the weight, as not only are they unstable, but the brakes are working very hard in hilly country.

As elsewhere in the civilised world insurance is a legal requirement, as it should be to protect all of us road users, and driving without it carries severe penalties. Reports in the Spanish Press indicate that as many as 25% of moped/scooter riders do not have insurance, possibly due to the relative high cost because of the low ages of most riders, and also the generally reckless driving habits of many in this group. One result of this has been that from December 2005, the minimum age to start riding was changed from 14 to 16 yrs but you will still see many underage youngsters in the pueblos riding around without a helmet on their 49 cc motos, reecognisable by the small number plates. The "problem" is that machines up to 49 cc are not considered to be motor vehicles in Spain. There are quite a few motorcar drivers without insurance due to cost and their low income, it is therefore doubly important that if involved in an accident with particularly one of these road users, and especially where they are injured, you obtain ALL details (refer to the accident report form at the back of this book and as supplied by your insurer) and also obtain the names of any reliable witnesses, which is not always possible easy due to language differences. If possible, take a photo of the other driver/s with your throwaway camera kept in the glove compartment, or mobile if so equipped.

Also recommended is the carrying of a throwaway camera kept in the car unless you have a very good camera on your mobile phone, of course. If someone is hurt, you must contact the *Guardia Civil* if on the open road, and the Policia Local if in a town, and a mobile phone is ideal for this. (GC tel. 062; policia local tel. 091)

But all can be contacted through one number, 112, (the equivalent of 999 in the UK, and 911 in the USA), and the chance of getting an English speaking person is much higher. It is an easy matter to enter this in your mobile's phone-book record ready for such an emergency. Do not forget to put "0034" if it is a UK phone account. If someone is injured you must have the police/GC present as per Spanish Law.

WARNING: UNLESS YOU ARE ABSOLUTELY SURE THAT THE INFORMATION FROM THE OTHER DRIVER IS CORRECT, DO NOT SIGN THE **ACCIDENT** FORM, EVEN IF THE POLICE/GUARDIA CIVIL ARE URGING YOU TO DO SO. SORT IT OUT LATER.

In Spain, whether you are at fault or not, if someone is hurt, you should always rely on a local lawyer to represent you to avoid any possible later charges and claims by the other driver. Your insurance covers these costs only up to a limit, so please check your policy and take advice. Also, the insurance company's lawyer works for the insurance company, not you even though you are paying the premium, so make sure that you get all evidence at the scene.

ACCIDENTS AND BREAKDOWNS.
(Tel. 112, Emergency or use SOS telephones).

PUT YOUR REFLECTIVE JACKETS ON BEFORE YOU GET OUT OF THE CAR.

In the event of an accident or a breakdown, if you are physically able, place the two triangles you must carry by law facing the traffic with one about 100 metres/yards away and the other about 10-20 metres/yards away, both facing the oncoming traffic. This is very important and the distance should allow for another driver or drivers, perhaps speeding, to be able to stop or slow down safely especially if on wet roads. It could save your life or at least prevent your vehicle being hit. So the speed limit on the road can determine the distances.

If the road is very narrow and two-way, place one facing the <u>traffic behind</u> about <u>75 to 100 metres away</u>, and one facing the other direction traffic on the opposite side of the road at a similar distance especially after dark. Give plenty of distance warning to allow adequate safe braking for the other traffic. Have your camera ready to take photos if an accident has occurred. If you do not carry a good camera (mobile phones are generally limited especially as far as being able to enlarge the picture clearly and using a flash in poor light conditions, then do what I have always done, carry a throw-away film cameras with a built-in flash. They cost about €6 to 10 and can be kept in the car.

You must always call the local police or Guardia Civil if on a main road outside town if <u>someone is injured, otherwise it is not necessary unless there is an altercation.</u> However, if the other driver/s are Spanish, you will find that they usually do call the police/GC as it solves for them the language problem if you are not fluent in Spanish. But beware of their actions, take their names and numbers and point out any evidence in your favour. This is where photos of skid marks, road signs and so on are very important. Fill in an accident report but do not sign it unless you are fluent in Spanish and fully understand the wording. See Anatomy of an Accident chapter in this book. If the police/GC are called, remember to obtain their <u>report number</u> from their office if they do not give you one on the spot. Show your driver's licence and insurance certificate: complete an insurance accident form with the other driver if possible. <u>Do not admit to any fault</u> regardless of what happened, and do not sign a statement other than the insurance report <u>if you fully agree with it</u> because it is in English (or if necessary, your lawyer agrees later). Note the safety condition of the other vehicle/s including tyres and for evidence of drink or drugs used by the other driver/s. Do not be bullied by the other drivers who will often adopt this attitude if they know they are in the wrong. Most importnat, do not get aggressive even if the other driver does. Stay cool especially if there are witnesses around and if the other man starts to look as if he is going to hit you, hold up your hands with palms open to show that you do not want to fight.

AS A VISITOR TO SPAIN.

Check that your insurance covers you fully in the countries you are to drive in and for the time you intend to spend abroad. Your insurance usually only covers you for up to three months in one year as a tourist in a foreign state. You must carry your policy certificate (used to be called the green card), and make sure that you have proof of payment for the cover. If you pay in advance for one year, it is shown on the certificate, but if you pay monthly by debit order, etc, you must have the receipt from your Bank showing the payment. It is also advisable to discuss with your insurance company extra public liability insurance as, if you are judged at fault in an accident and the other party/ies, or your passengers (but not close relatives) or pedestrians, etc., are injured and/or property damaged, the Criminal Court, can, and often does, set the amount of damages to be paid by the guilty party. It is important that you have adequate liability cover. No civil claim needs to be made at a later date unless the party awarded the damages considers that they are not enough, so it is very important to be represented by your own selected and appointed lawyer. The lawyer provided by the insurance company is usually there to protect the company more than you. Any fines and damages usually have to be paid immediately, and if insured, this is not a problem (except when your next premium is due).

imprisonment and/or impounding of your goods, usually the vehicle unless it is not worth enough.

Remember that the legal defence lawyer you may have paid for with your insurance premium, is always working for the insurance company, not you, and the first priority they have is to save the company money, which in turn, keeps premium costs down. However, you may feel annoyed when they decide not to go to Court to ensure the other driver is rightly found at fault.

The current law specifies for all drivers in Spain that they must have public liability for third-party body injuries of up to about €340.000 and for damages to other property, including walls, etc., about €100.000. In practice, you are advised to ensure cover for much more to avoid personal liability from your own assets, for example, €1.000.000 and €250.000. This extra cover is not usually that much more expensive. Please note that "bodily injury" claims do not normally include immediate members of your own family, but can include other non-related passengers.

It is also a good idea to have a bail bond facility so you do not spend "weeks" in jail because you cannot afford the set bail, although this is not a priority as it used to be. Your insurance agent will advise you on this facility if you are not familiar with it.

Another important point is that the insurance companies will usually pay only from €3.000 to €6.000 for your defence legal fees (check your policy), and remember that, although you are paying the premium, they look after the insurance company's interests first, not just yours. Their main task is to protect the company despite what you are told. Extra separate insurance may be a good idea here for this reason. The insurance company usually appoints their lawyer, and gives you no choice of yours.

It is worth remembering that in Spain, the "consortium of insurance companies" pays out Third Party damages on behalf of uninsured drivers, using the specified lower limits above, so it is worth ensuring that your and your family's own personal injury and liability insurance provides adequate cover for your own sakes as well as other parties. I am sure you will agree that any driver not insured at all should be considered a "parasite" by all of us who do pay, and end up paying for them also.

As part of the insured's premiums pays for the actions of the uninsured where it is impossible or impracticable to recover the costs from the uninsured. A recent report in the UK stated that the insurance companies charge €40 per policy issued to cover damages caused by uninsured drivers there. Here it is about €7 - 10.

INSURING A MOTOR VEHICLE IN SPAIN.

As in all European countries, there are basically three types of cover: Third Party only (*tercero solo*), Third Party Fire and Theft (*tercero, contra incedios y robo*), and Fully Comprehensive (*total riesgo*), and the minimum insurance is Third Party. All insurance must include the minimum public liabilityasadvisedintheparagraphabove.ManycompaniesinSpainwillnotissue Comprehensive, or even Fire and Theft cover for older cars, say ten years plus. Your broker will advise, your broker will advise, those who cater for expats have their policies and other important information in English to give to you.

It is important to insure with a good broker and company, and I always like to see the person I am dealing with when I buy insurance, although many claims are made in advertising that insuring over the Internet or by phone saves a you a lot of money. In practice, it is reassuring at the side of the road after a "bump", to know who you are phoning for assistance, and they know you. In Spain, I personally have used John Knight Insurance and they have many branches in the "English areas". JKI has been in business for nearly 30 years, and I hasten to add that I have received no payment for making this statement.

You may insure a foreign plated car here but not with a Spanish insurance company (not the broker or agent) based in Spain. The agent or broker may have an arrangement with an off-shore company, or even from outside the EU, but make sure that you have it in writing that you are covered for all the time you intend/are in Spain, as most policies are for 90 day's cover (as a tourist) only outside the country of the car's registration.   On older cars, most companies photograph the car if it is not new to prevent early false damage claims, -- such are the morals of some people. They will also check and report on the car's condition visually. If you have a UK registered car here "permanently", and drive it back to the UK occasionally, remember that it must have passed the UK- MOT to be legal there, and should have the UK, etc. road tax paid. The police know how to check the discs, and having a Spanish ITV done on a foreign EU vehicle, as some ex pats have done on their UK registered cars, will draw attention to the fact that it has been in Spain for a long time.

No Claims discounts / bonuses can be as much as 50 to 60% especially if you are over 55 years of age with maximum no-claims bonuses, and of good health, but I always think that the following check list is useful: -

⇒ The actual cost is the important point, not the percentage discount.

⇒ That the cover is the same when comparing costs.

⇒ That the agent/broker is available (local?) for act on your behalf when you have an accident. You do not have to rely on someone 500 kilometres away at the end of a phone whom you have never met.

⇒ It is therefore important to ensure that you keep this bonus by making sure that you are not to blame in an accident, even by false information from the other driver. I also recommend that you do not sign the accident form at the scene unless you are 100% sure of what the other driver has written.

We only supply the basic advice here, as your insurance broker and company can answer every detailed query.

MAKE SURE THAT YOU HAVE PROOF OF PREMIUM PAYMENT WITH YOU.

An example of a Spanish certificate paid for in advance for the year is shown, with what is paid for by the Premium. The final column shows that the premium is paid and you are covered until the certificate expires.

Example of an Insurance Certificate Schedule of Cover and Payment					
Importe Prima Neta (net premium)	IPS/Prima (Insurance tax)	Consorcio (Consortium)	T/Sin (Claims charge)	AV (Breakdown)	Total recibo (total receipt)
Basic Premium for all cover selected.	Tax, IVA	Consortium charge for cover for uninsured drivers' payouts.	Charge for administration of claim, including legal costs.	Breakdown cover for a GRUA, etc, as in policy	Receipt for total paid. This is OK as a receipt for the police if paid in full for the year.

If you pay by debit order or monthly, etc, you <u>must carry a current receipt</u> to show that you are in fact covered. I know that this is repeated, but I know of several people who have been fined for this omission. The fine is about €100 plus for this offence, and you still risk not being able to move the car from where you are stopped by the police or Guardia Civil, as well as having to prove at the police station that you have paid (if you have?).

Please remember that all Laws are made due to people in the past causing serious problems by, in this case, not having paid for insurance so they were not covered after an accident.

IN THE EVENT OF AN ACCIDENT.

As in any EU (or most others) country, it is vital that, where possible, you follow a procedure after an accident. The following applies: -

Stay calm and be polite, even if the other driver is angry. If you do not speak Spanish and the other driver does not speak English, say, "*No hablo Español*" (no ablo espanyol). (There is, of course, also the chance that the other driver may be German or French, etc., and this is where the pertinent phrase book is useful).

NEVER ADMIT THAT YOU ARE AT FAULT. Your insurance policy instructions usually specify this and your cover could be affected if you admit fault. Please also see the page on an actual accident in this book (Anatomy of an Accident) for more practical advice on what to do, especially at a later date.

If someone is injured, the police <u>must be called</u> as well as an ambulance. Telephone 112. On the Costas holidays areas, some policemen speak some English, and they are very helpful, -- unless you are abusive or drunk, of course. If they suspect you have been drinking or you are under the influence of some substance, the police/Guardia Civil well ask for a drug and alcohol test to be taken, and the penalty for refusal is often more than if you fail the test: a sizable fine for "civil disobedience" as well as licence seizure, and penalty points being awarded. Use the special accident report form issued by your insurance company, if a rental car, there will be one in the glove compartment and it will probably be in Spanish. Use a copy of the English one in this book to make sure you know what you are agreeing to at the scene.

IF YOU SIGN THE FORM, IT IS USUALLY ACCEPTED AS THE TRUTH, SO BEWARE.

The form is acceptable to any insurance company (in the EU) whether it is Spanish, English, German, etc. That is why it is the same layout in all languages. This form is called the *Declaración amistosa de accidente de automóvil*, or "Agreed friendly statement of facts on motor vehicle accident", and if you do not have one, either get one from your broker or photocopy the one in this book (three copies: need carbon paper) and carry them with you to either complete or to use with the other driver's form's Spanish headings at the accident scene. The other driver from an EU country may have his form in French, if he/she is from France, but the form may be completed in two languages, as long as it is agreed to be correct and is signed by both drivers. Exchange copies of the report forms. They are in three parts, one for the insurance company, one for you, and one for the other driver. Again, remember that the contents of the form are legally binding in Court if signed by both drivers.

They must not be altered once completed and signed. To do so renders them inadmissible, and the driver concerned may suffer a penalty his/her insurance company.

It is suggested that you familiarise yourself with all the forms and procedure occasionally. Make sure you are familiar with all paper work before setting out on your journey to or in Spain.

Keep a black, fine point ballpoint pen in the car for completing the form. It is also always a good idea too have a camera in the car. The "throwaway" ones are OK for this purpose, and I always have one in the car. They cost about €6 to €10 with a flash unit.

It is important to record the other driver's name, driver's licence number and place of issue, street home address, phone number and vehicle registration of the other driver, if possible, checked by looking at the vehicles official papers that must be kept in the glove compartments in all vehicles in Spain, and the other drivers' licence.

If you have a camera with you (I have already suggested that you should) take pictures of the vehicles' damages and accident area, including skid marks and proof of the speed limit in that zone. This action could greatly help your case especially if you are not at fault. If you are not able to do so at the time of the accident, if convenient, come back soon at a later time to measure and take photos.

DO NOT MAKE ANY ALTERATIONS ON THE ACCIDENT FORM AFTER IT HAS BEEN ACCEPTED BY BOTH ALL PARTIES AT THE SCENE OF THE ACCIDENT AND THE CARBON COPIES SEPARATED. SEND IT TO YOUR INSURER ASAP.

Check quickly to see if the other vehicle is un-roadworthy in anyway, e. g. worn tyres, windscreen excessively dirty, wipers not working properly if raining, driver tired or been drinking or on drugs (pupils dilated?), vehicle overloaded, etc. Please note that if there is such a fault, their insurance company will usually pay you out, but claim from the other driver, as they would with you if you were unfit to drive. Remember that drivers are not insured if their vehicle is not roadworthy or they are unfit to drive, but if he/she is at fault, <u>you will still get paid but you must insist that your no claims bonus is not affected.</u>

If you wish to make an official criminal charge (*denuncia*) for the other driver's dangerous driving, etc., you have up to two months to do so at the local police station (*Policia Local* or *Municipal*). If possible, do it at the side of the road.

Take the advice of your insurance agent who may use a local lawyer (*abogado*) who is a specialist in these matters and especially one fluent in your language. If a visitor to Spain, check with your own insurance company first for preferred representatives in Spain, but if none are forthcoming, obtain reliably recommended local lawyer's details.   It is also advantageous if they have E-mail as a communication method as this is by far the most reliable and inexpensive way today.

If the other driver/s is a foreigner, obtain passport number and place of issue, OR if they are resident in Spain, their *residencia* card / paper number (NIF or NIE) and (Spanish? – with their address in it) Driving Licence details.   You should also check the vehicle VIN number if it is a "late" model car. This is in the dash on the LH side and can be seen through the windscreen. Do not panic if the other driver is not insured as the consortium especially if you are back in your own country, still works as part of the EU Directives on the subject.   Many still only use fax machines. If resident in Spain, your insurance company can handle the legal details, and most have arrangements with companies in other EU countries for such work.

If possible, ensure that the car is taken to a reputable panel-beater / repair shop recommended by your insurance company who will be expecting to be advised of the accident within the time as stated in the policy anyway, usually not more than two days. Ask them as soon as possible about the recommended repair shops as delays may occur otherwise. Most will say take it where you want as it absolves them of any comebacks if there are problems with bad repair work. Remove all valuables and loose items, and avoid "hole in wall businesses". I have found that the best place to take the car is the local <u>official dealer</u> for your vehicle who will handle the repair for you and deal with your insurance company, as well as do good work.

If the damage to your vehicle is minimal and it was your fault, consider paying for the repair yourself to speed the repair time and eliminate a claim which is covered only by your insurance excess.   You should <u>still advise your company</u> though, as specified in the policy to avoid future problems, but stress that it is "<u>not a claim</u>" to keep your No Claims Bonus, and make sure that everything is in writing.

Litigation can take a long time, but it works, although at time of printing, a new criminal (as opposed to civil) system has been introduced called "fast trials" (*Juicios Rapidos*) which can result in a verdict within a very short time. If a you are a visitor, it is stressed again that it is important to have a local specialist lawyer who could save you wasted trips coming to Spain in the event of a Court case, and if you appoint one, remember to sign a **Power of Attorney** so he/she can represent you without having to constantly contact you for instructions while you are in your home country.

⇒ Your insurance company will pay for any hospital costs as a result of injuries caused by the accident if it is in your cover.

⇒ If you and your passengers have to go to the hospital for any treatment where you can leave the same day, the hospital may expect you to pay if you have no other medical insurance, and the vehicle insurer will then recompense you, so keep the receipts.

TRANSFERENCE OF INSURANCE COVER.

A question I was asked for the first time recently was what happens if a vehicle cover policy is in the husband's name, and he suddenly dies? Can the wife just carry on without her name on the certificate or what? The answer from my reputable broker was:

"Providing the surviving spouse requests that the Policy is changed into her (or his) name there should not be any problem. Some companies allow the current Policy to continue whilst others may require a cancellation and rebate provided against a new Policy."

So it is a question to ask your broker when taking out your insurance if applicable.

DRIVING LICENCE LOSS INSURANCE

This type of insurance has been around for probably 20 years or more where if due to losing your driving licence for whatever reason such as losing too many penalty points, except for drinking or drugging and driving which is considered a self-inflicted penalty, the cover will provide a driver so as a businessman you can carry on with your daily work. While the situation is nowhere as bad as it is in the UK where there are so many speed cameras around now and professional drivers who have been accident and penalty free for many years are being caught exceeding a speed limit somewhere and being heaviliy fined with the eventual problem of losing the driving licence for a period of time which often means losing a job as well. If this potential situation applies to you, contact your insurance broker to find out more.

If you need a lawyer though for a specific case it is better to personally employ (a local) one when the problem occurs, remembering that the legal aid supplied on the vehicle insurance policy works for both you and the company which means they always look to saving the company undue costs.

ANATOMY OF AN ACCIDENT

The following is an account of an accident in Spain, what occurred at the time and afterwards. It is in this book as an example of why you need to be very careful when you have an accident here (or anywhere), especially if the other driver is Spanish. It is a weekday at 10H30: visibility very good.

Imagine that you are at a Stop sign, at a <u>very busy rural main road junction</u> (not in a town) for at least 30 seconds waiting for heavy traffic to turn left across your path. Then after having looked and seen the way to your left was clear as far as you could see, 140 metres, and having been signalled by another driver with his hand, to your right who had right of way that he was letting you through, you quickly move through the Stop sign. You passenger, your wife in the RH seat suddenly says "This one is coming very quickly" so without even looking as you are halfway across the road, you accelarate as fast as you can. Then your car's left side rear wheel is hit by a speeding car with all four wheels locked in a panic braking action. The speed that it was travelling at was later proved by the skid marks to have been easily at 100 kph (62 mph) or even more, this within a 60 kph (37 mph) area and at a busy road junction where a good driver would not have been doing safely more than 30 kph (20 mph). The road to your left has trees casting a shadow across the road at about 120 to 140 metres (same in yards) and there is also a gentle curve as in the photo. The whole action of looking left, and then seeing the other driver wave you through and moving out takes <u>less than two seconds</u>.

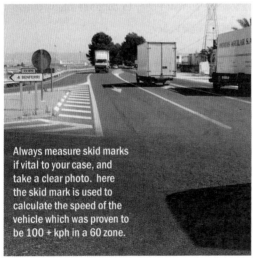

Always measure skid marks if vital to your case, and take a clear photo. here the skid mark is used to calculate the speed of the vehicle which was proven to be 100 + kph in a 60 zone.

Fortunately, no one is hurt, but you are more than a little annoyed because you know that the other driver must have been speeding and you could have 30 years of No Claims ruined. The skid marks on the road for the other vehicle, when checked later, measure 35 metres and continue another three metres AFTER having struck your car. If the other car, had not hit your car, thus slowing it down somewhat, the car would have travelled a total of about 40 to 45 metres to a full stop. But all are physically safe although the wife is badly shaken mentally.

The other driver, a señora, immediately phones for the Guardia Civil although this is not really necessary as no one is injured. Two officers on their motorcycles are on the scene within literally two minutes. You drive your car off the road after taking photos using the throwaway film camera carried for this purpose so the photos can be enlarged and still look clear, and the GC officers realising no one is hurt, assist the señora with the accident form carried for this purpose. As usual any other witnesses have left the scene not wanting to get involved.

You ask one of the GC officers to come and look at the skid marks, but he refuses stating that as you have gone through a Stop sign, you must be at fault. You politely disagree and having been trained in accident investigation at a police college and on another courses as a policeman in South Africa, if the other driver was speeding as the evidence proves she was then it could very

Accident point can be just seen about 170 meters away

well be her fault. After all, having checked the road was clear, you have to move through a Stop sign sometime. But even after asking three times, the GC officer finally says that <u>even if the señora was doing 150 kph, you are at fault</u>.

You take photos of the scene, including the speed limit signs at the approach to the junction some 170 metres away showing that the maximum is 60 kph with two signs, the first an 80 kph, followed soon after by the 60 kph sign as in the picture, so there can be no excuses. The photo shows that the señora must have seen the busy junction in good time. With all the traffic turning at this very busy junction, only an idiot would go through the junction at anything over 30 to 40 kph anyway! But she uses this road every day. If she had even been doing 60 kph, she would have been able to stop in 16 metres including the reaction time as later proven with official statistics. Look in car road test figures

It is a very hot day and the señora is thirsty so your wife offers her a drink of water which she gratefully accepts. The señora relaxes a little because the GC officer has told her not to worry as it is your fault. As it turns out later, she only has third-party insurance, so she needed to be worried! The señora then comments to your wife as she was giving her the water, as people do when they are relaxed, that she was "<u>late for work</u>"!

After putting your details on the accident form, you look at the sketch and alter it as it shows that the señora hit the front of your car, <u>not the rear</u> and this is important. You sign it as basically it is correct and this was a big mistake because it is <u>later interpreted</u> by your insurance company that you admitted fault. Moral, do not sign when the other details are in Spanish unless you are 100% fluent. Neither my wife nor I was then. As stated before, you take photographs of the scene including the skid marks which due to the road markings can be measured officially at a later date even if the skid marks have been rubbed away. Later you look in some car magazines where they road test the cars' braking abilities and find out that for a mixture of road cars and 4x4, the braking test figures show 60 to 0 kph gives an average distance of 12 to 14 metres, and, 100 to 0 kph gives an average of 35 to 41 metres, and these distances include reaction times, not just the "skidding" distance. Remember that the señora skidded 45 metres plus 3 more after she hit your car.

Your insurance broker later reads the Spanish comment written by the GC officer and states that you have signed that you "jumped the Stop sign", which is patently untrue as the evidence proves. It had been interpreted by you as there being a Stop sign there, which is true, but we all have to move through them eventually when it appears safe to do so.

Anyway, having had training in accident scene analysis while a police reservist, you prepare a report that proves, with the help of facts from the Internet, the speed that the driver must have been doing before reacting and braking was at least 100 kph.

Tests also show that if she had been doing 60 kph, she would have easily stopped before the junction, and in an similar saloon car the next day, the distance from 60 kph was proven not to be more than 11,5 metres actual braking distance (without reaction times) without leaving rubber on the road but with ABS brakes. In other words, at 60 kph, she would have stopped about 30 - 40 metres <u>before</u> the junction, but of course, if she had been obeying the posted limit, there would have been no reason to stop at all as she would have been seen coming in good time. The law states that you must approach any situation at a speed that allows you to take action to avoid any accident or dangerous situation, and with all the cars turning right across her path, 30 kph would have been far more sensible speed to approach the junction. But she was "late for work!"

So the evidence is very much against the other driver who can easily be proven to have been driving dangerously at excessive speed in an area clearly marked at 60 kph (maximum).

Moral:

⇒ NEVER SIGN the *declaracion amistosa* accident form at the scene if you are not 100% sure of what the other party has written. If written in Spanish, play safe is my advice.

⇒ Grab a witness if possible. Just get their name and phone number and have a Spanish friend phone him/her later for help.

⇒ Always carry a camera with you. They cost about €6 - 10 for a 24-shot film throwaway one, with a flash so you are ready for a night accident, and they give ideal results as the photos can be blown up an still be very clear. If you have a 5 + Mp digital this would be OK as well. But remember to have it with you whenever you drive.

$\Rightarrow$ Get the Guardia Civil (or police) officers' names and numbers. You can note them on the report form as I did.

$\Rightarrow$ Obtain a report number from the officer in charge for the insurance report if they have not entered it on the form. They usually supply it without being asked.

$\Rightarrow$ Use an insurance company where you get immediate action. The mobile phone is a blessing here and it is also far better that you have met the person you are speaking to at the insurance company.

$\Rightarrow$ AGAIN, DO NOT SIGN THE FORM unless you are 100% happy.

$\Rightarrow$ Finally, if you feel really strong about the other driver's culpability, as we did in this case. lay a civil charge against her if you can afford it; or take out legal insurance in addition to that offered with your vehicle insurance premium. After all, the lawyers there are working for the company with the main aim being to save money. This in itself is good as it keeps premiums down, but it is not good for justice.

FOLLOW UP.

As you may have guessed, I was the driver involved who was hit by the speeding car. I sent a letter in Spanish (obviously, and I headed it "Is This Justice?") to the chief of the Guardia Civil in that area, (Orihuela, Alicante) and a reply has been received, which has been passed to my insurance company. They took an interest especially as I was very upset after 30 years of no claims (NCB). With the report and photos they decided that they would not change my NCB status when the new premium was due in six months which is what happened. I also obtained a copy of a judgement from the UK for a similar case where the speeding driver was found guilty, and in that case, the magistrate actually went to see the accident scene. The insurance brokers said that problem is the Spanish Courts and the police / GC still have the "old fashioned" idea that if you go through a Stop street sign and you are hit by another motorist, even if he/she is driving at a provable dangerously high speed, you are still at fault. It needs a test case apparently.

IT IS OBVIOUS THAT UNTIL A TEST CASE IS DONE TO GET THIS MINDSET INTO THE 21ST CENTURY, WE MUST BE EXTRA CAREFUL FOR THE SPEEDERS WHO ARE LATE FOR WORK.

GENERAL NOTES ON BUYING/IMPORTING A VEHICLE IN SPAIN.

Buying a vehicle in Spain is useful even if you only have a holiday or a property here. You can bring your UK vehicle here whether or not you are resident, but eventually you will have to put it on Spanish plates if you wish to use it here full-time as a resident, although it is recommended to buy a LH drive spanish vehicle if you intend to do this.

Motorcycles are not a problem as far as the driving position is concerned, but the main differences with cars from the UK and Ireland are: -

- • The obvious one is that the steering wheel is on the opposite side of the car to those in mainland Europe. This is not a problem for good drivers who maintain a fair distance (2 seconds plus?) from the vehicle in front and overtake correctly. But when you are on your own and need to collect/pay for parking or at toll road cash booth, you must be able to easily stretch over the front passenger seat or you will have to get out. Also, to put the vehicle onto Spanish plates, the headlights, rear fog light and mirrors will/may need changing and also unless it is a "classic" it will not be worth much when you sell it here which according to the EU directive on the subject, is not allowed anyway. We see a few LH drive cars here on UK plates so they must be planning to move here or drive to here a lot. But with these vehicles if bought especially new in the UK or Ireland, beware of the way the headlights dip as often being sent there, the manufacturer installs the legal equipment for where the headlights dip left, and if fitted with a single rear fog-light, it may be installed on the right rear of the vehicle and will have to be changed to the left which often means new rear fog and reversing lights as they are "handed". The vehicle must also have two side mirrors but most do now anyway.

- • If it is a commercial, that is a van, truck, lorry or motor-home, whether LH or RH drive and it is on foreign plates, it will not be allowed to be re-register onto Spanish plates. There may be exceptions if the vehicle is not more than six months old and with the steering wheel on the left, but this new specification is intended to stop imports of older polluting vehicles into Spain. Do not buy until you have positively checked the situation for the specific vehicle. We may be able to help; see pages 287 - 288.

- • If it is a 4 x4 with a cab and load area at the back where a canopy may be fitted, this is also not acceptable for the same reason. (See picture.)

- • If you are already resident here, and the car has been bought since you became resident, check with Trafico and the tax office often called the "Hacienda" that they will allow you to import it without paying any import duties. Usually you are treated as an Spanish resident importing a car and will have to pay any taxes due which from January 2008 are based on pollution levels. Again, see pages 287 - 288.

- • If you did not re-register your personal vehicle/s within 30 days of APPLYING for residence, your vehicle may be treated as a normal import, not personal property, and the relevant taxes will apply. There may be ways to avoid this. See the back of this book.

- • 49 cc motos and those covered with an LCC driving licence such as light quadricycles are not considered to be motor vehicles but must still be re-registered.

- • Check that the vehicle is homologated for the whole of the EU. I have had one reader who brought in a UK registered 2-year old Yamaha 49 cc scooter without a homologation plate fixed to the frame, and the model is sold in Spain. It is not only the cost, it is the frustration at dealing with officials who do not speak your language (understandably) and *gestors* who cannot help either because too often it is a new experience for them.

- • If buying a vehicle in Spain that is on foreign plates, check that it is homologated. You can check easily using an expert for a small fee as listed at the back of this book, pages 287 - 288. But if you are not willing to do this, do not buy it unless it is for spares only and you are happy it is not stolen remembering that the engine and chassis numbers will be listed somewhere as stolen.

- • If you intend to keep the car in Spain for more than the six months per calendar year and use it as well for more than six months, you will be deemed as a resident and have to transfer it to Spanish registration plates but as stated elsewhere in this book, do it within the 30-day period from your notification of Spain being your official place of residence.

- • If it is used legally for <u>commercial reasons</u> such as a normal touring car while you are working with e.g. an estate agency, especially if covered in advertising, you may legally only use it for 30-days and then you must transfer it onto Spanish plates. I have seen several vehicles like this and advised them (if possible). They are "mobile fine generators".

- • If you only use it for the allowed six months, you will still have to go back to the country of origin to have it safety-tested (MOT), and also need pay any road-taxes liable there and these are often more expensive than Spain's equivalent. An ITV is only legal on a foreign plated vehicle during the transfer procedure to Spanish plates and many have tried during 2005 & 2006 to have UK cars ITVed thinking that would be OK. The ITV stations happily took the cash but it sent a message to Trafico, who administer the ITV stations, that the numbers of change of registrations and ITVs actually done did not match up in a big way. So they advised the GC and policia locales so they could inspect vehicles in a routine roadcheck that had an ITV with a foreign plates so they could check all documents to see if they were legal, which in most cases they were not. Result, a fine and 30-days given to put the vehicle onto Spanish plates. Plus if anything else was found wrong.... There are literally thousands of such vehicles driving around and every now and again, the authorities have a roadside blitz. If it is a commercial or a motorhome, etc, the chances exist of the vehicle being impounded until exported again.

⇒ The author has evidence where the police or *Guardia Civil* have issued fines of up to €300 for the use of a foreign plated car for more than one month where they can prove that you have taken up legal residence here. And this evidence can be on the documents carried in the car such as the insurance certificate with a Spanish address, or your Spanish identity i.e. residencia card or certificate. You must start the procedure as soon as you apply for the residence certificate.

⇒ You can avoid the 30-days rule if you only use it for short times in Spain and even though owning a property here by obtaining a Spanish local police certificate stating that you are not legally resident here as well as carrying current foreign receipts for water and electricity to show that you have a home outside of Spain, and if the car is used to travel back and forth, ferry receipts or similar.

⇒ Again, vehicles have even been impounded by the police where a roadside check has found that driver had *residencia* and also owned the vehicle. In one case, he was busy moving back to the UK in his Ford Transit van which could not be re-registered here anyway and was thence illegal as he was resident officially, was using a foreign plated commercial vehicle for moving furniture with a LH steering wheel. They are officially only allowed to be in Spain for one month at a time delivering goods to here and returning to the UK only. I was able to give advice that got him off the hook completely but he was a week late returning to the UK.

If you wish to sell a car on foreign plates car in Spain, unless it is a sought after classic (older than 25 years) you may have difficulties unless you can find someone who is moving back to the UK. Any offered buying price may be much lower than you expect.

I read the above and feel a little bad about listing all the "must" and "must not" rules, but if it saves us expats. unecessary fines and stress, it has to be good. Do you agree?

PLEASE NOTE:
I regularly receive enquiries about importing vehicles and other administrative worries, many from people who have not even bought this book. To take the pressure off (30 E-mails a week?) I have found an expert, who has retired from his profession as a university lecturer (languages) and who now does nothing else but vehicle and driving-licence administration, etc. and he has been "in business" since 1999 doing nothing else. Like myself, he is keeping busy during retirement but of course he charges for the service. As a billionaire boss I once worked for (well-known in the world, especially the UK, sadly dead now) told me once,

"*People do not appreciate what they do not pay for, whether it is in cash or deed, especially kids.* (It is a human being point). *Make them feel better by charging them something.*" My associate is very knowledgable and has excellent contacts at the Hacienda, Trafico and the councils. As such he says he can work for clients in any area in Spain as it is all on-line now.

PLEASE SEE PAGES 287 - 288 and my web-site for an easy free enquiry.

⇒ Motor cycle headlights need to dip right as well.

⇒ If the vehicle is from outside the EU, there are various technical specifications to which it must conform to (EU homologation) before it will be accepted for Spanish plates. By contacting myself via my web site, we can easily advise you in advance and even organise the import where possible.

⇒ This can cost you more money if the car does not conform and I have been advised that the Canaries are particularly difficult in this matter although the same laws apply there as in the rest of Spain. The main reported problems are the costs asked for by intermediaries (gestors?) who offer to do the re-registration for you. This is why it is good if you know what is involved as described in this book. You will then know if you are being "ripped off". This can be overcome if the manufacturer, or the main distributor who speaks English has exported similar models to Spain, even in small numbers, and they are the best people to contact. UK caravans are a good example where they are over 750 kg MAM (maximum authorised mass). In the UK and Ireland, they do not have their own registration so they do not have a V5C etc. document. From experience, you may need to get the UK manufacturer to instruct the Spanish main distributor to attend to the needed documents as caravans of this size have to be registered with its own "R" (remolque) registration plate in Spain as well as the tow vehicle's number plate (copy) attached to the rear of these trailers. More on this later in this chapter.

⇒ If a trailer under 750 kg MAM, you will need to take it to the COC office (usually near or at the ITV Station) where it can be certified and a small plate is attached by the engineer.  This will avoid any problems in a road-block check and legalise your trailer. But below a MAM of 750 Kg, the registration plate number is the same as the towing vehicle. The picture is for a small trailer with a MAM (MMA) of 300 Kg.

RIGHT HAND DRIVE MOTOR-HOMES, AND COMMERCIAL VEHICLES.

All such vehicles whether with LH or RH steering are now being refused transfer onto Spanish plates as part of the anti-pollution drive. Previously it was only those with the steering wheel on the RH side (UK & Ireland) for safety reasons. So it is better to sell it before you come and buy a vehicle, new or used, in Spain that already has Spanish plates. But for newer vehicles with a LH steering wheel we may be able to help. See pages 287 - 288

- • There are some enterprising dealers who are importing inexpensive left dipping pattern headlights from the Far East now. They usually advertise in local English language newspapers. Check the quality though remembering that headlights are supposed to be to EU-CE conformity standards, marked as such and not just on a paper sticker, and compare with the dealer's listed price. Most dealers will give less 10% for cash if you ask. As my father used to often say, "If you do not ask you won't get". And sometimes if we did not say thank-you, my brother and I would get a clip around the ear. We loved him though.

- • If you are importing a vehicle from especially the UK with tinted windows, be very careful. It is not so bad if the windows have removable film, but if the "tint" is in the glass, usually sandwiched, the glass will have to be changed. It is usually better to not import such a vehicle. See information in this book on Tinted Windows on pages 250-252.

PERMANENT EXPORTS FROM THE UK - SOME MORE NOTES.

Please remember that you should always check on the DVLA web site to see if there has been any changes of procedures and form numbers.

www.dvla.gov.uk.

If you are taking your vehicle out of Great Britain permanently you must notify the DVLA but do not do it until you have your Spanish registration finalised. If you have a Registration Document (V5) which is now obsolete since July 2005, (the V5C replaced it) you can do this by completing section C to show the intended date of export. The relevant section may then be returned to the DVLA or to a DVLA Local Office. In its place you will receive a Certificate of Permanent Export (V561) as confirmation of your vehicle's registration and export status. If you have a Registration Certificate (V5C) then you must notify export on the purple section (V5C/4), but you need to take your Registration Certificate with you as you may have to hand it over to the relevant authority when the vehicle is registered abroad i.e. In Spain this is Trafico who will then advise the UK DVLA or the relevant authority if another country. Please note that if your papers are older than the current V5C, then get them updated at the DVLA, as the V5C can be understood by all EU States as it is "multi-lingual".

THE PAPERWORK PART OF BUYING IN SPAIN.

You are settled here for a while or "for ever" and need a new or used car, this is no problem as long as you have the following: -

- • The necessary cash or credit facilities.
- • You are registered as a resident with your local town hall, the *Ayuntimiento, with* the certificate called the *Nota de Empadronamiento.*
- • You have an NIE (six-month form) or a *residencia certificate or the older obsolete card* ("permanent" – 2 / 5 year residency card).
- • A full copy of the *escritura* or property deed for your owned Spanish accommodation, or a current rental contract for at least one full 12-month year or more. You will need this to get the *Nota de Empadronamiento anyway.*
- • You will need the originals of the above and your passport.
- • Note, in 2007, Trafico (and all government departments) announced that there will be no need to submit photocopies anymore as the information is to be kept on their computer system as is usual now in most modern countries, with original documents being directly scanned in. (But do not expect all to be as it should be though.) So originals are essential and if you are posting them by Correos, they usually have a special, secure mail bag to ensure no losses occur. I have not had any problems.

The same applies as anywhere else. If your Spanish is not so good, you have three choices: take a Spanish friend or someone fluent in Spanish, pay someone who speaks Spanish to go to the dealer/seller to help you negotiate, or use a sales outlet where the people speak English. There are many of these in the expat and holiday areas. In all cases be very careful. TRUST NOBODY. Based on previous readers experiences, there are those who prey on the ignorant here and they are not all Spanish.

But my advice is that it is better to buy a local car in Spain if you intend to stay as it is difficult and costly, especially if the imported car is old and not worth much, to change a foreign non-EU car to Spanish plates. However, if you wish to go ahead and re-register your car, the step-by-step procedure is in the back of this book. If buying from a dealer where he is organising the transfer, keep back about 20 - 25% of the payment until all the documentation is completed correctly as described in this book and if you have a question, you can E-mail me for advice. Remember to put "Motoring in Spain question" in the subject line as I receive about 300 SPAMs every day so yours may be deleted as such if not easily identified. The E-mail address is at the front of this book.

When you are buying a new car, you can do what the author did. Car sales are slow in the summer months, and we decided to buy a new car after an accident to our older BMW where a Mercedes rammed us from behind (we only pick the best!). The local dealers have a maker's "corporate image" quotation form with the base car cost and then the options where the prices are inserted, the total being complete with local registration tax and the year's (or part of the year) road tax. Now the first line of this particular quotation form is the discount, and this often depends on what the manufacturer states to the Dealer the discount for that model for that month and is the same at all the big car dealers for any make.

I took the completed quotation form to two other main dealers, both of whom had the same maker's standard discount at that time) and obtained further substantial discount quotations in writing (same form). As a result, the car was bought at the English-speaking dealer at much less than the original price quoted as I showed the dealer the other lowest quote, and asked him to match it which he did. He needed the sale and we received another €600 discount.

Buying a used car is fraught with pitfalls if you are not fluent in Spanish. The Spanish people are nice to know but many seem to think that all foreigners are very wealthy so it is easier to buy from someone again who speaks English well if you do not have a good friend who can negotiate with you in Spanish. Used cars in good condition are reported to hold their values much more than in the UK. Also, I have had several E-mails where readers have been cheated by English dealers here, some well established, sometimes where they do not even transfer the ownership at Trafico once they have the cash, despite this being part of the sale as first agreed. Another complaint was that the car was not the model that the salesman said it was, but that is a problem that is common everywhere.

For example, In one case, the buyer bought an 800cc 3-cylinder car but thought he was buying the 4-cylinder 1.100cc version. The invoice stated sold "as is" so he had no comeback without an expensive Court case. As a non-mechanically-minded person, it would have paid to have a mechanic or a knowledgeable friend check it before buying it. So *caveat emptor,* 'Let Buyer Beware, and Trust No One. It is not only the "rip-off" that hurts, it is the indignation that you have been conned.

Also make sure that the vehicle is as you think it is or as you are told it is. Rental cars, ex-driving school cars and taxis are "no-nos" usually unless you are a mechanic and they are very cheap. They need ITVs much more often that private vehicles as in the table in this book on pages 97 & 98. Another problem although more for private sales that accredited dealers is where the vehicle has outstanding taxes and fines owing on it. If you do not pay traffic fines, Trafico puts the amount against the vehicle so when it is sold/transferred the next time, the transfer is conditional on these fines being paid, just as the ayuntamiento will set unpaid bills against your owned property. If you are the new owner, it is you that has to pay unless you can catch the seller. You can check the existence of any debts against the vehicle by using the Trafico TASA 3.050 enquiry form and pay about €9 for the information which will be the history of who has owned it from when and any outstanding debts. You may even find that the vehicle has been scrapped! And pay a visit to the ayuntamiento where the vehicle annual tax is paid. It will be the one covering the area where the address on the *Permiso de Circulacion* states. Check all payments are up to date and again reader's horror stories of unpaid bills on cars that have been sold even years earlier have been received. And the seller has to pay if the transfer has not been done since the time of sale. Could you afford a sudden and unexpected bill for €1.000? It has happened according to reader's advice.

WHERE TO BUY A VEHICLE. There are possibly three sources you can buy from.

⇒ A MAIN DEALER for the make of car and model you want. They may also have a demonstrator model (0 Km?) that you can buy for a good price with a full warranty, or one that has been traded in from a regular customer who has bought a new one. If the car is low mileage as it should be as a demonstrator model or one used by a dealer employee or director, the dealer may give you up to a year's warranty or even the two years in writing (in Spanish) on it, but have the terms (to be legal, in Spanish) checkcd by an expert if it is NOT the manufacturer's standard warranty. Some manufacturers also have an extended warranty that may be transferred. Note that the standard new vehicle warranty in all of the EU by law is now two years anyway. Many dealers supplying English speaking customers will have the warranties and operator manuals in English as the manufacturer stocks them anyway, or the latter may be available as a download off the manufacturer's web-site.

⇒ From a PRIVATE SOURCE. If you are experienced and can check the car yourself, go ahead, but be careful as *caveat emptor* (let buyer beware) applies here. If you are not a mechanical person, you can have the car checked by an expert, chosen by you, not the vendor, for a reasonable cost. This should include a fairly long 50 km road-test.

•• From a **CAR RENTAL COMPANY.** Official figures state that around 6% + of the cars registered in Spain are to rental companies. Spain has many rental agencies that sell off their cars from when they are one year-old to four year's-old, or sooner if the renting sales are down especially if it is not their busy time of the year. As this market is fairly busy, you can negotiate a good deal with a warranty, e.g. 3 months, to cover any serious problems. These cars are not as bad as you may think, depending on the company selling the car, but do ask for copies of the servicing records to be shown on the spot so they are not "made up" ready for you later. A used rental car can be obtained for a good price, as little as 50% or more of the new price if three years plus old and do not be afraid to make an offer below the asking price. Again, if you are not mechanically minded, get the car checked by an independent engineer. There are the equivalents of the AA & RAC in Spain and they are listed in this book. As it is a rental car, the owner can either rent it to you for a few days, or let you use it on test for free if you are a "good negotiator". You can then give it a thorough inspection by an expert (you?). There are also reliable British or Irish mechanics, with their own garages with whom you can easily chat who will check the vehicle over and give you a report as well as good Spanish experts who speak enough English. And they will all welcome your custom later but if possible, use reliable recommendations when selecting one.

However, be careful at some sales-rooms as they may trade on you ignorance and sell you an ex-driving-school (check for where the dual foot controls have been installed) or a taxi (usually white) vehicle without your knowledge. Check the *Permiso de Circulacion* and the *Tarjeta de Inspeccion Tecnica de Vehiculos* for the history, who was it first registered to (private or company) and have any ITVs been done before it was four years old which is a sure sign that it is not a private vehicle. If yes, the price should be negotiated down a way if you want still want it. Remeber as I have written already, it is a major purchase usually, so check before you pay. Use the Trafico TASA 3.050 form "*Solicitud de cuestiones varias* (conductores - vehiculos)" which means loosely translated, request for answers to various questions about drivers and vehicles. It may be the best €9 approximately you will have spent.

TRANSFER OF YOUR PURCHASE.

There are formalities to follow and the dealer or car rental agency will normally carry out these on your behalf. In the back of this book there are check lists and three pages of step by step instructions to help YOU easily carry out Trafico procedures, or you can pay a gestor to do it for you if you are not adventurous. But watch you are charged fairly especially in the Canary Islands according to reader's letters I have received from there where, especially for imported vehicles, very high charges are demanded. Ask for a breakdown of the costs, not just a lump sum. If the vehicle is coming up for ITV (the same as MOT in the UK) see that they will have it tested for you as part of the transfer. Do NOT rely on the testing procedure as being a sign that the car is in good condition though as the author has seen old cars that have just been passed (literally, on return from the ITV station), with the front wheels ready to fall off due to serious suspension wear. The addresses of all the ITV Stations in Spain can be found at the Trafico web site at : -

http://www.dgt.es/tramites/itv/itv.htm

BEWARE.

If the dealer is not a well-established company with a good, reliable reputation, it is highly recommended that you do not hand over more than an agreed deposit until all the procedures are completed. I suggest not more than 50 to 75%, with the understanding that the remainder will be paid when the vehicle is fully registered in your name. Do a check list based on the information in this book. If the dealer is not happy, walk away. It is not worth the potential aggravation when the deal goes sour because a "rogue or lazy dealer" has reneged on his part of the sale when he already has your cash and it happens as readers tell me far too often. There may be a good reason such as the vehicle was a taxi (if white in colour, be careful) or is an ex-driving school car (it has happened). These have the handicap of needing the annual and then six-monthly ITV inspection much sooner than the normal 10 years. Always get the sale-agreement terms in writing on the company's letter head in English if possible. This will ensure that the dealer will think twice about trying to cheat you as well as respecting you for not being a "fool".

I have received numerous mails and phone calls, especially from the Costa Blanca where people have bought cars and in one case a new scooter, and the transfer has still not been effected, in one instance up to two years later (in this case a used car where the owner only came to Spain on holiday for a couple of times a year). Several were from one dealer, incidentally not Spanish, but the stress and cost of employing legal people to chase these dealers is not acceptable, plus it can take over a year to get to Court so the dealer relies on you giving up. Once these unscrupulous people have your cash, they do not care. Fortunately they are few in number.

THE ABILITY TO PAY TAXES AND OBTAIN PERSONAL INFORMATION ON LINE.
USER'S CERTIFICATE OR CERTIFICADO DE USARIO

Spanish citizens and foreign residents who are registered as such in Spain can carry out many actions on line to save much time and money. However the ability to read and understand Spanish is really necessary to be able to use the full benefit. Actions such as paying taxes on line, obtaining information about yourself as listed on the State' records and much more is possible from the comfort of your home computer, in fact, using the secure "digital signature" called the Certificado de Usario means that you can only do it from one PC unless you are a registered gestoria or accounts company legally representing individuals or other companies who have authorised you to do so. Your local ayuntamiento can also do this on your behalf.

What is a digital signature? It is a code number made up of letters, numbers and symbols as on the standard (Spanish in this case) computer keyboard, which is issued by a specialist company as authorised in this instance by the Spanish government that ensures your on-line identity cannot normally be used by anyone else without your permission, and the fact that for the individual it can only be used on your computer where the system identifies the hardware details such as the serial number of your processor, means that your data cannot be compromised. When prompted to on the screen, the "certificado" number is typed into its box on the screen just like a PIN number and you are then allowed access to the particular action you wish to take.

What can you do with this Certificado de Usario or User's Certificate? Well one action is to pay your vehicle's transfer tax on line thus saving a day in the hacienda queuing and filling out forms. Another is to pay such taxes as the IBI, income tax if not already deducted by an employer, obtain information about your particular details as record by the ayuntamiento and the Agencia Tributaria (Tax Agency). You can also check how many traffic penalty points you have lost. Much you will not do unless you are fluent in Spanish or on the way to being so, but with the modern features on the Internet browsers where you can translate a page from Spanish to English at the push of a button or key, it is not as difficult as it used to be. I have included how to obtain your Certificado de Usario in this book, but it would take many pages to explain step by step how to do other actions. It is better that you do so when you are able to knowing the Spanish language adequately.

I have retained the manual method of paying the tax for when your re-register a vehicle either for import reasons or when you buy a new (or used) vehicle. Normally, if buying from a dealer, I would recommend that part of the deal is that the dealer organises the transfer (and the buyer retains say 20% of the payment until this has been satisfactorily completed). This will avoid the numerous complaints I receive from readers where once the seller has the cash, they lose interest in completing the paperwork. But if the seller is a private individual, even the Spanish are more likely to use a gestor for the convenience of it, but as the reader of this book, I think it is a very good idea that you know what is involved to avoid the odd instance of people trying to pull the wool over your eyes with excuses why the paperwork is not completed in good time.

OBTAINING YOUR CERTIFICADO DE USARIO.

Note this can only be done by those who have registered in Spain and have at least an NIE tax identification number for foreigners (*Numero de Identificaron de Extranjero*) with the correct address details etc. on the official computer systems.

Form 576 is the application form where the tax agency (commonly called the Hacienda, although they are trying to get rid of that unofficial name) works out the tax on your specific vehicle for any taxes to be paid. <u>It can only be completed now on line although this can be at the Hacienda offices</u>. The tax is based on the listing of all vehicle models and years, with the actual amount being 4% of the list price on their list. After ten years, the tax is a straight 10% of the original list price as in their lists and this list can be located via my web-site at: www.spainvia.com/vehicletaxlists.htm.

To obtain and complete the application form, you must:

Obtain a digital signature or as it is also know, a certificate. This is one issued to you so you can pay all taxes on line including local ones that and it is designed to eliminate any fraud such as people trying to register stolen cars, etc. by stealing your personal data. It can also be used for any transaction with any government department that uses the system. By using a code numvber or PIN issued via this web-site, the person applying can complete and sign forms without actually putting his or her normal signature on the form. FNMT.ES is a secure web-site that will issue you with this code or certificate.

The "signature" can be used with two methods:
1. Using a supplied credit-card sized key card with a PIN for "swiping" on suitable equipment.
2. Using a code number that can be typed in on relevant application forms.

The credit card would be used more by companies making many transactions than the individual who would use just the code number. There is no charge for the supply of the code.

Some examples of the services using this system by citizens and residents are:

⟹ Presentation of taxes, returns and claims.

⟹ Annual reading of the data of the population census and houses in a municipality.

⟹ Presentation and payment of local and national taxes on line.

⟹ Checking records in the municipal register (voter's roll) including adding your names.

- • Consultation of traffic and other fines.

- • Banking details of municipal taxes such as the IBI (the municipal rates charges called the Impuesto sobre Bienes Inmuebles), the vehicle road fund tax (Impuesto Municipal sobre Vehiculos de Tracción Mecánica), and more.

AFTER COMPLETING THE PROCEDURE DESCRIBED BELOW, IT TAKES 24 HOURS FOR THE CODE OR PIN TO BE ISSUED.

IT IS ALSO IMPORTANT TO REMEMBER THAT ANY APPLICATION AFTER THE INITIAL CODE HAS BEEN ISSUED MUST BE MADE ON THE SAME COMPUTER AS THE SYSTEM HAS THE ABILITY TO RECOGNISE IT AND WILL NOT WORK IF A DIFFERENT COMPUTER IS SUBSEQUENTLY USED.

To obtain the certificate via the Internet:

1. Go to www.fnmt.es: which is the web site for the "*Fabrica Nacional de Moneda y Timbre*".

2. Select "Ceres", which is the *Certificación y Seguridad en la Transmission de Datos*" or the certificate for the secure transmission of data).

3. Then click on "Obtenga certificado de usario" – Obtain the user's certificate.

4. In the second column at the top, click on "Obtener el certificado" under "Cuídanos" or citizens, as distinct from companies, etc).

5. Further down in that column, click on the line "1 Solicitud vía internet de su Certificado".

6. The next screen will show you a block where you must type in your DNI, NIE or if you are representing a ward of Court, or a person unable to legally conduct their own affairs, the CIF number. The number must have nine numbers and letters. If there are spaces left, insert zeros to make up nine to the left before your actual number.

7. Select the security strength e.g. 1024 which is the number of "bits". Computer experts will know what this is. 1024 is OK.

8. Select on the block "Enviar petición" or send application for the code or certificate as it is know in PC-speak.

9. The next day, go online to the same place as 5 above, and click on the line "Renovación de certificado". If it is ready, you will be supplied with the code / certificate to use for all your transactions with most government and municipal departments in Spain. If it is not ready:

10. Click on the line above "Verificar estado" and you will be advised if there is a delay and the reason (in Spanish). If no reason is given, wait another 24 hrs.

Obtaining the certificate from your local town offices. Find the local offices:

1. Go to www.fnmt.es: which is the web site for the "Fabrica Nacional de Moneda y Timbre".

2. Select "Ceres", which is the Certificación y Seguridad en la Transmission de Datos" or the certificate for the secure transmission of data.

3. Then click on "Obtenga el certificado de usario" – Obtain the user's certificate.

4. In the second column at the top, click on "Obtener el certificado" under "Cuídanos" (citizens, as distinct from companies, etc).

5. Further down in that column, click on the highlighted line "Oficinas mas cercanas" or closest offices.

6. You then go through to the data base which has all the addresses of the offices where your certificate can be issued by a "physical" person, that is if you are not computer literate, or do not understand Spanish, etc.

7. The top block has "Elige la provincia, población y calle que buscas en el mapa" meaning you need to insert your address in the order below as follows, using the drop down menus:

• • Provincia – Your province where you live e.g. Alicante, etc.

• • Población – The town, or village or area listed where you live.

• • Todas – The type of street or square, etc where you live as on your correct address.

• • Type in (only) the full name of your road without any "avenida, calle", etc.

• • The number of your home in the little square.

• • Click on Buscar (find) and a list of the offices the closest will be show on the next screen with street addresses and telephone numbers. Select the one that you can easily get to. Take all your documents with you to prove your identity and the address where you live, such as a current receipt for water or the telephone, etc. The office will supply you with your number but again, with a 24 hr wait (work days only).

• • The other block is for locations where there are no villages, etc. such as a farm or country estate. There you use the province, the closest main road and a Km number reading as on the autovias.

If anyone has problems with this procedure, please E-mail me with the details including where you live, as although the system is excellent, if any changes are made I can update them on the web-site after doing all I can to help.

One use for this code is to find out how many PENALTY POINTS you may have lost by referring to the Trafico web-site at: https://puntos.dgt.es/tramites/permisos/ppp_sin_cert.htm

Where is says Datos de Usario, enter your NIE or NIF number and in the next box your Certificate de Usario code. You will see how many points you have lost, if any. However, I have not personally been able to check this as I still have them all (by the Grace of the Almighty!) Also, if you have no user's certificate; click on "Aqui" below the boxes. In te next page you can also check by entering the date of the offence instead of a user's certificate as well as your NIE.

WINDOW TINTING - THE CAVEATS AND BENEFITS.

Why "tint" vehicle windows? The film that is used contains chemicals including aluminium in it that allows light to pass through but not heat, the degree of transfer, called the Visible Light Transfer or VLT, depending on the amount of the insulating and light transmission restriction materials used in the film. And less transmission usually means a darker film just like your sun-glasses. And many new cars now have this feature built into the glass at the manufacturing stage but never more than that allowed for the territories that the vehicle is destined for because in many countries it is not a needed due to the climate or the preponderance of vehicles being sold now with air-conditioning as a "standard option". Also, an important factor, the laws are different for each EU State as described below.

BEWARE. Imported UK vehicles that are legally tinted for the UK as far as which windows and the VLT are concerned, may not be legal in Spain, for here the windows forward of the pillars behind the drivers/front passenger doors and the windscreen are <u>not allowed to be tinted at all in Spain</u>. The specifications for most EU countries can be seen at:

<u>http://www.iwfa.com/iwfa/Law_Chart/EWFA%20Tint%20Laws.pdf</u>

WHAT DO THE FILMS DO? They restrict to varying degrees the amount of heat, and coincidentally light, that can be transmitted through a glass panel (window). The film can be installed at manufacturing time which means it is usually sandwiched between the glass laminations depending which window it is, or, by officially authorised installing companies who then also supply a certificate for the vehicle owner which in Spain, needs to be carried in the vehicle: or does it now as there seems to be some argument on this point? Also essential is a small homologation sticker which is put on the glass before the film is applied on each window. Certain films are also designed to reduce glare from the sun; good for other drivers.

The problem with the films is that they can restrict vision from inside the vehicle as well as into it, and for this reason specifications have been drawn up to make sure that the wrong films are not used so that, as with every walk of life today, the general public as well as the occupants of vehicles are safer. In other words, so drivers can see where they are going especially after dark.

First of all, throughout the EU the specifications allowed are not standardised, and Spain has the tightest regulations of all and owners must be very careful if importing a UK vehicle into Spain.   If you bring a vehicle from the UK to be re-registered here and even if it has passed through the COC (Certificado de Confórmate) and ITV inspections for re-registration here but the windows are not to Spanish specifications, as has happened to a reader where the vehicle had passed through the COC and ITV reregistering inspections, but he was subsequently ordered by the GC in a roadside check to have the film removed within 14 days. Very expensive if it is not a film but is in the glass itself as this vehicle's was.   The particular ITV Station that approved the reader's vehicle was obviously not awake that day. The UK standard is that you may use a 75% VLT (visible light transmitted) film on the windscreen and a 70% VLT film on the front side windows.   In Spain, vehicles are not allowed to have any percentage of restricted light transmission on these windows which basically means you cannot have a film fitted unless it is clear which could be for anti-shatter reasons. The differences are being disputed in Brussels or wherever the "great unelected" do battle on this subject for quite some time now to ensure we are all the same in the new Europe so eventually, I guess we will all have the same specifications.

WHAT ARE THE BENEFITS OF WINDOW TINTING? The first is that on a hot day, heat is restricted from passing through the glass, and most of the new buildings, the ones with dark windows everywhere especially skyscraper office blocks, have this feature otherwise the electricity bills for heating and air-conditioning would be "eye watering" when payment time comes. In a vehicle, the temperature is kept lower, the interior is less susceptable to fading, and the glass is less likely to shatter in the event of it being hit by a foreign object, especially if being hijacked. Very popular pastime in in South Africa.   You are allowed in Spain to install quite dark film on all windows except for the windscreen and the two front side-windows, as long as you have two side mirrors, and the other windows have no VLT restrictions and that is why here in Spain you see some vehicles where you cannot see into the rear passenger section.   The benefits also include the vehicle's air-conditioning system having a much easier time thus saving fuel in summer, as well as the vehicle being warmer in winter.

Table of the rules for Spain and the UK on next page>

WINDOW TINTING: SPAIN AND THE UK, THE DIFFERENCES

COUNTRY	Front – forward of the "B" Pillar. The "B" pillar is the vertical support for the roof just behind the drivers/front passenger's seats.	Rear of "B" pillar.	NOTES issued by the EWFA (European Window Film Association.)
SPAIN	NOT AUTHORISED No film (tinting) is authorised other that to the specification issued by the Spanish government. See column 3 on the right.	All windows with no limits on the visible light transmission (VLT). Provided that two approved side (wing) mirrors are fitted	The Spanish window film industry has filed complaints with the EU Commission to regularise the EU laws and allow film tinting as in other EU states. The Spanish government issued specifications for the film as requested in June 2001, setting technical requirements and testing conditions that so far no manufacturer or importer has been able to comply with to gain certification. In 2004, the industry filed a complaint with the EU and the discussions are proceeding (but do not watch this space!)
UK	Authorised. • 75% VLT for front windscreens. • All other windows within the visual zones • Forward of the "B" 70% VLT	All windows behind the "B" pillar, no limits of VLT	

PURCHASE TAX CHANGES PROPOSED FROM 2008 TO ENCOURAGE NEW CAR BUYERS IN SPAIN TO BUY LOW EXHAUST EMISSION VEHICLES.

Please note that at the time of publication, this information was correct.

The Spanish Government has announced changed <u>special purchase taxes for new motor vehicles</u> from January 1st. 2008 that are intended to encourage buyers with their choice of motor vehicle with the intention of reducing carbon emissions. This tax is not to be confused with IVA (VAT). At present there are two special taxes when you buy a new vehicle and they are 7% for petrol engined vehicles up to 1.600 cc and 2.000 diesel, and 12% over these engine sizes. The new scheme basically means that models with efficient clean engines as determined by the EU homolgation testing standards will be cheaper to buy and this benefits 63, 7% of vehicles based on the sales figures for 2006, the last complete year. But vehicles with higher polluting exhausts, the other 36, 3%, again with reference to the 2006 sales figures, will pay more. The new costs are announced at this time to be from the 1st January 2008, so sales of the smaller cars will be slow until January 2008 and the larger cars should be increased for these are the ones where prices will rise before that date. It is a fair guess that the new proportions will not cause any loss of revenue for the Spanish government.

The exhaust pollution is measured by the amount of CO_2 that is discharged by the vehicle's exhaust per Km based on controlled tests, so therefore the bigger the engine or the more powerful the engine, or the heavier the vehicle the more the pollution usually results. The pollution from diesel engines is different to that from petrol but the new figures allow for that fact. The exhaust systems for the latest diesel engined vehicles contain special "particulate" (carbon dust) filters to reduce pollution and will be legally set to higher standards in the years to follow.

TABLE OF NEW TAXES.

The taxes are going to be based on the emissions of each model based on the EU testing during homologation. These will be based on four new tax rates as in the table below. The sales figures are for 2006 and are given to show the splits for that year for comparison purposes. The percentages can be changed in future years to preserve the overall tax collected.

CO_2 Emissions (Gm/Km)	Registrations 2006	%-age of market pool.	New Special Tax (%)
>120	125.662	7,7	0
+120>160	915.718	56	4,75
+160>200	453.846	27,8	9,75
+200	139.309	8,5	14,79
Overall totals	1.634.595	100	

COSTS OF LEARNING TO DRIVE AND OBTAIN A DRIVING LICENCE IN SPAIN.

More and more families are coming to live in Spain for various reasons. One newcomer stated recently that one feature they noted before they decided to move here was the fact that children can still safely play in most residential streets without getting sold drugs, shot or stabbed and so on, but perhaps that is being a little cynical on my part. But I read the UK Press.

But the fact is that children grow up and need to get a two-wheeler licence first, and eventually a car licence. I have covered the basic rules elsewhere in this book, but most driving schools away from the expat. densely populated areas only speak Spanish, but some now in the "English areas" are inceasingly employing staff that can teach in English, and they even have the test theory questions re-written in English. Try obtaining instruction in Spanish in the UK. Is it possible?

The main problem for the English-speaking learner-driver in Spain is that, except in selected areas where there are many English-speaking residents with teenage children who are of the age to learn to drive, the lessons are not in English. If the "child" has lived in Spain for a few years this will not be a problem as childen soon learn a new language, but it is for the newcomers. I have suggested that the best way is to learn and take the test in the UK, but if you live on the Costa del Sol and the Costa Blanca, there are schools who will teach and arrange for the driving test to be taken in English. The cost is an important consideration. A recent survey stated that the costs are now high, from €550 to €950 depending on the location.

If you live in Malaga Province, namely Malaga City, Benalmadena or Marbella, then Javier Gomez of *Autoescuelas Torcal* is a well respected registered driving instructor who speaks English. He lived in the UK for 18 months and his phone numbers are: 600-950-685; 600-950-611, and the school office number is (Marbella) 952-86 86 64.

I would appreciate any more such contacts around the country, especially the Costa Blanca, so I can include them in the updates that support this book and other current news on my website .

www.spainvia.com/motoringinspain.htm

Go to the menu at the page bottom left.

SCRAPPING A VEHICLE IN SPAIN.

SPANISH-PLATED VEHICLES.   If you are to scrap your vehicle for whatever reason, it will cost you about €9 to advise Trafico unless it is older than 15 years where the cost is then nothing. Over ten years old and you receive a financial credit to go towards your next NEW car. This is part of Trafico's scheme, called PLAN PREVER* to encourage owners to scrap vehicles that do not have modern catalyst exhaust systems and also legally saving the authorities time and money removing them from the streets.   It is highly recommended that you advise Trafico when you are scrapping your Spanish-plated car otherwise your vehicle could be rebuilt by "cowboys" (what an insult to real cowboys!) and from then, using your original registration, and your car is totting up fines IN YOUR NAME, or if used in a Bank robbery....   You can also phone an official scrap yard and have them collect it and the drivers carry the correct forms for you and them to sign, you keep a copy and they are then responsible for advising Trafico. But TRUST NOBODY! Play safe and advise Trafico also to be safe. The phone numbers and addresses of all official scrapyards are at:

http://www.dgt.es/tramites/cards/cards.htm.

Click on the province required.

The Trafico form for scrapping is the TASA 9.060 and it can be downloaded from the Trafico web-site as advised in this book.

*PLAN PREVER. Claiming your cash.   You will be awarded from €480 to about €740 (at this time) by the government depending on the vehicles.   Be careful if you are selling the car through a dealer as a trade-in as he may keep the cash for himself trading on your ignorance. I would claim it as an extra discount once the final price has been agreed. The Agencia Tributaria form to use is No. 567, but unless you are fluent in Spanish it is best that this procedure is handled by someone who does it on a regular basis. Please see pages 287 - 288 for reliable help.

SELLING YOUR VEHICLE IN SPAIN.   When you sell your car/motorcycle, you can carry out the necessary paperwork yourself if your Spanish is up to it, or use the services of a *gestor,* or, if to a reputable dealer, they will do the work for you if you include it in the deal. Or with a friend who is fluent in Spanish, and the needs lists are in the back of this book to help you.   Note that under EU Laws it is illegal to sell a vehicle with foreign registration in any country other that the one it is registered in, but it does happen. You will see advertisements in the local English language Press offering small sums to take vehicles off your hands. If your vehicle has not been declared scrapped with the relevant authority, i.e. the DVLA in the UK, you are leaving yourself open to a future fine/s, especially if the registration number is used on another vehicle which possibly could have been stolen, or the vehicle is used to break traffic regulations such as camera speed traps. So be safe and do it the correct way by sending in the relevant page in the Form V5C for UK vehicles, and whatever for others.

It is very important to ensure that this procedure is completed correctly due to there being a transfer tax to be paid, which is normally paid by the buyer (but can by arrangement be by the seller and there are two different forms to allow this), but is also the responsibility of the seller to see that it is paid. If it is not done, the tax office will try and collect this transfer tax from you at a later date. In addition, if the transfer is not done correctly, any traffic violations committed by the new owner can be charged to you as the registered owner as well as you having to pay the taxes (including the 4% hacienda tax) normally paid by the buyer; and a fine for not transferring the vehicle.   AGAIN THE PROCEDURE FOR TRANSFERRING IS IN THE BACK OF THIS BOOK, AS WELL AS AN OFFER OF A AN EXPERT ADMINSTRATOR WHO DOES THIS WORK FULL TIME. HE KNOWS MANY SHORT CUTS.

If you do it yourself, as the seller, you will need the Trafico form TASA 9.07A, *Notificación de transmisión de vehiculos* (seller), which can be prepared on screen and printed out from this web site address, or the form can be obtained from Trafico.

http://www.dgt.es/indices/dgtHtm_Impresos_es.html

You will need a receipt for payment of the vehicle transfer tax, which is charged at 4% on the sale of second-hand vehicles, based on the tax authority's tables. This tax is paid to the local tax (also known as the *Hacienda*) office, and is called the *impuesto sobre transmisiones patrimonales y actos juridicos documentados, or* ITP in short. They have a list of values of all vehicles so they will set the actual amount to which the percentage for the tax is applied, which reduces each year until the car is ten years old, and then it is set at 10% of the original value. Up to the ten years, the 4% tax is based on this value and is normally paid by the buyer, although, and I write it again as it is very important to make sure the transfer is all done correctly, it is also the responsibility of the seller to see it is paid, so please be aware of this fact as unscrupulous buyers will try and avoid this action. The tax is declared on *Forma* 620, *compra/ venta de vehiculos usados entre particulares*, which, like most legal forms in Spain, may be bought at any tobacconists or *estancos,* or the tax office *(hacienda),* and the tax must be paid within 30 days of transferring the vehicle.

TELL TRAFICO WHEN YOU SELL THAT VEHICLE.

As a result of my weekly newspaper articles, I had a call from a worried lady in 2007, one of two similar problems. It appears that like most of us, she has trustingly sold her cars over the years and believed the buyers when they say they will attend to the transfer out of her name. My answer to that is, as I always say, **TRUST NOBODY!** Many people are full of good intentions but.... Others are just plain amoral. Anyway, she has just received notification from Trafico that she owes just over €1.000 in traffic fines and taxes as vehicles are still registered in her name and the period goes back ten years. Yes 10 years. Have you kept all your documentation and correspondence for that period of time when you have sold a vehicle? Most likely not! The person/s she sold them to never bothered to advise Trafico of the new owner so, as the government always gets its money in the end, and they are not bothered where they get it as long as it is according to the law, the seller can easily be the loser, plus it is an offence not to tell Trafico when a vehicle has been sold.

How do you do it? Download the Trafico form TASA 9.07/A which is on the Trafico web site, complete it remembering that the buyer's street address must be shown, not an Apartado de Correos, and if at your home and you do not know the buyer well, check that it is correct with a document shown by him, such as the permiso from his car, post it to Trafico certified post. Always keep an original copy signed by the new owner. Note that the form for the buyer to notify Trafico is the TASA 9.060.

Even if the buyer is a dealer, it does not matter what he/she says. TRUST NOBODY. It is easier to do it the right way at the time than spend time, money and endure the stress later when it has gone wrong and you have no record on either paper or in an accurate memory.

VEHICLES ON TOURIST PLATES IN SPAIN

There are two types of tourist plates. Those for: -

1.   Residents within the EU Community area covered by EU Customs

2.   Residents outside the EU area.

A. Residents within the customs area. This applies to all persons who have the following status: -

⇒   Their main residence is within the community but not in Spain.

⇒   They have no business activity in Spain.

⇒   That they (and their immediate family - spouse, parents or children) use the car only for private purposes.

Therefore, persons complying with the above conditions, where they are residing in the EU, but not in Spain, are allowed to keep their car on tourist plates by only paying a one off payment 16% IVA, and thereafter, the annual municipal ayuntamiento tax.

There are two exceptions where persons resident within the community area, but not in Spain, may qualify to have a car on tourist plates without having to pay the IVA:

⇒   Where the owner is about to transfer their principle place of residence to a country outside the community.   In this case three months are allowed for the transfer.

⇒   Where the owner is working in Spain for one or more of the following categories:

•   Correspondents for foreign newspapers in Spain

•   Teachers in schools established by foreign governments.

•   Employees without diplomatic status in embassies, consulates and international organisations located in Spain.

In these cases, there is no limit on the use of the vehicle.

LIVING IN SPAIN, TEMPORARILY OR PERMANENTLY.

As with any other country, to live in Spain permanently without any strings attached, you have to advise the authorities of your intentions. This <u>used to be</u> by applying for "residencia" at usually an office at the local Comiseria or National Police Forces offices, but from March 2007, all that is necessary now is to go to usually the Foreigner's Department at your local ayuntamiento (it may vary in the pueblos, please ask friends) and complete the form they will supply and after a short period (sic) you will receive a simple A4 certificate that confirms your residence. The Foreigner's Department may direct you to the correct office in your area if they do not handle this procedure. However, the certificate is not suitable as a form of identification so it is important that you carry some document that is "tamper proof" with your photo on it. I use my Spanish Driving Licence, but the foreign EU one will be OK, if it has a photo. We carry also photocopies of our passports, the *nota de empadronamiento also* issued by the ayuntamiento, an NIE (tax notification receipt) all folded up in my wallet, and being over 65, I also have a social security card for medical. As the UK passports now are worth their weight in gold to replace them, we only carry ours when we are travelling outside of Spain, and then safely in my body-belt. It is sobering thought that with the other associated costs, a new passport from October 2007 will cost in Spain (everywhere outside of the UK) as much as €250. But if you intend to stay in Spain, after five years you may apply to become a Spanish citizen (you will not lose your British citizenship) and get a Spanish passport which at this time costs under €20. Makes you proud to be British! (Who coined the phrase "Rip Off Britain"?) You do not now have to renew you residence every five years but should, if you leave Spain for good, advise the authorities of the action.

Now having written that, you do not need to personally take out a *residencia* certificate if: -

⇒ If you have a legal Spanish work contract or are officially self-employed in Spain with a registered company, a student or a beneficiary with the right to stay in Spain permanently. You will be registered through the company.

⇒ Family members of those noted above, as long as they live together with the qualifying family member.

⇒ Anyone who works in Spain but maintains a residence in a member EU State, and who travels to Spain every day or at least once a week.

The reasoning is that you will be registered with your employer or through your own company, and registered with the tax and other authorities so they know that you are legally entitled to live in Spain

Número de Identificación de Etranjero, or NIE is intended for those who do not live in Spain for more than six months of any year, and who are not holiday visitors.

TEMPORARY STAY, NON-EU CITIZENS.

These are usually only allowed to stay for 90 days on a visa, but if property is owned in Spain, you may stay for up to 183 days and must arrange this before leaving at the Spanish Consulate in your country of origin. If visiting relatives who qualify for full Spanish residence, it is not unknown for the three-month visa to be extended to six months in Spain or more with proof of this relationship provided, and the accommodation and needs (accommodation, food, full medical cover, etc.) proven by the relatives living here. Proof of adequate medical insurance is needed and you must apply at the Spanish Consulate in your home country before leaving with, preferably, a notarised in Spain letter from your relatives. Some non-EU citizens have been known to visit say Morocco for a few days and then return for another 90 days in Spain after obtaining another Spanish visa there, but this is not morally correct and could be queried by the authorities with possible future problems in coming to Spain.

Theft or loss of your Driving Licence. If you lose your DL for any reason, you must:

Spanish licence. Report the loss to the local police station or if away from home, the Guardia Civil. Obtain a police report number. Complete a TASA Form 2.23 which can be downloaded from the Trafico web site and the check list is at the back of this book.

Foreign EU Licence. If you are resident here, you will need to obtain a Spanish DL and this is explained at the back of this book. If just visiting, it is advisable to contact the local British Consulate and obtain a letter to that efect in case you are stopped. Hopefully, you will have a copy of the DL. When you return home, you will need to obtain a copy of the DL as explained in the DVLA web-site at www.dvla.gov.uk. It can be done on line.

"PERMANENT" RESIDENCE, EU CITIZENS.

Under various EU Directives which resulted in the Spanish Royal Decree - 240-2007 - dated 16th February 2007, which has been reproduced in my web-site courtesy of the team of David Burrage and Peter Woodman who both run the excellent web site:

www.ukgovabusesexpats.co.uk/

--- the following applies. Basically as an EU citizen you cannot be refused residence in a member state. You need to be registered for tax via at least an NIE, and need to have medical insurance cover if you have not paid into the Spanish State system for 15 years minimum. But if you have reached pensionable age, men 65 yrs. and women at this time, 60 yrs. (but the female age is currenty increasing each year for non-civil servants) and qualify for free State medical treatment in your home country in the EU, you then qualify for the Spanish "Seguridad Social", and the necessary forms must be obtained from the Pensions Office in the UK or the similar offices in your home country. There is a reciprocal agreement where you qualify for the same here free of charge. See web-site addresses below. And most important, if your wife has not reached UK pensionable age, she also qualifies for the medical services under your name as a pensioner but will not receive a widow's pension until her actual retirement age is reached. However, the receipt of this need must be organised with your home country government health organisation as in the following web -sites noted below for the UK.

http://www.thepensionservice.gov.uk/ *and* http://www.dh.gov.uk/Home/fs/en

-- are useful sources of up to date information.

Another vital source is the excellent UK Gov. abuses of expats web-site, and this link provides more detailed information on the subjcet of residence, being a translation of the Spanish decree.

http://www.ukgovabusesexpats.co.uk/Articles/Translated%20Directive%20-%20240.2007.htm

For those living in Valencia, this link is very useful:

http://www.ukgovabusesexpats.co.uk/Articles/health-care-applications-04-07.htm

After 15 years of paying the requisite taxes in Spain, you may also qualify for Spanish State pension (reduced). The full pension is after 30 years.

After registering at the local health offices here, You will be issued with a card with with a smart chip in it. Carry it with you in case of accident or a health need.

There are books sold in Spain, in English, that go into these matters more deeply than we have space for here and this book is not intended to fully cover the subject as the title implies. Visit the local English book store who should have these books in stock, along with this book, of course.

If your local shop does not stock this book you are reading, please E-mail me with the shop details, including phone number, and I will try and rectify the local supply problem.

A list of stocking bookshops is in: **www.spainvia.com/bookshopslist.htm**

LIST OF SOME MOTORING BREAKDOWN ORGANISATIONS IN SPAIN.

Name	National Tel. No.	Web Site
Real Automóvil Club de España (RACE)	902 40 45 45	www.race.es
Ayuda del Automovilista (ADA) H/Off. Madrid	914 13 33 30	www.ada.es
Europ Assist.	902 15 85 85	www.europ-assistance.es/
RACC - Real Automobil Club de Catalunya	902 15 10 80 24 Hrs.	www.racc.es info@racc.es

STANDARD EMERGENCY PHONE NUMBERS IN SPAIN		
Authority required	Tel. No.	Why call this number.
Emergency, General	112	Emergency, as 999 or 911.
Policia Local	092	Accident, etc in town.
Guardia Civil	062	Accident on a main arterial road.
Vodaphone	141	Mobile Phone Service Provider's Emergency Numbers.
Movistar	404 or 506	
Amena	2221	

A SIGN THAT CONFUSES MANY DRIVERS INCLUDING SPANISH ONES.
WHAT IS IT?
THE ANSWER IS IN THE SIGNS PAGES.

CHECK-LISTS FOR TRAFICO APPLICATIONS.

The following lists are for you to use to ensure that you have the correct paperwork, etc. for the actions as noted below. The descriptions of each document are in the relevant pages in this book. Please note that application forms may also be obtained by going to the *Dirección General Trafico* web-site and printed from there and this will save you time in completing the form with a Spanish friend if your Spanish is not good, and also queuing at Trafico. The web site address is:

http://www.dgt.es/indices/dgtHtm_Impresos_es.html

Note that the form name "TASA" is Spanish for "Rate" as in cost. Trafico will provide you with a return envelope and this is included in the charge. Also in march 2007, we were all advised that there is no need to send photocopies anymore. This is great, but beware. Make sure that Trafico has the correct details for you on their system including your residence details, *Nota de Epadronamineto* and the correct address, all matching each other.

Please note that any changes to this information after printing will be noted in my web-site.

PHOTOS. Trafico will not accept photos printed on an ink-jet printer as they will run with water on them. The photo must be printed on a film type of paper or with a laser type of colour printer (as used at the photo shops now) so it cannot smudge when wet. The background must be white.

DOCUMENTS THAT MUST BE CARRIED IN THE CAR.

⇒ Circulation Permit or *Permiso de Circulacion* for the vehicle. This should have your correct address and other details on it. If not, the official may pick it up on the new PDA system at the roadside and issue a fine.

⇒ *Tarjeta de Inspeccion Tecnica de Vehiculos,* with the ITV inspections stamped as done at the ITV station if the vehicle is old enough.

⇒ The sticker in the upper right hand corner of the windscreen showing when the next ITV inspection is due if applicable. It is still a finable offence not to display this.

⇒ Current receipt for the municipal tax or the *Impuesto de Circulacion (IVTM)* paid to the local *ayuntamiento* each year.

⇒ Current year's insurance certificate with payment receipt. If you pay monthly, the current payment must be proved with, for example, a Bank payment slip. For a year paid in advance, it is noted on the certificate.

⇒ Valid driving licence. Spanish or foreign EU. Remember the medical rules if the latter although most police staff will not know enough to check this yet. They will just look at the dates of expiry, but if you have an accident then you could be in trouble if you have not had the mandatory medicals.

⇒ Not legally needed but very useful, the accident report form as supplied by your insurer.

EXAMPLES IN ENGLISH ARE AT THE REAR OF THIS BOOK ON PAGES 274-277.

⇒ ORIGINALS or certified photocopies, as explained above, must be presented when required by, for example, the police or *Guardia Civil*. You must have them with you while driving at all times and you do NOT get any time to present them at a police station, etc. as in, for example, the UK.

NO DOCUMENTS: YOUR VEHICLE WILL BE IMPOUNDED AT THE ROADSIDE.

ACCESS TO TRAFICO FORMS.

If you have problems going directly to the Trafico forms page on their web-site, use this path:

1. Go to www.dgt.es

2. On the Home page that appears, click on "Conductores" under "Tramites" in the middle top of the screen.

3. On the left side of the next screen click on " "Modelos e Impresos".

4. You will be in the correct listing page. Click on the dot to the right of the TASA (rate) form you need as described in this book on page 142.

5. You can type in most of the information needed before you print it, or you can print the form out and fill in by hand. You receive two A5 printed forms on an A4 sheet of paper and both contain the same typed in information.

6. Send off with the correct payment which can be made at the post office. From January 2008, the payments will be listed in my web site. The PO clerk will know what to do and at our post office they are placed in a special, secure bag which only goes to Trafico.

7. Carry copies of the forms and documents sent along with the Correos receipt in case you get stopped on the road.

8. It normally takes 3 to 5 weeks to get the new document back from Trafico depending on how busy they are. If you have been waiting say 3 months, check on why you have not been sent, or you have not received, the needed documents.

Exchange of EU Driving Licence for a Spanish one.

⇒ Application form, TASA 2,4.

⇒ Residence card or new certificate (from March 2007).

⇒ Original of driving licence to be exchanged.

⇒ One colour passport type photo, size 35 x 25. Blank white background and the head filling the photo.

⇒ If applicable due to age (see page 124) you may have to take an official periodical medical. If age 70, then yes.

⇒ The fee, currently about € 20. If over 70 yrs. old, no charge.

Renewal of Driving Licence (DL) .

Please note that you do not have to change your legal FOREIGN EU DL for a Spanish one until it expires (at age 70, or 60 if a vocational one), but you do need to, as a resident in Spain, have the periodical medicals the same as Spanish drivers do. These are shown in the table on page 124. If you do not take the medicals your DL will be deemed to have expired regardless of the actual date on the DL.

If you have a foreign EU driving licence and it has expired bcause you are 70 or 60 if a vocational classification, it will be exchanged for a Spanish one, so also please refer above.

⇒ Application Form TASA 2,220/T. Please note that the costs vary, depending on how long it has to be extended due to the need for a medical every five to one year depending on age. Refer to main section on driving licences for more information.

⇒ If over 45 years old, a medical certificate from official centre may be needed.

⇒ Photo, passport size, 35 x 25 mm.

⇒ Residence certficate or older card.

⇒ Original of driving licence to be renewed.

⇒ The fee, currently about €20, or proportional if applicable as advised on the *Aviso* letter.

PLEASE NOTE that if you have a foreign EU driving licence an you are resident here in Spain, and you do not have the periodical medicals, despite what date is on your licence, it will be legally declared expired. Many of the police and GC at the roadside are not aware of this yet, but the lawyers and Courts are.

See Para 3 at web site: www.spainvia.com/drivelicenceletteradsl.htm

Exchange of Non-EU driving Licences.

In addition to the list in the exchange of a foreign EU driving license for a Spanish one (above), the applicant may need a *Certificado de Equivalencia (CE)* if the licence is not an EU "ring of stars" type. (The CE is an official translation to Spanish of their licence). You may also be expected to take an approved medical as described in this book, depending on your age.   Although the old paper "non-ring of stars" driving licences are still legal, it would be better to exchange it for a new Spanish driving licence which is recognised everywhere in the EU. Be aware that because of lapsed or non-agreed foreign agreements with Spain, some foreign non-EU licenses are not being exchanged at all. Please refer again to Driving Licence section in this book for more on this subject.

Vehicle Transfer of Ownership
⇒ Application form TASA 9,050 if by the buyer, TASA 9.07A if by the seller.
⇒ *Permiso de Circulación.* The new one will have if petrol or diesel. Note your vehicle's fuel used on the application.
⇒ Current municipal tax receipt, the *impuesto municipal sobre vehiculos de tracción mecanica.*
⇒ Receipt for the payment of transfer tax. This is the 4% tax based on the *Hacienda's list* and paid at the *Hacienda* using a Form 620, which can also be bought at most *tabacs* or tobacco shops.
⇒ Current vehicle ITV inspection certificate, if applicable.
⇒ Original of sellers ID, e.g. DNI card or residence certificate.
⇒ Originals of buyer's *Residencia* or Residence Certificate (March 2007) or NIE.
⇒ The current fee payable at the cash window in Trafico. Remember that the cash window normally closes 30-minutes before the office does, i.e. in summer, 13H30 (for siesta?). It makes it a long day if you are there personally. Addresses, telephone numbers and times of opening for all Traficos are in the Trafico web-site at:

http://www.dgt.es/tramites/donde_realizar/donde.htm

Advice of Sale of Vehicle
Sellers advice form TASA 9,07/A . Also, remember to advise the *ayuntimiento* in writing and get a signed or stamped and dated receipt. You will also need the buyer's original ID document as well as your own.

Register of an EU Driving Licence.

This is to register your foreign EU driving licence with the Spanish Trafico main register. It is now NOT A LEGAL REQUIREMENT. Despite what you may be told by officials, the EU Directive on the matter specifically says that you do not need to register it, but a benefit is that if you do, you should then receive *avisos* when a medical is due or it is about to expire at age 70 or less for the vocational classifications. I have had readers contact me for advice after forgetting that their licence had already expired say 18 months before when they were aged 70.

⇒   Application Form TASA 2,4.

⇒   Driving licence and a copy.

⇒   Medical certificate from official centre, if applicable due to age.

⇒   Residence card or NIE and photocopy.

⇒   *Certificado de Empadronamiento.*

De-Registration (*Baja*) of a Vehicle.

The book explains the importance of this action to save future fines and problems. For vehicles more than 15 years old, there is no fee, and if buying a new car, you can receive a cash sum for scrapping the old one. (Plan Prever.) If you need to declare your vehicle scrap because it has been stolen, you may make a temporary declaration (temporada) until it is found or the insurance company has paid you. The temporary *baja* will ensure that the registration cannot be used for another (usually stolen) vehicle, with you perhaps later receiving fines.

⇒   Application Form TASA 9,060.

⇒   *Permiso de Circulación* and ITV card for the vehicle, or a declaration (police report, vehicle stolen?) that you do not have them.

→   Current Municipal Tax receipt.

⇒   Residence card or NIE.

⇒   Payment of € 9,00. This amount is fair and well worth the peace of mind from having your registration number stolen.

Note that if the vehicle has been stolen, or you need a temporary *permiso de circulación* for this reason until the insurance company declares that it has been stolen, take an original stamped copy of the police report with you. It is better that you carry certified copies in the vehicle.

Note also that the costs noted here in these pages might change slightly as they were correct only at the time of printing.

You can also have any vehicle legally scrapped by the local scrap yard (desguace) that is registered with Trafico.

See a list at, www.dgt.es/tramites/cards/cards.htm.

The GRUA will visit you home or place where the vehicle is, collect it and the driver issue you with a receipt which they are then supposed to register with Trafico, but do not rely on this, check that it has been done a few weeks later. You will be charged for the collection unless you are a good negotiator.

Replacement of Lost or Damaged Driving Licence.
⇒ Application Form TASA 2,23.
⇒ Damaged licence or declaration of loss on the form.
⇒ Medical certificate from official centre if applicable.
⇒ Photo, passport size, 35 x 25 mm.
⇒ Residence card or NIE.
⇒ *Certificado de Empadronamiento.*
⇒ Fee, currently € 17,20. If over 70 yrs. old, no charge. If stolen, no fee but need police report number.

Replacement of Lost or Damaged *Permiso de Circulacion.*
⇒ Application Form TASA 2,23.
⇒ Damaged *permiso* or declaration of loss on the TASA.
⇒ ITV Certificate. If this is lost, obtain a copy from the ITV office.
⇒ Residence card/certificate or NIE.
⇒ *Certificado de Empadronamiento.*
⇒ Fee, about €9. If stolen, no fee but need police report number
⇒ If over 70 yrs. old, no charge.

Change of Address on Driving Licence (Spanish) if applicable.
⇒ Application form TASA 2,23
⇒ Original driving licence (*Permiso de conduccion*) to be changed.
⇒ Photo, passport size, 35 x 25 mm.
⇒ Original Residencia card, or new certificate, or NIE.
⇒ Original *Certificado de Empadronamiento* showing new address or residence certificate.
⇒ Fee, currently about € 9. If over 70 yrs. old, no charge.

Change of Address on foreign EU Driving Licence.

This cannot be done. The only way is to exchange the foreign licence for a Spanish one, but my new (May 2007) Spanish DL does not have the address on it. Also, when your foreign licence expires, you must change it for a Spanish one if you are resident here. Start the change procedure about three months before it expires which for a UK one is age 70 for normal, age 60 for vocationals.

REGISTERING A FOREIGN EU VEHICLE IN SPAIN.

The following is the procedure and the reader must, of course, locate the various local offices and check opening times when planning the work. Make sure that the car conforms to the Continental driving and mechanical layout as far as the lights (right dipping), left-hand door mirror and rear, single (?) fog-light (on the LH side) as applicable, etc. are concerned, before you start. If you are not mechanically minded, there are places you can take the car to be checked. And you must legally do this transfer within 30 days after registering for residence, (registering your permanent arrival in Spain by applying for a residencia certificate).

⇒   Take your car to the local ITV Station and ask for a form to "*cambiar de residencia/ matriculation*".

⇒   For the UK, there are two forms to register the permanent export of a motor vehicle. If your older vehicle registration document is not a Form V5, you will have to contact the DVLA in Swansea for a Form V756 or download it from the DVLA web-site, complete it and send it to the DVLA for acknowledgement and return. The V5C has the same layout as in all the EU and allows those who do not understand English to still complete the administration as the information is in the same place for all countries. For the UK - Form V5, now superceded by the multilingual V5C, send them the completed section "Notification of Permanent Export" in the form set. If you wish to have a record of the forms, photocopy them before you hand them in because *Trafico* (the Spanish Government Department that deals with all traffic matters) will keep the originals.

⇒   You will have to go to your local ITV (*Inspección Tecnica de Vehiculos*) station where motor vehicles are periodically checked for mechanical safety, and the address is either in the Yellow Pages or on the Trafico web-site at: http://www.dgt.es/tramites/itv/ itv.htm. Have the vehicle checked for the *Certificado de Conformidad (CEE),* or that it is EU type approved (homolgated) and often this can be legally done by the representative at, or near, the ITV station for a fee. Ask at the ITV station. If you have a vehicle already type approved, this is a simple check. If you have a trailer or caravan from the UK, use the information in this book on the subject as these and trailers generally are not registered in their own right as in Spain and on much of the Continent.

⇒ After you have obtained a "*Satisfactorio*" (pass) certificate from the ITV and the CEE, take them to your local *ayuntamiento* or council offices, where the details will be entered on their computer and you can pay the "road tax", as mentioned above (*impuesto...,* etc). You may have to take a form to a specific Bank to pay this, depending on the local *ayuntamiento*, and the amount varies depending on the engine size of the vehicle as shown in my web-site at www.spainvia.com. However it can also be paid on line as described in this book using a *Certificado de Usario* secure digital signature.

⇒ Go to the local Irish or British Consulate with your car documents and ask for a *Baja Consular*, this being the declaration that you intend to import the vehicle permanently into Spain. I HAVE ADVISED ELSEWWHERE THAT YOU GET THIS DONE BEFORE YOU LEAVE YOUR HOME COUNTRY (LOCAL TOWN HALL) AS ESPECIALLY THE BRITISH CONSULATE IN SPAIN FEES ARE VERY HIGH NOW. These duties/taxes normally only apply if the vehicle is less than three months old or has done less than 3.000 km. If you are over the time limit, you may be able to state a date on the form (and I did not recommend this!) that is within the month allowed.

⇒ Go to the *Hacienda* or tax office with the original Irish or UK DVLA (etc.) vehicle registration document plus a photocopy, and very important, the original Bill of Sale or Invoice showing that VAT or sales tax was paid. If you do not have this invoice you will probably have to also pay VAT/IVA based on their valuation of the vehicle. (The EU is currently discussing a "split VAT" payment to this rule.)

Checklist: take the following documents with you: -

⇒ The ITV and CEE certificates mentioned above.

⇒ *Baja Consular* OR import certificate from the British Consulate OR your home council offices.

⇒ Original *residencia* or NIE documents.

⇒ You will need a Form *Modelo* 576 which is only available on te Internet and ths is where it can be very difficult as you need a *Certificado de Usario*. See pages 266 to 268 for more information on how to shortcut this procedure saving a lot of time and travel.

⇒ Go to the counter where the *sellos* or (revenue) stamps are to be bought. It should be identified by the sign "*Espacio reservado para le etiquita identificada.*" These are to be stuck on the form. If in doubt, you may ask the clerk if she/he does not speak English (with a bit of practice) "*Por favor, puedo tener algunos etiquetas identificativa*" and point to the top left-hand side of the Form 576. You will be asked to show your residencia certificate or NIE as applicable, and if you do not have this document, you can show the official receipt for the application for the same. You will be given a sheet of "*etiquetas*" (stickers/stamps. I have been advised that this procedure is likely to stop and if it does, watch my web site for news. The form 576 is now expected to be only completed on a PC to cut out as much paperwork as possible.

⇒ Go back to the "*sellos*" counter (if you have left it to stick on the stamps) with your form and all documents and they will certify the "*libre de impuesto*" (tax exempt) box on your form if all is in order. If not, you will be asked for payment of the tax.

⇒ The next stop is the Trafico offices, where you must have the following documents, and I will repeat them because it can be very frustrating if you have forgotten any and have travelled a long way.

⇒ The completed *Hacienda* Form *Modelo 576*, as the receipt for it..

⇒ Original DVLA registration document (V5C or V651).

⇒ * ITV and COC certificates. (C.O.C.= Ceat. of Compliance)

⇒ * Residencia certificate/NIE or a copy of the application for either.

⇒ The road tax receipt *(impuesto municipal sobre vehiculos de traccion mecanica)* after payment at the Bank or the local *ayuntamiento* as applicable.

⇒ The registering (*matriculation*) fee in cash, currently about €70 at time of printing.

⇒ Do not forget to save queuing at Trafico, down-load from the Internet the form *Solicitud de Matriculación*, Form number TASA 9.03 at the web-site address: -
htp://www.dgt.es/indices/dgtHtm_Impresos_es.html

⇒ You will need Adobe Reader software to do this. You need two copies of the form but they are printed two A5 sizes on one sheet of A4 paper, completed as a "carbon copy" set. When you arrive at Trafico, (tip, they usually close early on a Friday, especially the cash desk which closes 30 minutes before the other desks do anyway every day) if there is one get a queuing ticket from the machine immediately to book your place in the queue when you hand in the documents listed below.

⇒ If you do not have a form via the internet, you will normally have to go through three queues, the FIRST, the *Informacion* counter to get a form TASA 9.03 which you will have to complete there. The SECOND, the cash counter to pay the fee, and the THIRD, the counter or desk where the clerk processes your application. He/she will hopefully accept them as being correct, give you a receipt for them and you will be asked to return probably the next working day, or if you want to risk the wait (due to the postal services), they can send the documents to you. You may be offered "P" plates to drive in the meantime. These can be placed at the front and rear inside the car so they can be easily seen outside.

⇒ When you next return, go to the cash counter and show the receipt and you will be given a "queue number" ticket. Then go to the appropriate window (if you are lucky and do not have to join a long queue) and hand over the receipt and you will be given your registration document, the *Permiso de Circulación - Certificado d'Immatriculación* with all the other documents except for the original Irish or UK (or any foreign similar) registration document which you no longer need. These are sent back to your vehicle's country of registration organisation, e.g. the DVLA in the UK.

⇒ Return to the ITV centre where you will be given a *Tarjeta de Inspeccion Técnica* document and if your car is over four years old, or five if a motorcycle, you will be given an ITV sticker to place in the top RH side of your windscreen showing when the next inspection is due, month and year.

⇒ Go to the local number plate maker and have the new plates made up to fit your car: cost should be about €25 - 30, and then fit them securely with screws and nuts.

CONGRATULATIONS, YOU ARE FINISHED.   The total cost for a vehicle, will depend on the circumstances, and the value, including whether or not it is a personal property import or otherwise. If you wish to have the above carried out by a *gestor* or Spanish business advisor, depending on where you live the "labour and travel" costs although may at first seem hjigh, by the time you have travelled backwards and forwarsd several times, they will seem quite reasonable if you use the services of a reputable qualified and skilled administrator. Please see pages 287 - 289 for such a person.

THE STANDARD INSURANCE REPORT FORM.

The common in Europe accident report form, known in Spain as the *Declaracion Amistosa de Accidente de Automovil* is used to ensure that the details of any accident are recorded on the spot immediately after the accident, if possible. The least it does is to provide a check list of the essential details needed to process any claim. However, beware because in Spain, you have a potential problem. The chances that the accident will involve a Spanish speaking person are very great for the obvious reason and the reader is warned <u>NOT TO BE COERCED OR ENCOURAGED</u> in any way to sign the form except when <u>you are absolutely sure</u> that the details are correct on it. You do not have to sign it at the scene especially if, for example, further investigation is needed such as measuring skid marks at the scene and analysing other data to hopefully prove that you were not at fault.

DO NOT SIGN THE FORM UNLESS YOU ARE COMPLETELY SATISFIED .

If the investigation finds that you either were not at fault or were half to blame, but the Spanish information from the other driver states that you were 100% to blame, your case is seriously prejudiced even in Court. The form is in English on the next four pages to ensure that you have a translation with you when you carry this book in your car. I suggest you look at it occasionally so you are familiar with it as it is better than learning it at the road-side when you are "stressed".

I also strongly recommend that if you do not carry a mobile phone with a good quality camera in it (at least 2 Mp + flash), carry a throwaway film camera with a built-in flash so you always have a camera on hand. They cost about €5 to 10, last two plus years in the glove compartment, and the quality film photos are invaluable for supporting your case, especially if there are skid marks showing the other vehicle was speeding and distances are involved that would break up into "pixels" with a digital camera or phone when enlarged. Grab a witness if you can. I hate to write this but if the "officials" are Spanish, they may support the other Spanish person, even if he/she (a pretty senorita?) is at fault as shown by the evidence at the scene, and I speak from experience. If during working hours, phone your insurance broker for help, especially if you do not speak Spanish, as they will help you, and there are also some useful phrases in this book. Outside of working hours, phone the insurance supplied 24-hour breakdown company as someone there should speak English at the main office, the number for which is on the card supplied by the insurance company. They then contact the closest company in their network to send help (a GRUA) and they are usually quite quick. If not, you can complain via your broker whose mobile telephone number you should have.

AGREED STATEMENT OF FACTS AFTER MOTOR VEHICLE ACCIDENT

Does NOT constitute an admission of liability, but a summary of identities and of the facts which will speed up the settlement of claims.

Must be signed by BOTH drivers

1. date of accident	time	2. place (exact location of accident)	3. injuries even if slight

3. injuries even if slight   no ☐   yes ☐ *

4. property damage other than to the vehicles A and B   no ☐   yes ☐ *

5. witnesses names, addresses and tel. nos. (to be underlined if it relates to passenger in A or B)

vehicle A

6. Insured policyholder (see insurance cert.)

Name (capital letters)
First name

Address

Tel. No. (from 9 hrs. to 17 hrs.)
Can the insured recover the Value Added Tax on the vehicle?   no ☐   yes ☐

7. vehicle

Make, type

Registration No. (or engine No.)

8. insurance company

Policy No.

Agent (or broker)

Green Card No. (if issued)

Ins Cert. or Green Card } valid until

Is damage to the vehicle insured?   no ☐   yes ☐

12. circumstances

Put a cross (X) in each of the relevant spaces to help explain the plan.

1	parked (at the roadside)	1
2	leaving a parking place (at the roadside)	2
3	entering a parking place (at the roadside)	3
4	emerging from a car park, from private grounds, from a track	4
5	entering a car park, private grounds, a track	5
6	entering a roundabout (or similar traffic system)	6
7	circulating in a roundabout etc.	7
8	striking the rear of the other vehicle while going in the same direction and in the same lane	8
9	going in the same direction but in a different lane	9
10	changing lanes	10
11	overtaking	11
12	turning to the right	12
13	turning to the left	13

vehicle B

6. Insured policyholder (see insurance cert.)

Name (capital letters)
First name

Address

Tel. No. (from 9 hrs. to 17 hrs.)
Can the insured recover the Value Added Tax on the vehicle?   no ☐   yes ☐

7. vehicle

Make, type

Registration No. (or engine No.)

8. insurance company

Policy No.

Agent (or broker)

Green Card No. (if issued)

Ins Cert. or Green Card } valid until

Is damage to the vehicle insured?   no ☐   yes ☐

9. driver (see driving licence)

Name
(capital letters)

First name

Address

Driving licence No.

Groups _____ Issued by

valid from _____ to

14		reversing
15		encroaching in the opposite traffic lane
16		coming from the right (at road junctions)
17		not observing a right of way sign

← State TOTAL number of → spaces marked with a cross

13. plan of the accident

Indicate: 1. the layout of the road - 2. by arrows the direction of the vehicles A, B- 3. their position at the time of impact - 4. the road signs - 5. names of the streets or roads

10. indicate by an arrow the point of initial impact

11. visible damage

14 remarks

9. driver (see driving licence)

Name
(capital letters)

First name

Address

Driving licence No.

Groups _____ Issued by

valid from _____ to

14		reversing
15		encroaching in the opposite traffic lane
16		coming from the right (at road junctions)
17		not observing a right of way sign

10. indicate by an arrow the point of initial impact

11. visible damage

14 remarks

15. signatures of the drivers

A

B

Do not alter anything in the statement after signature and the separation of the copies for the two drivers.

For insured's accident report see back →

*In the event of injuries or in the event of damage to property other than to the vehicles A and B, give information overleaf.

MOTOR ACCIDENT REPORT

To be completed by the Insured and sent immediately to his Insurers (Use a separate sheet of paper where necessary)

Insured

1. Occupation (if more than one state all)

2. Make/Model/Type | C.C. | If commercial vehicle state carrying capacity and g.p.w. | Date of first registration as new | Registration mark

Please give/confirm instructions on my/our behalf (where appropriate) for the repairs

3. Are you the Owner?   Yes ☐   No ☐   If no, state Owner's name and address

Insured Vehicle

4. Exact purpose for which vehicle was being used at time of accident

5. Is the vehicle still in use?   Yes ☐   No ☐   If no, state where it is at present   Tel. No.

6. Name and address of Finance Company (if any)

Driver or Person in charge of Vehicle

7. Date of Birth | Occupation (if more than one, state all) | Date driving test passed | Was he driving with your permission? Yes ☐ No ☐ | Was he your employee? Yes ☐ No ☐

8. Give details of any impairment of sight or hearing and of any other disability

(If the Insured complete this section as appropriate)

9. Full details of all driving convictions including pending prosecutions

Date	Offence	Penalty

10. Name(s), Address(es) and approximate Age(s) | Injuries Sustained | If Vehicle Occupants state in which vehicle | Were seat belts being worn?

276

	Injuries Sustained	Nature of Damage	If Vehicle Occupants state in which vehicle	Insurer's Name and Address (if known)	Were seat belts being worn?

Injured Persons

10 Name(s), Address(es) and approximate Age(s)

Damage to Property & Vehicles (other than vehicles 'A' & 'B' overleaf)

11 Owner(s) Name(s) and Address(es) | Details of Vehicle or Property | Nature of Damage

Police Action

12 Was the accident reported to Police? Yes [ ] No [ ]

If yes, give station and P.C's name and number

13 Was warning of prosecution given? Yes [ ] No [ ]

If yes against whom?

Accident Details

14 Weather Conditions

15 Speed of vehicles A [ ] B [ ]

16 What warnings were given by driver or other party?

17 Were street lights illuminated? Yes [ ] No [ ]

18 What lights were displayed on your vehicle/the other vehicle(s)?

19 If your vehicle is commercial state weight of load carried at time of accident

20 State how accident happened, indicating width of roads, speed limits, etc.

Declaration

I/We declare the foregoing particulars are true in every respect

Insured's Signature _____ Date _____

ARE YOU BEING SERVICED (PROPERLY)?

It has been reported regularly that many (most?) of Spain's vehicle workshops do not obey the EU laws on servicing where the customer's rights are concerned. The %-age figures below refer to an official report in 2006.   The EU laws are that all servicing garages must:

⇒ Display the costs of basic servicing for motor vehicles on a board in the customer reception area. For example, in a tyre shop, the costs of the different types of wheel alignments, balancing, etc. In a garage it would be for standard services.   55% of workshops were not doing this.

⇒ Not displaying the times of opening and closing. 40% were found at fault.

⇒ Not advertising the official complaints book* availability as in all establishments where the public buy goods or services. 62% at fault.

⇒ No giving the work done guarantee (warranty) on the invoice. 64% at fault.

⇒ Offering fairly <u>accurate estimates</u> for work as requested by customers, and these estimates must apply for a minimum of 12 days, but preferably 30 days. The quotes must be written and include the vehicle details and be broken down into <u>labour parts</u> and <u>consumables</u> such as oils, etc. IVA must also be stated as a favourite trick is to give an estimate that a normal customer (not a company) would expect to include IVA (VAT), and then when the bill arrives after the work has been completed, IVA has been added inflating the estimate cost by 16%. 70% at fault.

⇒ New parts fitted are, under EU law, warranted (guaranteed) for 2 years and this should be stated in the terms on the invoice, usually the reverse side in the small print.

⇒ Charging much higher hourly rates than those laid down nationally, often by charging for more hours than the work took to complete and not the vehicle manufacturers' published job times. Most manufactures have a manual for each of their vehicles where the time that each task can be properly and economically completed is laid down.   Often, a good mechanic will better those times while still doing a good job, but the customer will pay the stated times and there is nothing wrong with this because the times are fair anyway and the estimate cost is then the charge cost as far as labour is concerned. The idea is that the mechanics must be trained properly to do the particular work and then the times are fair to all parties.

*Complaints Book or *Hoja de Reclamación*, book kept at all companies where complaints can be recorded and you keep 2 copies. Take to the local *Oficina Municipal de Información al Consumid* who will investiaget and take action. This is covered in Spanish Law.

But unscrupulous dealers will disregard these laid down times and charge what they think they can get away with and most of the members of the public do not know about these stated times. Generally, manufacturers' main dealers stick to the laid down manual times as customer complaints to manuafcturers could lose them the franchise.

The EU Law, since 1986 is, in simple terms, that all workshops dealing with the public must obey the above conditions as a part of "FAIR TRADING". The differences found in actual charges were extreme. For example, hourly labour rates varied from €20 to €57: to change a car battery varied from €44 to €114: a basic car service from €15 to €147. In all, in 2004, the *Spanish Organisacion de Consumadores y Usarios* (Consumers and Users Organisation) received over 6.600 complaints, but most people (but not me, I refuse to pay and threaten to involve the Law as it is a criminal offence to cheat) usually just say, "Not going there again!", and that is if you know that you have been cheated. How many of us do complain strenuously? It is a question really of shopping around and listening to trusted friends who have used the best (or the worst) and making sure that you are not cheated. In my experience, a good sign of a workshop that is probably in good order and managed well is one that is always clean and tidy: and carries out the dictates of the law as detailed above.

A problem that can cause great stress and cost is where you take your vehicle to a registered servicing workshop and serviced at the manufacturer's recommended periods, and then a failure occurs which should have been seen and corrected or even changed as part of the service schedule but the dealer than refuses to compensate the customer for his error. If the dealer is a franchised company, then the manufacturer can be involved, otherwise it means complaining to the local comsumer affairs representatives and their location is to be found via the local *ayuntamiento*.

Remember that under EU laws, new vehicle warranty (two years) cannot be affected if you take the vehicle to other than a manufacturer's franchised dealer and this law is intended to avoid such dealers charging excessively because they have a monopoly. It pays to keep accurate records of all vehicle costs. I use Microsoft Excel so I can work out easily the costs per Km. as well as average fuel consumptions, and when services and repairs were done and at what mileage. Having had cars such as a Toyota Corolla from new and which was sold after eleven years at 220.000 km still with neglible oil consumption between the self-imposed 10.000 km oil changes using the best synthetic oils, it really pays to service and use your vehicle properly.

REGISTERING HISTORIC VEHICLES IN SPAIN

Please note that copyright © exists on this information as written in English. Explanation of some terms/names for new residents.

- **TRAFICO** is the sub-department of the Ministerio Del Interior that looks after all Traffic related matters including driving licences, vehicle registrations, driving tests and accident statistics. Trafico has offices in all Provinces and residents should always apply to the Trafico in their Province.

- **TASA** means "rate" or the amount charged and for each Trafico application form there is a different rate, so the form title is called "TASA ..."

- **AYUNTAMIENTO**. The local council administration in Spain. Unlike the UK, for example, the ayuntamientos set and collect the equivalent of the UK Road Fund Taxes, and because of this, they often vary from one district to another.

- **NOTA DE EMPADRONAMIENTO**. The receipt, usually a printed A4 sheet that shows that the foreigner who either owns property or is renting property for long term with a contract is registered with the local ayuntamiento and that he/she resides there with the street address details.

- **RESIDENCIA, AND FROM 28th MARCH 2007, RESIDENCIA CERTIFICATE**. The state of being registered with the Spanish government as being officially resident in Spain for 183 days plus each calendar year. The residencia card has been replaced by the simple certificate from 28th March 2007 and card holders must apply for this replacement when their card expires. Registration is now done at the local ayuntamiento offices and has been made much simpler, although positive ID is required such as a driving licence and passport. It should be remembered that in Spain, unlike the UK, for example, it is legally necessary to carry positive identification on your person at all times while in public.

- **ITV or INSPECCION TECNICA DE VEHICULOS**. The equivalent of the MOT in the UK.

Mauricio Yeo, Pesident of the Clasicos Balcon de Europa Club, based in Nerja, Malaga Province has provided information on the certification and checked the text here for accuracy. He is also able to do all the work for you for a fair fee. His address follows.

The Spanish government though Trafico, has a classification where a vehicle that is deemed of "historic value" and as such should be maintained for historical interest, may be classified as such and issued with a special historic registration, including a special plate number. Historic value virtually means any old car that could be maintained in very good condition so that in the years to come, it shows the history of transport. However, it is an owner's choice as many classics have not been registered, perhaps due to the cost of doing so.

WHAT ARE THE BASIC RULES AND BENEFITS?

1. The vehicle has to be at least 25 years old since the first registration.

2. To qualify, it must be inspected by authorities who will certify that it deserves within the rules to be classified as such.   These include:

$\Rightarrow$ A qualified vehicle engineer who checks that the vehicle is roadworthy and safe.

$\Rightarrow$ An appointed recognised official historic expert usually associated with a historic car or motorcycle club who will check and approve the vehicle's papers and that the vehicle is original and has no modern modifications except when specifically called for by law for safety reasons.

You also require a certificate from any one of the authorized Official Laboratories (Mauricio Yeo advises that he uses the Madrid based Institute for Applied Automotive Research) who check the Club and the Engineers' Certificates. The Lab Report is the most expensive document being about €500. The total cost is usually around €1.000 and this needs to be added to the value of the vehicle.

3. After you have had the certificates approved by Industria in Sevilla, and they have been approved, you can move to the next step which is the ITV station when the vehicle is going through its registration process and you will need the above documents to take to the ITV station as part of the registration process.

4. The registration of the vehicle is otherwise basically the same as a normal one using Application /Solicitud Form TASA 9.03.

4. The benefits MAY include no ayuntamiento taxes each year (impuesto municipal sobre vehiculos de traccion mecanical) but this depends on the individual ayuntamiento, i.e. Malaga City has a 100% discount, Nerja 50%, but councils such as Madrid do not allow any discounts. One argument put forward is that there are many cars in Spain in daily use that barely pass the ITV each year, and they are not being maintained as "classics".

Rate for the Official form request. (Form available in www.dgt.es; refer to this book for details on how to download all forms) The Trafico rate in 2007, (TASA) fee is €69, 40, except for mopeds/scooters up to 49 cc engine capacity, €17, 80.

TRANSLATION OF TRAFICO WEB PAGE ON THE RULES FOR REGISTERING HISTORIC VEHICLES.

With thanks to Mauricio Yeo of Clasicos Balcon de Europa Club.

Trafico web address: http://www.dgt.es/tramites/vehiculos/pdf/mathisto.pdf

The registration must be applied for at the local Trafico office in the Province where the owner lives.

You will need:

1. Identification of the applicant, such as a DNI, NIE, Spanish driving licence, or Passport.

2. A document that legally proves the applicant's home address such as a *nota de empadronamiento.*

3. For legally constituted groups such as a company or a club, etc. that owns the vehicle, the registered number of the company with the identity as listed above of the responsible person representing the group or company.

4. Minors or incapacitated persons, the details of the father, mother or guardian with their DNI and a document that proves they are legally empowered to act on the applicant's behalf.

5. A "resolution" document from the legally competent authority (Industria in Seville in the case of Andalucia) that proves that the vehicle is registered as a classic. See web site at http://www.industria.es/

6. The vehicle documentation, *permiso de circulacion*, or in the case of a restored very old vehicle where papers may not exist, proof of legal ownership, along with any supporting documents.

7. *Tarjeta de inspección técnica* from the Province which states that the vehicle is of historic interest, inclusive of blue and pink pages.

8. Four good colour photographs of the vehicle from the front, rear and both sides.

9. If already registered as a Spanish vehicle, the *permiso de circulacion* and the ITV receipts for previous inspections, if applicable, i.e. the vehicle has been submitted in the past for these inspections.

10. If the vehicle is being imported, the original and a photocopy of the registration documents.

11. If the documents do not have the current owner's name on them, legal proof of ownership which could be a notarised letter from the person/s shown on the registration documents, along with a translation into Spanish which needs to be notarised here in Spain.

12. An invoice from the previous owners if a registered company.

13. An invoice if both seller and buyer are registered companies.

14. If a transport vehicle where the MAM is 6 tonnes and the tare (load) weight is more than 3, 5 tonnes, a certificate of transport.

TAXES.

- Acurrent receipt from the ayuntamiento that the Impuesto municipal sobre vehiculos de traccion mechanical has been paid. Original and photocopy.

- A completed form 576, 06 or 05 from the Agencia Estatal Tributaria (Tax Office) if the vehicle has NOT been previously registered in Spain. (This applies to all new imports during the re-registration onto Spanish plates.)

- A receipt or exemption certificate for the transfer tax if a contract between registered companies applies.

- A "*Documento Único Administrativo*" (DUA) issued by the Spanish Customs authority if the vehicle has been imported from outside the European Union.

Long established classic or vintage vehicle clubs have the official ability to assist in the certification of the classic vehicle and it is recommended that the services of these are used because they have the experience, the contacts and the knowledge of the old vehicles to do the work quickly and economically. It should be noted that quickly in this case could mean a total of three months.

On such person who can assist in this matter here on the Costa Del Sol is Mauricio Yeo who is fluent in Spanish and English, and who is President of the Nerja Classic Car Club (*Clasicos Balcon de Europa*)   Tel. 952 52 66 45: 658 926 509: E-mail,

CLASICOSBALCONDEEUROPA@telefonica.net

COSTS.

At this time the first two certificates are about €150 each, but the registration at the Paritos (Industria in Seville for the Region of Andalucia) can cost up to another €500 to 60 depending on the vehicle.   If readers in other Provinces including the Gran Canarias know of other such classic vehicle clubs including for motorcycles, please send me an E-mail with the details the E-mail addresses and the names of Presidents or committee members and I will find out information there and include them in my web-site for the information of others in those areas. See my web-site www.spainvia.com/classicclubs.htm

Other countries, as found on the Internet.

BELGIUM: 25 plus years. Not to be used as your everyday transport, travelling abroad is only allowed to meetings and old-timer events. No road tax, cheap insurance.

FRANCE: 25 plus years. You must stay in your department (Province) and those next to it. Not to be used as your everyday transport, travelling abroad is only allowed to meetings and old-timer events. Huge discounts apply for insurance. The "Contrôle Technique" (equivalent of ITV or MOT) is a lot easier.

UNITED KINGDOM: 25 plus years. No restrictions, no road tax.

UNITED STATES OF AMERICA: 25 plus years.

GERMANY: 30 plus years, very cheap road tax, simplified technical control but your vehicle must be original. You must also own another vehicle which is fully taxed.

NETHERLANDS: 25 plus years after 1st registration, not manufacture.

GERMANY: 30 plus years, very cheap road tax, simplified technical control but your vehicle must be original. You must own another vehicle which is fully taxed.

NETHERLANDS: 25 plus years after first registration, not manufacture.

ITALY: seems to be a major headache, like having to be a member of a classic car club to qualify.

SPAIN: a vehicle is considered as historical 25 years after the official date of manufacture. It must preserve the original looks and parts.   ITV is every two years until age 35, then every five years. It is highly recommended to join an OFFICIALLY REGISTERED classic car club. The certifying can take as long as 9 months.

 Notes to readers. Any other factual information you can provide so that others can benefit will be welcomed. My E-mail address is bjdeller@spainvia.com.

   PLEASE PUT "RE-HISTORIC VEHICLES" IN THE SUBJECT LINE SO IT IS NOT DELETED AS SPAM.

SUGGESTIONS FOR THIS BOOK.

This Third Edition has grown from the first, which was published in 2004, with information requested by readers that normally would probably not be considered to be pertaining to the laws, but as in the principle that the "customer is always right" I am happy to oblige. On point that many of us should remember is that the driving test and traffic laws have changed and grown enormously since many of us first started to drive, and a recent TV show in the UK showed that there are many of us mature drivers (65 plus?) who do not know all the road signs and laws which is quite naughty really. After all, driving is a privilege, not a right, and as such just as lawyers and doctors have to keep up to date with their professions, I believe that it is important that we should all keep up to date with our skills. There are moves afoot throughout the EU to remove as many vehicles as possible off the roads for overcrowding and pollution reasons, and the older retired members of the public are one target.   Official seminars have been presented on this subject in EU countries and we are being prepared with promised driving tests and stricter medicals for older drivers so it is up to us to keep "on top of the job".   After all, we really have earned the freedom to take a ride into the country or to visit relatives after a lifetime of hard work that has resulted in the economy's current prosperity.

THE AUTHOR'S SUPPORTING ACTIVITES.

The author is retired and as many others in a similar position who do not have their own private jet or ocean going yacht have found, touring the white villages and so on gets very boring, especially when a totally different retirement was planned in a different country. So in addition to this book, which was origianlly started as a hobby, I also am motoring correspondent on REM.FM Radio (Radio Europe Mediterraneo) which broadcasts to much of Spain including the Canaries. The spot I am invited to take part in is hosted by the popular and professional presenter Mary Harboe. The programme consist of new legal news and a phone in facility for listeners to ask questions. To find out the frequencies, see www.rem.fm

Mary Harboe and the auth[or]

In addition, short advice interviews are given out on **Coastline Radio** which is broadcast to the East of Malaga as far as Nerja and Granada along with Colette Hall.

The web site is: www.coastlinefm.net.

WEEKLY ARTICLES IN THE PRESS.

The **Round Town News**, which is published to cover the Costa Blanca down as far as Murcia and Almeria and the Canaries. A weekly publication, the articles are mostly legal matters but some technical matters written without the jargon as asked for by readers are included occasionally. The association with this paper has been for over three years now (as in late 2007).

The web-site is: www.roundtownnews.com

The **Costa Del Sol News** which covers that area. Again a first class weekly publication which by virtue of the fact that it costs a small amount, not free as many others are, it tends to have a discerning readership. It is a "sister paper" to the Costa Blanca News.

www.costadelsolnews.es.

The author also gives talks to organisations when invited and if close to his home or if visiting another area. He and his wife live near Marbella.

SERVICE TO ENSURE YOUR VEHICLE IS IMPORTED QUICKLY AND CORRECTLY

Due to continuing requests for actual help which I do not personally have the time to carry out, I have "vetted" an expert whom I am able to approve with no fear of any problems or repercussions, who does this work full time and has been doing so since 1999. He is highly qualified and until retirement, was a university lecturer in languages, so he is fluent in English, Spanish (of course), Persian and Arabic, and he can understand French and German when written. We have formed a businss relationship to ensure the best service.

His full-time work is solely attending to:

⇒   Transfer of all foreign vehicles onto Spanish registration.

⇒   Transfer of ownership, Spanish to Spanish vehicles.

⇒   Attending to motoring and general fines (multas).

⇒   All driving licence administration matters.

⇒   Organising NIE numbers and Residence Certificates. ITVs of vehicles, Vehicle technical and legal surveys before a purchase decision is made.

⇒   Advising and arranging tecnical inspections of vehicles before purchase with a report in your language. (Costa del Sol only at this time. Watch my web-site, please)

⇒   Free estimates for the above services

 Our expert is able to overcome many of the problems that vehicle owners can encounter as he has all the necessary official contacts and knowledge of all shortcuts and "pulling strings".

Once we have the requested and supplied information as below, he will supply a quotation based on that information. If there are any subsequent problems due to incorrectly supplied information or any other reason, he will re-advise the new cost explaining the reasons.

He is based in Fuengirola in Malaga Province but with the administration work now capable of being completed on-line, it means that he can carry out the service for anywhere in Spain.

This is how it works:

You wish to import a vehicle or quickly complete transferring of one you have just bought in Spain or for any of the services above, you complete the form on my web-site which is then E-mailed to me by clicking on the "SUBMIT" button. I check it to see if there is enough information, if not, I send you an E-mail for what else may be needed. I then pass the information to my associate who will then advise you of any potential problems as described in the book, Motoring in Spain, Third Edition, if necessary. We will then advise you what needs to be done if we are going to carry out the work to get you on the road legally in the shortest possible time.

If you live further away, anywhere in Spain, you can carry out the simple tasks of taking the vehicle to the ITV Station for the physical checks and paying the ayuntamiento tax thus saving you the costs of paying others to do it for you, and a simple advice list will be sent to you with instructions in English, and Spanish for the staff at the ITV Station and ayuntamiento, to make it very easy for you and the staff to follow.

Please note that as specified in the Data Protection Act, we acknowledge that your information supplied will be kept confidential and will not be supplied to any other party/ies for any reason without your written permission.

Please note that this application form and information is on my web-site at

www.spainvia.com/service.htm.

It is easier and far quicker if you have a computer and you have access to the Internet to complete the form and send it instantly to us.

TO TAKE ADVANTAGE OF THIS SERVICE, PLEASE COMPLETE THE ENQUIRY FORM ON MY WEB-SITE FOR MY INSTANT RECEIPT AND FAST RESPONSE.